A SUSTAINABLE WORLD

A Sustainable World

Defining and Measuring
Sustainable Development

ॐ

Edited by Thaddeus C. Trzyna

with the assistance of Julia K. Osborn

Published for
IUCN - The World Conservation Union

by the
International Center for the Environment and Public Policy
CALIFORNIA INSTITUTE OF PUBLIC AFFAIRS
Sacramento and Claremont

A publication of IUCN - The World Conservation Union

Published and distributed in North America by the
International Center for the Environment and Public Policy
P.O. Box 189040
Sacramento, California 95818, USA
Telephone (1 916) 442-2472; fax (1 916) 442-2478

HC
79
. E5
S869
1995

Distributed outside North America by
Earthscan Publications Ltd
120 Pentonville Road
London N1 9JN
Telephone (44 171) 278 0433; fax (44 171) 278 1142

Published in cooperation with Development Alternatives, New Delhi, India

Cover design © 1995 L. R. Caughman, The Press Box (1 909) 626-4334

Printed on recycled paper

LIBRARY OF CONGRESS CATALOGING-IN-PUBLICATION DATA

A sustainable world: defining and measuring sustainable development / edited by Thaddeus C. Trzyna with the assistance of Julia K. Osborn.
   p.   cm.
   Includes bibliographical references.
   ISBN 1-880028-02-6
   1. Sustainable development—Congresses. I. Trzyna, Thaddeus C., 1939-   . II. Osborn, Julia K. III. IUCN - The World Conservation Union.
   HC79.E5D442 1995   94-25490
   338.9—dc20   CIP

Earthscan ISBN: 1-85383-267-7

The World Conservation Union

INTERNATIONAL CENTER for the
ENVIRONMENT and PUBLIC POLICY   **Development Alternatives**

Contents

Foreword   7
ASHOK KHOSLA

Related Publications   10

About the Sponsors and Contributors   11

Introduction   15
THADDEUS C. TRZYNA

**Part I: Sustainability and Sustainable Development:
What Do They Mean?**

Sustainability: Rhetoric or Reality?   27
DAVID A. MUNRO

Knowledge for Sustainable Development:
What Do We Need to Know?   36
STEPHEN VIEDERMAN

Authentic Development: Is It Sustainable?   44
DENIS GOULET

Sustainabilism and Twelve Other "Isms" that Threaten the
Environment in Latin America and the Caribbean   60
NICOLO GLIGO

Part II: Measuring Progress

Monitoring for Sustainability   77
ERIC RODENBURG

Toward Environmentally Sustainable Development:
Measuring Progress   87
JOHN C. O'CONNOR

The European Sustainability Index Project   115
TJEERD DEELSTRA

Assessing Progress toward Sustainability: A New Approach   152
IUCN INTERNATIONAL ASSESSMENT TEAM

Part III: Indicators of Sustainability

Limitations in Measuring Ecosystem Sustainability   175
RICHARD A. CARPENTER

Environmental Indicators for Latin America and the Caribbean:
Tools for Sustainability   198
MANUEL WINOGRAD

National Economic Indicators and Sustainable Development   216
FULAI SHENG

Poverty Alleviation and Sustainability: The Case of Zimbabwe
238
CALVIN NHIRA

Learning Our Way Out: Indicators of Social Environmental
Learning   239
MATTHIAS FINGER AND JAMES KILCOYNE, JR.

Linking Sustainability Indicators to Performance Goals at National
and Subnational Levels   255
WALTER H. CORSON

Bibliography   265

Index   269

Foreword

The concept of sustainability has now acquired such a pedigree that no contemporary discussion on environment and development is considered complete without it. It was not, however, always a part of our conservation vocabulary.

That environment and development could not for long be in conflict gradually became apparent after the 1972 United Nations Conference on the Human Environment held in Stockholm. Already, "environmentally sound development" or "ecodevelopment," vague though such terms were, had acquired some currency as societal goals to which we should aspire. Although it was not easy to define what kind of development was implied by an "ecodevelopment," most thoughtful people knew that it had to be different from the kind of development currently in vogue. But for some time these had to remain visions, dreams without much content.

During the first ten years of its life, the United Nations Environment Programme worked hard to define a terminology that would capture the need to go beyond the rather simplistic—and unrealistic—either/or implications of the environment-development nexus. In the beginning, there was not even much expectation to operationalize the concept, or to put numbers to it: It was simply a question of trying to define some kind of a process that would lead to a better world and a better path of development. The terminology evolved to talk about "environment and development," "development without destruction," "environmental management," and other such broader and more holistic concepts.

The first major breakthrough in conceptual insight came from IUCN - The World Conservation Union. Working closely with the World Wildlife Fund and the United Nations Environment Programme, and under the Director Generalship of David Munro, we formulated the first *World Conservation Strategy*. This was launched all over the world in March 1980, and was a major attempt to integrate environment and development concerns into an umbrella concept of "conservation." Although the term "sustainable development" did not appear in the text, the *Strategy*'s subtitle, "Living Resource Conservation for Sustainable Development," certainly highlighted the concept of sustainability.

By bringing the element of time directly into the environment and development debate, the Strategy discovered a truly synthesizing factor in sustainability and was able to provide a concrete focus to what had earlier been a rather diffuse idea. Time and continuity provided an integrating platform that made space for a whole range of issues including efficiency, distribution and equity, conservation and resource management, and, of course, inter-generational responsibility. It may well go down as one of the major intellectual breakthroughs of the twentieth century.

The theme was picked up a few years later by the World Commission on Environment and Development, the Brundtland Commission. It became the leitmotif of the Commission's report, *Our Common Future,* which basically stated that the main goal of governance and of society was to achieve a development that was sustainable, and it identified some economic, technological, social, and political prerequisites for this.

In the meantime we at IUCN, together with our two main partners, pushed forward the need for strategies: global, regional, national, local, sectoral, and so on. Over time, these strategies became more and more strategies for sustainable development, rather than for the environment or pure resource conservation, and we were able to extend the propositions of the *World Conservation Strategy* into important new domains.

By the time we got to the Earth Summit in Rio, twenty years after Stockholm, we had a whole spectrum of interesting initiatives going on in the world to bring "sustainability" closer to becoming an operational guide for designing a better future. On the implementation front, there are now myriad grassroots experiments, some of which through a Darwinian process will no doubt survive and grow to become models that have widespread application. Some government and private sector organizations, and most independent organizations, have pioneered technological, institutional, and financing innovations that will certainly promote a more sustainable development. It is only through such activities that we can hope to meet our conservation goals.

On the planning and design front, considerable attention has been focused on indicators of sustainable development. The IUCN Commission on Environmental Strategy and Planning has its own activities in this field, as do the International Institute for the Environment and Development, the World Resources Institute, the Worldwatch Institute, the United Nations Environment Programme, and others concerned with redefining development priorities. The United Nations Development Programme has brought out one of the more useful annual series of publications, the *World Development Report*, and the World Development Index is fast becoming an accepted representation of where countries stand with respect to sustainable development. Even the World Bank has its Social Development Indicators reports. So there was a growing, snowballing effect in which mainstream development people—and not just mavericks like Hazel Henderson and Herman Daly—were beginning to look at the question of where we are, and where do we want to go with so-called development.

How do we measure these areas which constitute sustainable development? How do we put numbers or colors or other descriptors to these indicators of the quality of life or of well-being? One answer to that is, perhaps, do we need to? Another question we must address is: Are there indicators that are not amenable to quantification? And if we do try to quantify them, do we fall into the same trap as the economists have fallen into for the last one hundred and fifty years—that is, in believing that only things that have numbers mean anything? Clearly, this is not the route to take.

So we have a broader context for our discussion here. When we are talking about particular kinds of indicators, we must not lose the forest for the trees by trying to quantify everything, as there will be many things that need not and, indeed, cannot be quantified. My own feeling is that in twenty years' time, we will be much more concerned with the process than with the numbers. I think it is the decision-support systems, the decision-making processes of society, and the transparency and participation of these decision-making processes that are more likely to lead to better solutions for development than simply a methodology that can be put into a computer which will churn out the results.

But even so, we do need to have an analytical framework, and the purpose of the papers in this volume is to get into that black box of "sustainable development" and try to find out as much as we can about the methodological nuts and bolts inside.

ASHOK KHOSLA

Related Publications

The IUCN Strategies for Sustainable Development Handbook Series

Strategies for National Sustainable Development: A Handbook for Their Implementation. By Jeremy Carew-Reid, Robert Prescott-Allen, Stephen Bass, and Barry Dalal-Clayton. Earthscan Publications, in association with IUCN and IIED, 1994. (Available from Earthscan, 120 Pentonville Road, London N1 9JN, England.)

The first in a series being produced by IUCN and its partners to assist countries and communities implement Agenda 21, the action program of the United Nations Conference on Environment and Development. The series will include handbooks on local strategies for sustainable development, assessing progress toward sustainability, biodiversity action plans, involving indigenous peoples, and integrating population and resource planning; and regular companion volumes of case studies addressing the key issues of concern to strategy implementation.

For current information on titles available in this series, contact the IUCN Strategies for Sustainability Programme, IUCN, Rue Mauverney 28, CH-1196 Gland, Switzerland; telephone (41 22) 999-0272; fax (41 22) 999-0025; Internet: mail@hq.iucn.ch.

Other Publications

Caring for the Earth: A Strategy for Sustainable Living. IUCN/UNEP/WWF, 1991. The successor to the *World Conservation Strategy,* published in 1980, this global strategy for a sustainable society restates current thinking about conservation and development and is oriented toward practical action. (Available from IUCN and Earthscan.)

What Works: An Annotated Bibliography of Case Studies of Sustainable Development. Edited by D. Scott Slocombe and others. International Center for the Environment and Public Policy, 1993. A project of the IUCN Commission on Environmental Strategy and Planning. (Available from ICEP, P.O. Box 189040, Sacramento, California 95818, USA.)

About the Sponsors and Contributors

Sponsors

IUCN - The World Conservation Union

Founded in 1948 and formally known as the International Union for Conservation of Nature and Natural Resources, IUCN - The World Conservation Union brings together states, governmental agencies, and a diverse range of non-governmental organizations in a unique world partnership: over 850 members in all, spread across some 130 countries.

As a Union, IUCN seeks to influence, encourage, and assist societies throughout the world to conserve the integrity and diversity of nature and to ensure that any use of natural resources is equitable and ecologically sustainable.

This volume is a project of the Commission on Environmental Strategy and Planning, one of six IUCN commissions that draw together a worldwide network of expert volunteers. With some 270 members in 65 countries, CESP works to improve the process of making and implementing policies for environmental protection and sustainable development.

Address: IUCN Headquarters, Rue de Mauverney 28, CH-1196 Gland, Switzerland; telephone (41 22) 999-0001; fax (41 22) 999-0002; Internet: mail@hq.iucn.ch

Development Alternatives

Founded in 1982, Development Alternatives is an Indian non-governmental organization that designs options and promotes sustainable development through programs of economic efficiency, equity and social justice, environmental harmony, resource conservation, and self-reliance. It works through innovation and appropriate design of technologies, institutions, decision-making systems, knowledge structures, and societal paradigms. DA functions as an agent of change for people in villages and aims to transform the opportunities offered by technology into solid rewards for the people.

Address: B-32 Tara Crescent, Qutub Institutional Area, New Delhi 110016, India; telephone (91 11) 66 53 70; fax (91 11) 686 6031; Internet: sdn@doe.ernet.in

International Center for the Environment and Public Policy

The International Center for the Environment and Public Policy works to improve policy-making on environmental and related issues. The Center provides the secretariat for the IUCN Commission on Environmental Strategy and Planning, conducts an international project to build systematic consideration of values into decision-making to promote sustainable development, and publishes studies and reference books, including the *World Directory of Environmental Organizations*.

ICEP is a program of the California Institute of Public Affairs, founded in 1969 and affiliated with The Claremont Graduate School.

Address: P.O. Box 198040, Sacramento, California 95818, USA; telephone (1 916) 442-2472; fax (1 916) 442-2478; Internet: cipa@igc.apc.org

Contributors

Richard A. Carpenter, a consultant based in Charlottesville, Virginia, was formerly a senior staff member at the East-West Center in Honolulu. He prepared his paper for the United Nations University.

Walter H. Corson, a sociologist, is a Senior Associate with the Global Tomorrow Coalition in Washington, D.C., and lectures at American and George Washington universities.

Tjeerd Deelstra, an architect and planner, is the Director of the International Institute for the Urban Environment in Delft, The Netherlands. He has worked at The Netherlands' National Planning Agency and has taught at various universities, including Harvard and MIT.

Matthias Finger, a political scientist and expert in adult education, is Professor of Management of Public Enterprises at the Institut de Hautes Etudes en Administration Public in Lausanne, Switzerland.

Nicolo Gligo, an agrarian engineer, is the Coordinator of the Joint Development and Environment Unit of the UN Economic Commission for

Latin America and the Caribbean and the UN Environment Programme, based in Santiago, Chile.

Denis Goulet, a development ethicist and planner, is the O'Neill Professor in Education for Justice at the University of Notre Dame in Indiana, USA. He has worked and conducted field studies in Algeria, Brazil, Canada, France, Guinea-Bissau, Lebanon, Mexico, Poland, Spain, Sri Lanka, and the United States.

Ashok Khosla is President of Development Alternatives in New Delhi, India. A physicist by training, he is a former IUCN Vice President and has directed INFOTERRA, the International Environmental Information System of the United Nations Environment Programme.

James Kilcoyne, Jr., is a master's student in adult education at Teachers College, Columbia University, New York City.

David A. Munro is a consultant based in Sidney, British Columbia, Canada. A former Director General of IUCN, he has also held senior positions in the Government of Canada and the United Nations Environment Programme, and has been Project Director, Caring for the Earth.

Calvin Nhira is a social scientist at the Center for Applied Social Sciences of the University of Zimbabwe in Harare.

John C. O'Connor is a Senior Adviser in the Environment Department of the World Bank. He was formerly Chief of the Bank's Socio-Economic Data Division and has also been with the International Monetary Fund.

Julia K. Osborn is a program coordinator at the International Center for the Environment and Public Policy and Assistant to the Chairman of the IUCN Commission on Environmental Strategy and Planning.

Eric Rodenburg is the Research Director for the publication *World Resources* at the World Resources Institute in Washington, D.C.

Fulai Sheng is an economist in the Sustainable Resource Use Program of World Wide Fund for Nature International, Gland, Switzerland. He was formerly Assistant to the Chinese Executive Director of the World Bank.

Thaddeus C. (Ted) Trzyna chairs the IUCN Commission on Environmental Strategy and Planning. A former U.S. Foreign Service officer, he is the President of the California Institute of Public Affairs and a Senior Associate at the Center for Politics and Economics of The Claremont Graduate School.

Stephen Viederman is President of the Jessie Smith Noyes Foundation in New York City, which supports grassroots organizations working on environmental and reproductive rights issues in the United States. A historian by training, he has held senior positions with the Population Council and the United Nations Population Fund.

Manuel Winograd, an ecologist, is with the Centro Internacional de Agricultura Tropical in Cali, Colombia. He wrote his paper while he was Director of the Ecological Systems Analysis Group in Bariloche, Argentina.

Introduction

"Sustainability" and "sustainable development" have become the guiding principles of environmental policy and international development, but many questions are being asked about these concepts. What do they really mean? How can we get beyond generalities and put them into practice? How do we know if we are moving toward a sustainable world?

This book, sponsored by IUCN - The World Conservation Union, is designed to clarify the issues and remove some of the ambiguity surrounding these ideas. The contributors represent diverse backgrounds and a variety of perspectives. From five continents, they include biologists, planners, economists, humanists, and social scientists. They work in international organizations, policy institutes, and universities. In different ways, all of them have been grappling with the meaning and implications of sustainability in an international context.

The term "sustainable development" originated in the 1970s and was first promoted in the international environmental and development communities with publication of the *World Conservation Strategy* (1980). It was popularized by the Brundtland report, *Our Common Future* (1987), and has been further elaborated in two other major documents, *Caring for the Earth* (1991) and *Agenda 21* (1992). (See Note 1 for full references and additional background.)

Nowadays, the two most widely used definitions of sustainable development are those in *Our Common Future* and in *Caring for the Earth*. The former document states that "Sustainable development is development that meets the needs of the present without compromising the ability of future generations to meet their own needs" (p. 43). *Caring for the Earth* defines sustainable development as "Improving the quality of human life while living within the carrying capacity of supporting ecosystems," while sustainability is "a characteristic of a process or state that can be maintained indefinitely" (p. 211).

But although sustainable development is now part of the vocabulary of policy research and policy-making—not only in international circles, but more and more at national and local levels as well—many people misunderstand the concept or are uncomfortable with it.

Let me draw on my own experience. Over the past several years, I have taken part in a number of meetings in various parts of the world where leaders and experts have come together to talk about what they can do to move toward sustainable development in their countries or local areas. Invariably, much of the time in these meetings is devoted to arguing about what sustainable development means, and only rarely is there a consensus. This, in turn, hinders discussion of the three other questions that usually arise: How can sustainable development be measured (and how do we know when we have it)? How do we translate the concept into action? Which issues should we concentrate on, out of the great range of problems that cry for attention?

A meeting late last year on moving toward sustainability in Spain's Basque Country was typical. Near the end of a two-day session that examined many different aspects of the topic, a local political leader stood up and remarked that he still didn't "have a clue" as to what sustainable development was about. Those around him nodded in agreement.

I find the same discomfort among many leaders in the world conservation movement. A Canadian colleague recently wrote to me that he is convinced the term "sustainable development" is "as ambiguous, unhelpful, and ill-defined as ever, that it is not supported by a concrete body of theory, and means all things to all people." A senior staff member of an international conservation organization wrote that he has "gone off the concept of 'sustainable development.' I think it's an oxymoron." He added, no doubt with tongue in cheek, that he is now promoting something called "mutual enhancement."

Part I: Sustainability and Sustainable Development: What Do They Mean?

The authors of the four papers in Part I of this book face these issues squarely. Sustainable development is increasingly misunderstood, David Munro states, but this is because people miss the point. Sustainability is not a precise goal but a criterion for attitudes and practices; it is a "continuous or iterative process, through and throughout which experience in managing complex systems is accumulated, assessed, and applied."

Sustainability is not a technical problem to be solved, writes Stephen Viederman, but a "vision of the future that provides us with a road map and helps to focus our attention on a set of values and ethical and moral principles by which to guide our actions."

One of the main characteristics of sustainable development is that it forces us to look at many dimensions of a situation, at the total picture over the long term. If sustainable development, in the words of *Caring for the Earth,* is improving the quality of human life while living within the limits of natural resources, then, as Munro points out, it has social and environmental, as well as economic components.

For Denis Goulet, "sustainable authentic development" includes three other dimensions. He separates the political and cultural from the social, and adds what he calls the "full-life paradigm," beliefs about the ultimate meaning of life and history. He questions whether such authentic development is compatible with a globalized economy or with widening economic disparities. Sustainable development, he concludes, is a "monumentally difficult" task.

Nicolo Gligo describes a number of attitudes prevalent in Latin America—but certainly not limited to that region—that interfere with efforts to grapple with environmental problems. Notable among them is "sustainabilism," the "increasingly frequent and overly casual use of the term 'sustainable development.'" Many claim to practice it but few do, he writes. It "is brandished as a new standard by those who do not really wish to change the current pattern of development."

In addition, several of the authors of papers in Parts II and III of the book discuss definitions of sustainable development.

Part II: Measuring Progress

Part II looks at measuring progress. If sustainable development is our objective, then we need to know if we are moving toward a sustainable world.

Eric Rodenburg claims that the environmental information needed to monitor for sustainability is scarce: "There are no global programs that adequately monitor the conditions and trends of any environmental sector, and such programs rarely exist at regional or national scales." He introduces us to the highly complex field of environmental monitoring and calls for systems and indicators that will serve specific needs defined by policy, rather than scientific objectives.

John O'Connor reports on his efforts at the World Bank to develop an annual "report card" on global progress toward environmentally sustainable development, also factoring in social and economic indicators. For him, the main challenges are information overload, rather than a lack of basic data, and deciding which among many indicators are most meaningful and useful. Ideally, an overall "grade" would appear on the report card each year. However, in practice, this is "unlikely until far more insight has been gained into how ecosystems prosper and perish, and how human interventions affect those processes."

Tjeerd Deelstra describes his effort to put together an index of sustainability in European cities, using such indicators as rates of recycling, number of cars per resident, and voting in municipal elections.

The IUCN International Assessment Team's paper outlines a new approach to determining whether sustainable development strategies are working. These strategies also go by such names as conservation strategy, environmental action plan, or national or local Agenda 21.

Part III: Indicators of Sustainability

In Part III, we take a closer look at several kinds of indicators of sustainability—ecological, economic, and social—and how indicators can be linked to performance goals.

In summarizing the state of the art in measuring *ecological* sustainability, Richard Carpenter concludes that, as a practical matter, *un*sustainability is easier to identify at the project level. However, opportunities to improve monitoring and understanding of ecosystems are at hand. He argues that investing in such efforts would be highly cost-effective because better measurements would "permit the realization of a greater and more dependable productive potential from natural resources and even, perhaps, sustainable development."

Manuel Winograd outlines a set of *environmental* indicators for Latin America and the Caribbean that covers the causes of problems, the quality of the environment, social response and action, and land use.

Fulai Sheng writes that national *economic* indicators, in their present form, fail to measure economic sustainability, let alone accurately reflect social and ecological aspects of sustainable development. We should be concerned about these indicators because they conceal the true costs of economic activities and lead to overall unsustainability.

He makes specific recommendations for reforming national accounts and calls attention to the key role of non-governmental organizations in pushing for reform.

Calvin Nhira takes a historical look at *poverty alleviation measures* in rural Zimbabwe and argues that empirical indicators fail to capture people's motivations and their impacts on the environment.

Walter Corson reviews efforts at *linking sustainability indicators to numerical performance goals,* focusing on the national level in Canada and several European countries, and on the subnational level in the United States. He concludes that linking indicators and goals is a useful practical tool.

Finally, Matthias Finger and James Kilcoyne, Jr., propose to measure *social environmental learning,* or "learning our way out," as they put it. Three kinds of markers are needed to do so, they say: indicators of involvement (e.g., an annual inventory of stakeholders in a given situation); indicators of community-building (e.g., emergence of new sustainable social units); and indicators of transformation (e.g., awareness of sustainability issues).

Three Conclusions, Three Challenges

I can't speak for all the contributors to this volume, but I believe most of them would agree with three broad conclusions, each of which raises a tough challenge: (1) Sustainable development requires cutting across many professions and disciplines; how can we break down the barriers between them? (2) Among other things, sustainable development is a social process; what works? (3) Above all, sustainable development is a moral principle; how can we build it into decision-making?

A Cross-cutting Concept: How to Break Down the Barriers?

That sustainable development is a cross-cutting concept is both a strength and a weakness. It forces us to get beyond our usual compartmented thinking and consider the interrelationships between ecology, economy, and society. But this requires bringing together people who have very different backgrounds, mindsets, and agendas. Getting them to understand each other is not easy.

Denis Goulet has written elsewhere that three distinct rationalities, or basic approaches to logic, converge in development decision-making. These are technological, political, and ethical rationality:

> Problems arise because each rationality approaches the other two in reductionist fashion, seeking to impose its view of goals and procedures on the decision-making process. The result is technically sound decisions which are politically unfeasible or morally unacceptable or, in other cases, ethically sound choices which are technically inefficient or politically impossible (Goulet 1986).

This is an example of what the late philosopher Abraham Kaplan called the Law of the Instrument: The surgeon cuts, the carpenter hammers; a problem is seen as lending itself to one's own resources.

How can we break down the barriers between professions, disciplines, institutions, sectors?

A Social Process: What Works?

Sustainable development is a social and political process. The ultimate challenge is not a scientific or technical one, but one that requires changing human behavior. As I talk with people on the front lines of the sustainability movement around the world, however, I find them with a sense of isolation. They unfailingly express a strongly felt need for models or success stories. They want to learn from others who are struggling with the same issues elsewhere. How can they avoid making the same mistakes? What works?

Fifteen years after the *World Conservation Strategy* introduced the concept in the international community, there is a large and rapidly growing literature on sustainable development, but case studies are surprisingly few and hard to come by. The literature is long on policy proposals, descriptions of projects, and technical guidance, and short on relating practical experience with social process. The case studies that do exist are widely dispersed, often in reports and journals that have very limited distribution.

A bibliographic project of the IUCN Commission on Environmental Strategy and Planning (Slocombe and others 1993) identified a clear need for more and better case studies and more effective ways of communicating them. A few organizations recognize the need for sharing on-the-ground experience, notably IUCN with its Strategies for Sustainable Development Handbook Series (see page 10), and the International Institute for Environment and Development, with such publications as *The Greening of Africa* (Harrison 1987) and *The Greening of Aid* (Conroy and Litvinoff 1988).

One thing is clear: Sustainable development requires leadership and a new architecture for political and social organization—fundamental change, not just more information and still more sets of paper plans and strategies.

A Moral Principle: How to Build it into Decision-making?

Above all—as Stephen Viederman states so eloquently—sustainable development is a moral principle. It is not so much about what *is,* but what *should be.* It has to do with value choices.

It has become commonplace for those who speak and write in this field to stress the importance of values in motivating people to care for the world around them and call for a new "global ethic." Moreover, there is a growing literature on the ethical dimensions of sustainable development (e.g., Daly and Cobb 1989; Engel and Engel 1990; IUCN/ UNEP/WWF 1991; Rockefeller and Elder 1992; D. Brown 1994; N. Brown 1994; Engel and Denny-Hughes 1994; UNED-UK 1994). However, there has been little consideration of how moral ideas translate into policies and decisions that will move the world toward sustainability.

Transforming public attitudes and internalizing ethical values— through schools, religious groups, and the media—will be important in the long run, but we can get results much more quickly by institutionalizing the process of taking ethics into account. In other words, we need to make careful articulation of value choices an explicit part of policy formulation and decision-making.

Several of the contributors to this volume, along with others, have been involved in a parallel effort over the past two years to organize an international program to build values into decision-making to promote sustainable development. As this book goes to press, we are preparing to launch the program as a partnership of IUCN and non-governmental organizations in Africa, Asia, Europe, North America, and Latin America. We are under no illusions that the task before us is an easy one.

About the Book

Most of the papers in this volume were presented and discussed at a workshop on defining and measuring sustainability at the 19th General Assembly of IUCN - The World Conservation Union, held in Buenos Aires, Argentina, in January 1994. The articles by Tjeerd Deelstra and Matthias Finger were written later at our request. The paper on a new approach to assessing progress toward sustainability is the product of a parallel effort by IUCN and others to find effective ways of monitoring and assessing sustainable development strategies. That effort began with a meeting in Neemrana, India, in December 1993 that was organized by Ashok Khosla and his colleagues at Development Alternatives.

Panels at the Buenos Aires workshop were chaired by Ashok Khosla; Boyman Mancama, Chairman, Zimbabwe National Conservation Trust; and Patricia Waak, Director, Human Population and Resource Use Department, National Audubon Society, USA. Commentators were Youssef Barkoudah, President, Biologists Association of Syria; William Y. Brown, Vice President, WMX Technologies; Ana Cazzadori, National Coordinator, National Environmental Study, Office of the President of Uruguay; Marc Dourojeanni, Chief, Environment Protection Division, Inter-American Development Bank; Juan Mayr, Executive Director, Fundación Pro-Sierra Nevada de Santa Marta, Colombia; and John Robinson, Vice President for International Conservation, Wildlife Conservation Society.

Two other presentations were made at the workshop that are not represented by papers in this volume. Jane Lubchenco discussed the Sustainable Biosphere Project of the Scientific Committee on Problems of the Environment (SCOPE), a program of the International Council of Scientific Unions. In seven regional case studies (e.g., the Amazon Basin, the Himalayan/Hindu Kush mountain system, and the Southwestern Pacific islands), this long-term project is evaluating the ecological, economic, and social limits to the sustainable use of ecological systems and identifying effective policies and management practices. Lubchenco, Professor of Biology at Oregon State University, is the project's co-chairman.

Hassania Chalbi of Tunisia, program head of the group Femmes/Environnement/Développement, described her work to involve women in the development process in North Africa and called for more attention to the knowledge and role of women in managing ecosystems and genetic resources.

The workshop and this volume were a project of IUCN's Commission on Environmental Strategy and Planning, which I have the privilege of chairing. Among those who participated in the project, Brown, Khosla, Munro, Waak, and I serve on the Commission's steering committee, and Carpenter, Cazzadori, Corson, Deelstra, Finger, Gligo, Goulet, Mancama, Sheng, and Winograd are all members. Many others on the Commission commented on the draft program and suggested speakers. John Williams was the IUCN Secretariat liaison for the project.

The project was cosponsored by Development Alternatives and the International Center for the Environment and Public Policy. It was supported by grants from IUCN, the United Nations Environment Programme, and WMX Technologies.

I greatly appreciate the help of all who contributed to this effort. Special thanks are due to Julie Osborn, who had the major responsibility for organizing the workshop and putting together this publication. We hope its readers find it useful in considering how to move toward a sustainable world.

THADDEUS C. TRZYNA

Sacramento, April 1995

NOTES

1. The origins of the concepts of sustainability and sustainable development have been traced by Charles V. Kidd (1992). The term "sustainable development" achieved currency in the international conservation and development communities with the publication in 1980 of the *World Conservation Strategy* by IUCN - The World Conservation Union, the United Nations Environment Programme, and the World Wide Fund for Nature (IUCN/UNEP/WWF 1980). It was popularized by *Our Common Future,* the widely circulated report of the World Commission on Environment and Development, also known as the Brundtland Commission after its chairman, Norwegian Prime Minister Gro Harlem Brundtland (WCED 1987).

   The concept of sustainable development has since been elaborated further in two major international documents, *Caring for the Earth: A Strategy for Sustainable Living,* a successor to the *World Conservation Strategy* produced by the same three partners (IUCN/UNEP/WWF 1991), and *Agenda 21,* the action plan adopted by the United Nations Conference on Environment and Development held in Rio de Janeiro in 1992 (United Nations 1992).

   At least seventy definitions of sustainable development are in circulation. For a useful discussion of attempts to reconcile them, see "The Concept of Sustainable Development" in *Making Development Sustainable* (Holmberg 1992, 20-31). For an iconoclastic view, see "'Sustainable Development': Is it a Useful Concept?" (Beckerman 1994).

REFERENCES

For references from this introduction, please see the Bibliography on pages 265-268.

PART I

Sustainability and Sustainable Development: What Do They Mean?

Sustainability:
Rhetoric or Reality?

೦ଃ

DAVID A. MUNRO

Sustainability is now widely regarded as an essential characteristic of most human activities. The concept is derived from that of *sustainable development,* first given currency by the *World Conservation Strategy* (IUCN 1980). Since the publication of the Brundtland Report (World Commision on Environment and Development 1987), both terms have become buzzwords for everyone concerned with environment and development. And since 1987, further stimulated by the publication of *Caring for the Earth* (IUCN/UNEP/WWF 1991) and the adoption of Agenda 21 at the Earth Summit in 1992, awareness of the need to balance environmental and developmental concerns has increased dramatically. The terms *sustainable development* and *sustainability* have been used to characterize almost any path to the kind of just, comfortable, and secure future to which everyone aspires. But like other suddenly fashionable words and phrases, these have been misunderstood and misused with increasing frequency. Even worse, they have been used to misinform so as to gain advantage for narrow and special interests. One may well ask, do they still have any meaning beyond rhetoric?

I believe they continue to stand for a valid and vital concept. But what it means in operational terms—how it may be applied—is by no means clear. Accepting the importance of sustainability as a guiding principle for the attitudes and practices that must prevail in future, this workshop has a vital role to play in clarifying the meaning and underlining the reality of the concept.

If the workshop is to meet the objectives outlined by the Chair, it should start from a common understanding of what the terms mean. While we could easily spend all our time debating them, I would suggest that we give highest priority to discussing operational issues— practical applications of the concept. With that in mind I offer the following definitions and observations as a basis for the discussions to follow.

Development is any and all kinds of activities or processes that increase the capacity of people or the environment to meet human needs or improve the quality of human life. The product of development is people who are healthy, well-nourished, clothed, and housed; engaged in productive work for which they are well-trained; and able to enjoy the leisure and recreation we all need. Thus development includes not only the extraction and processing of resources, the establishment of infrastructure, and the buying and selling of products, but also and of equal importance activities such as health care, social security, education, nature conservation, and supporting the arts, among other things. Development is a complex of activities, some with social, some with economic objectives, some based on material resources, some on intellectual resources, all enabling people to reach their full potential and enjoy a good life.

For development to be *sustainable,* it must continue, or its benefits must be maintained, indefinitely. This means that there must be nothing inherent in the process or activity concerned, or in the circumstances in which it takes place, that would limit the time it can endure. It also means that it must be worthwhile; it must meet the social and economic objectives just noted. To characterize an activity as sustainable, or to refer to sustainability, is to predict the future—an activity that is risky at best. It follows, then, that sustainability is inevitably an uncertain characteristic and that the best we can do in seeking to achieve it is to chose activities that careful analysis tells us are likely to be sustainable. There are many grounds for such choices as well as for rejecting activities that are clearly unsustainable.

To summarize then, *sustainable development* is the complex of activities that can be expected to improve the human condition in such a manner that the improvement can be maintained.

At this rather simplistic level, the concept is easy enough to understand and it would seem to have widespread and powerful support. But applying the concept makes things more complex. *Caring for the Earth* begins to reflect this when it offers a more precise definition of sustainable development—namely, "improving the quality of human life while living within the carrying capacity of supporting ecosystems." It thus clearly defines an environmental or ecological constraint on development that must be respected if it is to be sustainable. To apply the *Caring for the Earth* definition, we need to know what supporting ecosystems are and what carrying capacity is.

Ecological Sustainability

Supporting ecosystems are the sole sources of the necessities of life, including air, fresh water, food, and the materials necessary for clothing, housing, cooking, and heating. In addition and equally important, it is only within ecosystems that vital life-supporting processes can take place: these include the regeneration of soil, pollination of plants, and the global circulation of carbon, oxygen, and other elements necessary for life.

To delimit supporting ecosystems for nations or communities is not a simple matter. The people of the Kalahari and a very few others who "lack development" may find all that they need within their immediate surroundings. This was once the case for all human communities, but now practically all the world's peoples depend upon ecosystems that are extended to greater or lesser degree, often virtually to the global level, by trade and technology. For example, the shops of high-income countries are filled with fresh, dried, and frozen produce of land and sea from all over the world. Phenomena that disrupt ecological processes have similarly extended effects—in the case of the destruction of the stratospheric ozone layer, to the limits of the globe itself. Other examples are acid precipitation, which kills trees thousands of kilometers from its points of origin, and pollution by heavy metals, which reduces the productivity of downstream waters thousands of kilometers from its sources. Despite the widespread occurrence of ecological impacts, it is nevertheless possible and instructive to define the origins and destinations of a community's imports and exports, including not only goods and services in trade, but also ecological benefits and damages. On the basis of such an analysis, the limits of its supporting ecosystem could be drawn. If this were to be done for the most highly industrialized nations, it would be evident that the supporting ecosystem is the world itself.

Having defined the limits of a supporting ecosystem, the next step is to define its *carrying capacity* for people. The notion of carrying capacity probably originated with the pastoral tribes of prehistoric times when they noted that their herds could not long subsist on just one grassy hillside; they had to move onto another one once the forage on the first had been lightly cropped, lest overgrazing should reduce its capacity to recover. It was no doubt also obvious to the pastoralists that the carrying capacity of a particular hillside depended on the characteristics of the forage species, the quantity and temporal distribution of rainfall, and the qualities of the soil and the slope of the land, among other factors. Furthermore, they must have noticed that the impact upon carrying capacity or, to put it another way, the stress on the land, was a product of the numbers and species of animals and the amount of forage that they consumed. In recent times, carrying capacities of habitats have been calculated for deer, elk, and other game species on the basis of quite precise measurement of all the factors involved, and these calculations take account of not just one, but a desired mix of species. *Caring for the Earth* attributes a new and broader meaning to carrying capacity in considering it to be the capacity of an ecosystem to support healthy organisms while maintaining its productivity, adaptability, and capability for renewal. This expanded meaning is important because it reflects the significance of ecological processes and the notion that carrying capacity for any species, including humans, must be determined within the context of the health and productivity of other species.

There has been much speculation about the carrying capacity for humans of regions, nations, and the earth itself. Some observers, noting widespread environmental deterioration, loss of species, and seemingly irreversible depletion of resource stocks, claim that global carrying capacity for people has already been exceeded. They are correct if we start from the premise that the costs of environmental deterioration, species loss, etc., outweigh the economic and social benefits that flowed from the activities that caused those losses. The vast majority of the people act as if there were no immutable limits to carrying capacity. Some of this majority justify their behavior on the basis that new technology and resource substitution offer infinite possibilities for cleaning up the environment and providing raw materials and that carrying capacity is, therefore, practically infinite. This seems logically impossible. We know that the carrying capacity of a field for cows is limited; it has objective reality, the factors involved are relatively few and simple, and it can be expressed in quantitative terms. While there may be some scope for expanding it, for example, by using fertilizer or better forage plants, the possibility is limited. But carrying capacity of the earth for people is subject to a multitude of complex, interacting factors. To cite a couple: With what populations of other animals do we wish to co-exist? How much wilderness do we want or need? It is clearly very difficult to define human carrying capacity on objective grounds since any definition would need to reflect the goals of the world community in terms of nutrition, living space, all sorts of amenities, and so on. Could we reach a global consensus on "how much is enough"? What sort of safety margin should be left? Almost certainly, the best approach to staying within the limits of carrying capacity, whatever they may be, is to do what we can to maintain the health and productivity of all ecosystem components.

While the document *Caring for the Earth* does not explicitly define socioeconomic constraints on development to ensure its sustainability, its postulation of the principles by which a society must abide if it is to be sustainable include those that relate to ethical, economic, and social factors as well as the ecological factors already referred to. These principles include the duty to care for other people and other species now and in the future and to improve the quality of human life. These duties are in addition to conserving life-support systems and biodiversity, ensuring that the uses of renewable resources are within the capacity of those resources for renewal, and minimizing the depletion of non-renewable resources. To take full account of these principles, a determination of the sustainability of any development activity must, therefore, reflect social (including ethical) and economic, as well as ecological, factors. Even though social and economic factors are interwoven (employment, unemployment, and poverty, for example, have both economic and social aspects), it is helpful to analyze them separately.

Social Sustainability

Let us begin by asking if there are social constraints on development analogous to the ecological limits set by carrying capacity. *Social sustainability* reflects the relationship between development and current social norms. An activity is socially sustainable if it conforms with social norms or does not stretch them beyond the community's tolerance for change. Social norms are based on religion, tradition, and custom; they may or may not be codified in law. They have to do with ethics, value systems, language, education, family, and other interpersonal relations (including between sex and age groups), hierarchies and class systems, work attitudes, tolerance, and all other aspects of individual or group behavior that are not primarily motivated by economic considerations. Most of these norms are difficult to define and measure, and social limits are therefore hard to determine and evaluate. It is also significant that we live in a world of fast-moving social and economic change: behavior that was unacceptable yesterday may now be or soon become fully acceptable. Social norms may persist in the short term, but most will almost certainly change in the longer term.

That social norms are not immutable, particularly in countries where change is a pervasive characteristic of society, is also shown by the changing roles and status of women in many industrialized societies; that they are not easily altered is testified by the slow pace and the limited extent of those same changes. Some very persistent social norms relate to property, or, to use a less limiting term, heritage. Among many traditional societies, high values are attached to the natural environment as a whole or to its major components, such as the land itself, water, fish, or game. In many communities some or all of these resources are considered as common property and, while traditional users' rights may be recognized, the resource itself is considered inalienable.

Social norms should be thought of as a net—an interconnected group of related beliefs that support and sustain groups and individuals in good times and bad. In periods of change and stress, as beliefs are lost or seem to lose their validity and are not replaced by other beliefs of similar, lasting utility, the net grows looser and weaker. In such unstable times, people feel deprived or insecure, and become less willing to contribute to or protect the common good. This is what seems to happen when development proceeds too quickly, when political processes rely on force, or even when incomes rise too fast. One example of this sort of regression is the increase in violent crime all over the world. A moment's reflection will suggest that the sudden loss of stabilizing beliefs, once enshrined as social norms, is not to be lightly dismissed. To put it another way, the need to maintain social norms within a pattern of gradual evolution is a social constraint on development.

The main consideration in assessing social sustainability is that even though social norms may change, many are highly persistent, and any activity which would breach existing social limits will fail because the people who must be involved with it will resist or oppose it. This leads clearly to the question of how to define the social limits that must be respected to achieve sustainability. It is clear that they cannot be measured. In fact, history reveals that the specific things that define the limits, such as a seemingly worthless tract of land, an undeveloped river, a time-honored dance or form of drama or a traditional way of making a living, often cannot even be comprehended by anyone other than a member of the society concerned. To define the limits, there is, therefore, no alternative to exploring the issues in question collaboratively with the group or community concerned. This means learning what is valuable by asking and observing, providing full information about all aspects of the issues, and testing the limits by explaining and discussing alternative courses of action.

Economic Sustainability

Are there economic constraints on development analogous to the ecological and social constraints just discussed? Clearly there are. *Economic sustainability* depends upon the relationship between benefits and costs; more precisely, it requires that benefits exceed or balance costs. It is more easily measurable than social sustainability because it can be defined in numerical terms, primarily units of currency. But it is at least as difficult to predict since it is affected by so many variables.

Economic sustainability is conditioned mainly by the availability and cost of inputs, the cost of extraction and/or processing, and the demand for the product. All these factors are highly variable over time and among the world's regions. For those whose approach to sustainability is driven by a concern for the natural environment, key constraints on economic processes are the need to use resources in ways that do not damage the environment nor impair the capacity of renewable resources to continually replenish their stocks. The imperative to reduce costs must not be an excuse to circumvent these constraints since they affect long-term economic, as well as ecological, sustainability. If meeting such environmental requirements results in added costs, those added costs must be reflected in prices. Also among the costs of economic activity are those for the necessary investments of capital and labor. These, along with the costs of material inputs, must be met by returns from satisfying the demand for products. A predictable demand is therefore just as important as a predictable supply since sustainability will be threatened as much by a decline in demand as by a decline in supply. Economic sustainability is constrained by anything that upsets a viable balance between benefits and costs.

From Rhetoric to Reality

It seems, then, that sustainability depends upon many factors; most are little-understood or poorly defined, practically all are difficult to predict. Is there, then, any point in trying to determine whether a policy, program, or project will lead to a sustainable situation? I feel sure that there is—if the determination of sustainability is looked upon as a continuous or iterative process, through and throughout which experience in managing complex systems is accumulated, assessed, and applied. The key is to develop a *protocol for assessing sustainability* and to follow it consistently to ensure a comprehensive, careful, and deliberate decision-making process. Such a process will almost certainly ensure the prediction and avoidance of much that is unsustainable, even though it is most unlikely that it can be used to ensure sustainability. Understanding the concept of sustainable development as a complex construct that can provide a basis for thinking about and planning for the future and as a way of approaching uncertainty so as to minimize risk is itself, however, of considerable value.

A protocol for sustainability would consist of questions to be answered about the expected ecological and socioeconomic impacts of a proposed activity. Answers should always be sought from a broadly representative group, and, so far as possible, the opportunity for participation should be made available to all stakeholders. A useful checklist of such questions, put together by the Department of Environment Affairs of the Republic of South Africa, is arranged according to twelve general and thirty-four specific headings, each of the latter embracing from two to more than twenty individual objects of question. The generic question is: "Could the proposed development (or activity, program, policy, or law) have a significant impact on or be constrained by . . . ?" Examples of the objects of the question include river flow, dispersal or influx of pollutants, survival of rare and endangered species, rate of soil erosion and sedimentation, and quality of the landscape on the ecological side; and distribution of income, job creation and economic opportunity, incidence of disease, adequacy of facilities for primary health care, and cultural or lifestyle stability on the socio-economic side.

All development activities and policies should be monitored and evaluated: first, to decide whether they should be continued without change, modified, or dropped; and second, to enable the identification or verification of indicators of sustainability and to facilitate reaching better decisions with respect to comparable activities in future. Monitoring should be continuous or periodic to determine not only short-term but also long-term cumulative and synergistic effects. Since sustainability must be the main criterion for judging ongoing or completed development activities, monitoring should aim to answer the same questions as those included in the initial protocol.

The conclusion, I believe, is clear. The concept of sustainability and the notion of sustainable development as an achievable goal are not just elements of rhetoric. Let me repeat that sustainability must be the main criterion for judging development. More profits, jobs, and goods will be to no avail if they are gained at the cost of sustainability. Defining sustainability may seem like a philosophical game; but achieving it is an imperative. There is in this vocabulary a reality that we can and must strive for. The full flower may always elude us, but so long as we continue to search, consult, and face up to hard choices, we may yet make the lives of our grandchildren tolerable.

REFERENCES

1. IUCN. 1980. *World conservation strategy: Living resource conservation for sustainable development.* IUCN, Gland, Switzerland.
2. World Commission on Environment and Development. 1987. *Our common future.* Oxford University Press, Oxford and New York.
3. IUCN/UNEP/WWF. 1991. *Caring for the earth: A strategy for sustainable living.* IUCN, Gland, Switzerland.

Knowledge for Sustainable Development: What Do We Need to Know?

ᗒᗕ

STEPHEN VIEDERMAN

On January 17, 1994 a major earthquake rocked Los Angeles. That event, combined with chronic problems of water and air, underline the obvious: that Los Angeles presents a textbook example of technology and science winning out over common sense. This bears directly upon our concerns today: knowledge for sustainability.

There are those who see sustainability as a problem of science. Harvard scholar and science statesman Harvey Brooks (1992) has written:

> There is a need for a relatively value-neutral definition of sustainability that permits consensus among people with widely differing value perspectives and world views to agree on whether or not the objective criteria for sustainability have been met in any given development strategy or project, but without necessarily endorsing that strategy or project in terms of their value system. In other words, whether or not a given development path is sustainable should, in principle, be a scientific rather than a trans-scientific question...

Robert White, President of the U.S. National Academy of Engineering, has similarly argued recently that scientists are more capable of creating "rational" public policy than the public-at-large (White 1993).

Sustainability is not a technical problem to be solved or an "uncertain characteristic," as suggested by David Munro in his article in this volume. Sustainability is a vision of the future that provides us with a road map and helps to focus our attention on a set of values and ethical and moral principles by which to guide our actions, as individuals, and in relation to the institutional structures with which we have contact—governmental and non-governmental, work-related, and other. I have argued elsewhere that sustainability is a community's control of capital, in all of its forms—natural, human, human-created, social, and cultural—to ensure to the degree possible that present and future generations can attain a high degree of economic security and achieve democracy while maintaining the integrity of the ecological systems upon which all life and production depend (Viederman 1993).

We must begin by recognizing that many of the problems that we face today, as Barry Commoner observed many years ago, are not the result of incidental failures but of technological and scientific successes. Witness nuclear power and the problems of agriculture. The problems of environmental justice are also products of technological successes, without comparable social and moral development. Witness Los Angeles.

Science can describe, with different degrees of precision, what is, and to a lesser degree, can help us to assess what can be. Science cannot tell us what should be, and that is the key issue of sustainability. Science is a form of know-how: it is a means without consideration of ends. It underlines the differences between knowing how to do something, and knowing what to do.

Many have argued for new thinking about science at different times in this century. Einstein observed that "we cannot solve the problems that we have created with the same thinking that created them." John Maynard Keynes remarked that "the difficulty lies not in new ideas, but in escaping from old ones." And Friedrich Hayek, in his Nobel address, noted the irony that economists of his time were being called upon to solve the very problems which they had helped to create. Each of these observations should become an internal guide for each of us as we think about the role of knowledge in sustainability.

With this as introduction, let us return to the assigned question: "What do we need to know?" It may not come as a surprise to you by now that I think that is the wrong question on at least two counts.

First, the problem of sustainability is not a problem of lack of knowledge. Focusing on "need to know" as an issue assumes that lack of knowledge is the problem and suggests that there is a cure—namely, more and "adequate" knowledge. But as David Orr (1991) has correctly observed, "As important as research is, the lack of it is not the limiting factor in the conservation of biodiversity." The problems of sustainability are primarily problems of power, on the one hand, and political will, on the other hand. Debates over international whaling and wetlands in the United States reflect this. These issues, however, go beyond the purview of the task assigned to me, so I will focus more on my second concern, which relates to the nature of science and the limitations that are encountered in addressing issues of sustainability.

Sustainability confronts us with a situation where, as Funtowicz and Ravetz (1991) have observed, "facts are uncertain, values in dispute, stakes high, and decisions urgent." This is not a set of circumstances where conventional science excels, to say the least. Investigator-initiated, peer-reviewed research, as suggested by the proponents of the U.S. National Institutes for the Environment, is not likely to be responsive to such circumstances.

The problems of sustainability are systemic in nature. In a system there are no by-products, there are no side-effects, nor are there any externalities, all of which are rather products of too narrow a paradigm. In a system there are only effects and products. Conventional science reflects the narrower paradigm, however, and is, therefore, often ill-equipped to deal with issues of significance for sustainability. Again, investigator-initiated, peer-reviewed research is unlikely to deal effectively with the system issues.

What, then, do we need?

First, I think we need to restate the question to conform with one of the key principles of sustainability. This is the humility principle, which states that we should recognize the limitations of human knowledge. The question then becomes: What is our tolerance for ignorance and uncertainty in order to act in a timely fashion with the highest degree of certainty possible while avoiding harm and doing good in the short- and long-term? That is what Ravetz (1986) has called "useable ignorance."

Yes, there are immutable laws of nature. But despite the mythology of science, they are not always knowable to us, and most certainly not knowable—or rarely knowable—in the time frames necessary to right the wrongs of the past and prevent future harm. Yes, we humans are always dominating nature. We have no other choice, in many respects. The issue is do we dominate in ways that destroy nature, such as is the case of conventional agriculture, or in ways that can contribute to sustainability, as organic and sustainable agriculture are assumed to do. Can we dominate without or at least while minimizing adverse repercussions? This brings us to another dimension of the knowledge base—economics, which is increasingly being recognized as part of the problem of sustainability.

There are no immutable laws of economics. Nor are there what Nobel laureate Paul Samuelson has called "inexorable economic forces." Economics and the economy are human constructs. The assumptions and assertions that are part of conventional economics are key issues that we need to address if we are to achieve sustainability. Among these are the mantra of growth; the assumption that rising tides raise all ships; that increasing national wealth effects distribution and equity within a country; that comparative advantage and specialization apply in an economy where capital is mobile; that the market can deal with all issues, including equity; and that competition is good and natural, in all cases. The need for a new economics—an ecological economics—is clear.

What then are some of the things that we might need to know to achieve sustainability, along the lines of the definition that I have offered above that includes economic security, democracy, and ecological integrity? This is clearly not a research agenda. Rather, my purpose is to suggest questions that I believe are quite different from those more normally asked.

☐ How can we design an economy that honors economic security, democracy, and ecological integrity? What would an economy look like that goes beyond socialism and beyond capitalism?

☐ What can be done, working with indigenous peoples to help them to preserve their lives and cultures, as well as their habitats?

☐ Can we begin technology development and product design with the question of need foremost in our minds, rather than simply worrying about how to do it better and in a less-damaging way, as important as that is? What is appropriate technology? Does "industrial ecology" really deal with the fundamental issues, or simply postpone the ultimate problem?

☐ What are appropriate measures of work and wealth that value sustainability? Ponder for the moment that the word "asset" once connoted "having enough." Can we move from "excessities" to necessities? How?

☐ What determines the sustainability behavior of individuals and institutions, and how can it be encouraged? Finger (1993), for example, has completed empirical research in Switzerland that suggests that only environmental action, with values of equity and justice, lead to environmental behavior. Environmental experiences, linked to fear and anxiety and awareness about environmental problems do not appear to translate into environmentally responsible behavior. This runs counter to the usual suggestion that knowledge, values, and attitudes taken together create new behaviors.

☐ How do we achieve a sustainable agriculture, one which includes sustainable communities? Is there such a thing as sustainable forestry? What are appropriate measures of production in agriculture and industry that reflect concern for sustainability? For example, why do we measure crop yields in terms of units of land, rather than in terms of, or in addition to, units of water used, land degraded, workers and consumers harmed, etc.?

☐ How can we live in peace within and between families and communities and nations?

I would urge us all to add to the list, while recognizing that in many—in most cases—we sadly cannot wait for the answers. We must proceed with caution, respecting the two other principles of sustainability, beyond the humility principle already referred to. These are *the precautionary principle:* When in doubt (which, taken together with the humility principle, means most of the time) move slowly and think deeply; and *the reversibility principle:* Do not make irreversible changes.

We must make clear our own values, assumptions, and assertions and demand the same of others, in terms of the problem definition, the scientist's response, the methods and models used, and the policy climate. We must understand the politics of knowledge, and the political economy of science. There are no knowledge products independent of institutional setting, financial support, scale, place, pace, and person. Fortunately, scientific bodies seem to be more accepting of this analysis now than has previously been the case, although the acceptance is far from universal.

Of particular importance is the recognition that much of the discussion of sustainability—all too often narrowly defined as ecological sustainability—has taken place in and is driven by northern elites. The South, no less interested in the concept of sustainability, has, however, spoken more of issues of poverty and inequity and justice. Only recently has there been a joining of the concerns.

But the northern paradigm of science still prevails. The prestige of southern institutions is still measured against a northern standard. Molecular biology is more highly valued than taxonomy as David Ehrenfeld (1989) has pointed out. As a result, what is taught, how it is taught, and what is researched all too often are designed to meet international standards rather than national needs. Thirty years ago Ali Mazrui referred to African universities as multinational corporations rather than national institutions (Mazrui 1975). The same is still too often the case all over the South. I have serious doubts that this contributes to sustainability.

The northern tradition of science has generally failed to value indigenous and experiential knowledge. While this is changing among some groups of scientists, the change is slow.

Knowledge generation for sustainability also demands that we involve stakeholders in the process because sustainability is more than ecological or economic. Sustainability is a statement of values; in effect, it is a vision of the future. Stakeholder involvement is also essential because, as I have noted earlier, "values are in dispute." In a democracy, value dispute requires participation.

In speaking of science for sustainability, it is important to observe that the corporate world has been stating its support for environmentalism more and more frequently in terms of support for "good science" rather than emotion. I suggest that is a smokescreen for inaction. The "good science" they want before they act—the exact answers to unanswerable questions—sounds good but is destructive. For example, the effects of the toxic soups that we are each exposed to by modern life cannot be assessed in a manner that reflects human variation.

We do need science and knowledge to address the realities of sustainability, but it will be a new science, an issue-driven science. It will not pretend to be either value-free or ethically neutral, although it will certainly need to remain objective and unbiased in its approaches and continue to be based on rigorous hypothesis testing. The scientific enterprise in this new paradigm will have to accept the world as it is, rather than try to recreate it in ways that are more susceptible to its research needs. The circumstances that demand this new paradigm are worth repeating: "Facts are uncertain, values in dispute, stakes high, and decisions urgent"(Funtowicz and Ravetz 1991). As a result, the new paradigm will focus attention on the qualitative assessment of the quantitative data available, recognizing that uncertainty exists. It will also extend the peer community involved in assessment to all stakeholders, as the only way to arrive at decisions that are both scientifically sound and politically tenable.

An "issue-driven" science would, therefore, begin with a problem orientation that is non-disciplinary or trans-disciplinary, recognizing at the outset that it is fraught with uncertainties. This distinguishes it from curiosity-driven science, where the effort is to minimize uncertainties. In this respect, the new paradigm is "post-normal," to differentiate it from the scientific paradigm that is now considered "normal." The characteristics of this new paradigm will include:

□ *Pragmatism and plurality.* Tools and conceptual frameworks will be appropriate to the solution of the problem, rather than being limited by the tools and conceptual frameworks of a particular discipline.

□ *Acceptance of uncertainty as a given.* It is acceptable to ask questions about the real world that at present we do not know how to answer.

□ *A focus on data quality* rather than data completeness.

□ *Use of a systems approach* that is comprehensive, holistic, global, long-term, and contextual.

□ Explicit concern for *future generations, sustainability, and equity.*

□ A concern for *dynamics, non-equilibrium, heterogeneity, and discontinuity.*

□ Expression of *social points of view,* as well as individualistic points of view.

☐ *Concern for the processes* through which the behaviors of individuals and institutions change.

I would like to close with two observations. First, history teaches us that we should expect the unexpected. We should, therefore, study history as part of the knowledge base for sustainability, as a constant reminder of humans' incapacity to manage the planet.

Second, knowledge is obviously better than ignorance. But wisdom is even better. We should proceed with caution and humility, and try to avoid doing something that cannot be undone.

REFERENCES

Brooks, H. 1992. The concepts of sustainable development and environmentally sound technology. *ATAS Bulletin* 1(7): 19-24.

Ehrenfeld, D. 1989. *Forgetting.* Orion.

Finger, M. 1993. When knowledge is inaction: Exploring the relationships between environmental experience, learning, and behavior. Paper available from author at IDHEAP, B.P. 209, CH-1257 Croix-de-Rozon, Switzerland.

Funtowicz, S., and J. Ravetz. 1991. A new scientific methodology for global environmental issues. In *Ecological economics: The science and management of sustainability,* ed. R. Costanza. Columbia University Press, New York.

Hayden, G. 1991. Institutional policy making. In *Ecological economics: The science and management of sustainability,* ed. R. Costanza. Columbia University Press, New York.

Mazrui, A. 1975. The African university as a multi-national corporation. *Harvard Educational Review* 45(2): 191-210.

Orr, D. 1991. *Conservation Biology.*

Ravetz, J. 1986. Useable knowledge, useable ignorance: Incomplete science with policy. In *Sustainable development of the biosphere,* ed. W. E. Clark and R. E. Munn. Cambridge University Press, Cambridge.

Viederman, S. 1993. The economics and economy of sustainability: Five capitals and three pillars. Talk delivered to Delaware Estuary Program. Available from Noyes Foundation, New York.

White, R. 1993. Regulations shouldn't be relics. *Technology Review* 96(4): 66.

Authentic Development:
Is It Sustainable?

ॐ

DENIS GOULET

Introduction

Although it is usually assumed that the two terms "sustainable" and "development" are compatible, this is not self-evident. As the economist Paul Ekins (1992) observes:

> There is literally no experience of an environmentally sustainable industrial economy, anywhere in the world, where such sustainability refers to a non-depleting stock of environmental capital. It is therefore not immediately apparent that, on the basis of past experience only, the term *sustainable development* is any more than an oxymoron. (p.412)

Sustainability calls for limits on consumption and resource use (Elgin 1981; Pirages 1977; Rifkin 1980). But development, as conventionally understood, requires continued economic growth, which may render sustainability impossible by further depleting non-renewable resources and polluting the biosphere. One cannot decide whether development is sustainable until two prior questions are satisfactorily answered: What is genuine wealth? and What is authentic development?

Defining Wealth

In development circles *wealth* means the accumulation of material, or economic, goods. It is identified with mass consumption, or at least, with a society's access to an ever-increasing supply of ever-more diverse material goods. Genuine human riches may lie elsewhere, however; it is perhaps more accurate to assign only instrumental value to economic riches and to posit other, qualitative, kinds of goods as constitutive of true human wealth. This quite different view of wealth appears from various sources.

Writing in 1934 on *Technics and Civilization,* Lewis Mumford concluded that:

> Real values do not derive from either rarity or crude manpower. It is not rarity that gives the air its power to sustain life, nor is it the human work done that gives milk or bananas their nourishment. In comparison with the effects of chemical action and the sun's rays the human contribution is a small one. Genuine value lies in the power to sustain or enrich life . . . the juice of a lemon may be more valuable on a long ocean voyage than a hundred pounds of meat without it. The value lies directly in the life-function: not in its origin, its rarity, or in the work done by human agents.(p.72)

Early Fathers of the Christian Church—John Chrysostom, Gregory of Nyssa, and Basil the Great—often preached sermons on the difference between material and spiritual riches. Material goods are by nature limited and cannot be shared without diminishing the advantages each one derives from them. In contrast, spiritual goods grow in intensity and in their capacity to satisfy as they are shared. Genuine wealth, the Fathers contend, resides in the internal freedom which makes one use material goods instrumentally to meet needs, and as a springboard for cultivating those higher spiritual goods which alone bring deeper satisfactions: virtue, friendship, truth, and beauty.

The psychologist Erich Fromm (1976) observes that people always choose one of two modes of living.

The alternative of *having* versus *being* does not appeal to common sense. *To have,* so it would seem, is a normal function of our life: in order to live we must have things. Moreover, we must have things in order to enjoy them. In a culture in which the supreme goal is to have—and to have more and more—and in which one can speak of someone as "being worth a million dollars," how can there be an alternative between having and being. On the contrary, it would seem that the very essence of being is having; that if one *has nothing,* one *is nothing.*

Yet the great Masters of Living have made the alternative between having and being a central issue of their respective systems. The Buddha teaches that in order to arrive at the highest stage of human development, we must not crave possessions. Jesus teaches: "for whosoever will save his life shall lose it; but whosoever will lose his life for my sake, the same shall save it. For what is a man advantaged, if he gain the whole world, and lose himself, or be cast away?" (Luke 9:24-25) Master Eckhart taught that to have nothing and make oneself open and "empty," not to let one's ego stand in one's way, is the condition for achieving spiritual wealth and strength.

For many years I had been deeply impressed by this distinction and was seeking its empirical basis in the concrete study of individuals and groups by the psychoanalytic method. What I saw has led me to conclude that this distinction, together with that between love of life and love of the dead, represents the most crucial problem of existence; that empirical anthropological and psychoanalytic data tend to demonstrate that *having and being are two fundamental modes of experience, the respective strengths of which determine the differences between the characters of individuals and various types of social character.* (pp. 15-16)

These and similar texts present a normative conception of genuine wealth[1] whose components are:

☐ the societal provision of essential goods to all;
☐ a mode of production which creates "right livelihoods" for all;
☐ the use of material goods as a springboard to qualitatively enriching human riches of a spiritual nature;

☐ the pursuit of material goods in function of their capacities to nurture life and enhance the being rather than the having of people; and

☐ a primacy given to public wealth which fosters, more than do personal riches, the common good.

Any evaluative ethical judgments one makes about wealth and the institutions devoted to creating it need to be rooted in philosophical conceptions as to the broader purposes of human existence. These broader purposes relate directly to the way in which true wealth is defined and reveal that the good life (the fullness of human good) is not necessarily the abundance of goods.[2]

Defining Development

No less diverse than definitions of wealth are the multiple notions of development in circulation. No consensus exists as to how development is defined, what its goals are, and what strategies should be adopted to pursue it. The economist Keith Griffin has evaluated six development strategies: monetarism, open economy, industrialization, green revolution, redistribution, and socialism. He assesses the resulting performance yielded by each strategy in different countries on six registers: resource utilization and income level; savings, investment, and growth; human capital formation; poverty and inequality; role of the state; and participation, democracy, and freedom. The indecisive results lead Griffin (1989, 242) to conclude that "there is no best path to development."

There is indeed no single path to development, applicable everywhere and at all times. Nevertheless, four identifiable general orientations have guided the choice of particular strategies as catalogued by Griffin: growth, redistribution, Basic Human Needs, and development from tradition.[3]

Growth

Growth strategists aim at maximizing aggregate production so as to "create a bigger economic pie." The way to create wealth quickly is to marshall domestic *savings* to the maximum or, if these are insufficient, to obtain foreign capital in some form (investment, loans, grants) and apply it to productive *investment*. Because growth comes not only from widening the base of productive assets, but from higher productivity in utilizing factors of production, great importance is placed on incorporating modern technology—the single greatest multiplier of productivity.

Inequalities resulting from growth are deemed unavoidable: to redistribute wealth through revolutionary or reform measures is merely to redistribute misery. Growth theorists argue that the benefits of growth will either trickle down to poor people at a later time or, if they do not, corrective welfare measures can be adopted by political authorities to assure equity.

Redistribution

Advocates of "redistribution with growth" argue that distributive justice—the elimination of great inequities in wealth—cannot result from trickle-down processes or even from corrective welfare policies. Equity has to be planned as a direct objective of development strategy. Accordingly, they seek not to *maximize* economic growth, but to *optimize* it in the light of equity objectives. Within this paradigm investments in education, job creation, health, and nutrition are treated, not as consumer goods, but as productive investments. Nutritious food and good health services add productive wealth to the nation's work force, leading to decreases in idleness caused by illness or absenteeism and to increases in economic demand among the poor classes. Champions of this approach contend that a high level of growth is compatible with equitable distribution.

Basic Human Needs

The Basic Human Needs (BHN) strategy goes beyond the redistribution model by specifying the quantifiable content of equitable redistribution. The priority task thus becomes neither to maximize nor to optimize aggregate growth, but to satisfy the basic needs of those segments of a nation's population which lie under some poverty line. Basic needs embrace goods and services relating to nutrition, health, housing, education, and access to jobs. The BHN paradigm does not assume that equity is necessarily compatible with high rates of economic growth. If basic needs can be met with little or no growth, so be it: genuine development is not measured by growth.

Even under the BHN formula, however, the ultimate *goals* of development are *accepted as being* those endorsed in the first two strategies: economic welfare for large numbers of people, technological efficiency, and institutional modernity. For BHN advocates, the best means to achieve these goals is to target scarce resources toward providing for the poorest as a first priority.

Development from Tradition

Development from tradition departs radically from the three pathways just outlined. Its central premise states that the goals of development, and not only its means, are not to be borrowed from countries already "developed": any such mimetic development is spurious and distorted. In "development from tradition," the goal of development suited to a particular society should be sought within the latent dynamism of that society's value system: its traditional beliefs, meaning systems, local institutions, and popular practices. Given that culture's understanding of the meaning of life and death, of time and eternity, and of how human beings should relate to the forces of the cosmos, certain ideal images of the good life and the good society emerge. Although modern ideas, behavior, and technology are not repudiated on principle, they must be judged critically to determine whether or not they contribute to the sound development of individuals and communities as defined by the traditional value system.

Traditional values are not immune to criticism, however. Gandhi himself, when evaluating the caste system or the spiritual authority of Brahmins of India, recognized that such modern values as rational inquiry and the democratic equality of persons before the law lay bare the inhuman characteristics of certain ancient beliefs. Consequently, traditional images of the good life and the good society should be critically confronted with modern alternatives to see which are more truly developed.

Both the BHN and "development from tradition" orientations assume varying forms. The BHN approach is variously labelled as "endogenous" or "self-defined" (auto-centered), self-reliant, or bottom-up development. As for the "tradition-rooted approach," it sometimes takes the form of an outright rejection of development. The French economist Serge Latouche (1986) urges us to discard development because, he argues, it is a tool used by advanced western countries to destroy the cultures and the autonomy of nations throughout Africa,

Asia, and Latin America. For the Mexican economist and planner Gustavo Esteva (1992), development is:

> A loaded word, and one doomed to extinction . . . From the unburied corpse of development, every kind of pest has started to spread . . . Development has evaporated . . . It is now time to recover a sense of reality. It is time to recover serenity. Crutches, like those offered by science, are not necessary when it is possible to walk with one's own feet, on one's own path, in order to dream one's dreams. Not the borrowed ones of development.(pp.6; 22-23)

Ivan Illich sees "development" as "modernization of poverty" and the "radical disempowerment" of people to define and meet their own needs. An army of expert professionals has captured a radical monopoly over diagnosis and prescriptions for society, by appropriating sole legitimacy to do so via a privileged "filtering" system of certification and "credentialization."[4]

Authentic Development

Development generates multiple value conflicts over the meaning of the good life. Ursula K. LeGuin's (1975) science fiction novel *The Dispossessed* contrasts two models of the good life. One model prizes collaboration, friendship, health, and a high degree of equality, achievable in an austere communitarian regime of disciplined resource use. The other values material comfort, individual selfishness, and competition, with its resulting inequalities, and depends on abundant resources.

A second conflict bears on the foundations of justice in society. Are justice and legitimacy to rest on inherited authority, majority rule, on some social contract? Should political rights and individual freedoms enjoy primacy over collective socioeconomic rights aimed at assuring that needs are met and that society's common good is served? Are human rights a purely instrumental value, or ends in themselves worthy for their own sake? A third set of conflicts centers on the criteria a society adopts to frame its stance toward nature. Is nature viewed simply as raw material for exploitation by humans, or as the larger womb of life in which humans live, move, and have their being, and whose rhythms and laws they must respect? Should the human stance toward nature be extractive and manipulative, or harmony-seeking?

Providing satisfactory conceptual and institutional answers to these three questions is what constitutes authentic development. It follows, therefore, that not every nation with a high per capita income is truly developed.[5]

Any adequate definition of development includes six dimensions:

(1) an *economic component* dealing with the creation of wealth and improved conditions of material life, equitably distributed;
(2) a *social ingredient* measured as well-being in health, education, housing, and employment;
(3) a *political dimension* embracing such values as human rights, political freedom, legal enfranchisement of persons, and some form of democracy;
(4) a *cultural element* in recognition of the fact that cultures confer identity and self-worth to people;
(5) *ecological soundness;* and
(6) a final dimension one may call the *full-life paradigm,* which refers to meaning systems, symbols, and beliefs concerning the ultimate meaning of life and history.

For any society, authentic development means providing optimal life-sustenance, esteem, and freedom to all its members. Therefore, the destruction of life-giving resources, the irreversible violation of nature's environments, and the indiscriminate adoption of technologies which alienate human freedoms constitute destructive, not creative, development. Like the colonial political system, however, spurious development breeds opposition, contradiction, and self-destruction: *it cannot be sustained.*

Sustainability must be assured in four domains: economic, political, social, and cultural. Long-term economic viability depends on a use of resources which does not deplete them irreversibly. Political viability rests on creating for all members of society a stake in its survival: this cannot be achieved unless all enjoy freedom, inviolable personal rights, and believe that the political system within which they live pursues some common good and not mere particular interests. And if development is to be socially and culturally sustainable, the foundations of community and symbolic meaning systems must be protected. Otherwise, they will be steamrolled into oblivion under the pretext of submitting to the requirements of scientific and technological "rationality."

A sound development strategy will be oriented toward a form of economic growth whose production package centers on basic needs, job creation (largely through adoption of Appropriate Technologies),[6] decentralized public infrastructure investment to produce multiple "poles" of development, an adequate social allocation ratio of public expenditures devoted to what the UNDP (1991, 5-6) calls "human priority concerns," an incentives policy to favor increased productivity in low-productivity sectors, and selective linkage and de-linkage with global markets, with primary emphasis on domestic markets.[7]

In its report on *North-South, A Program for Survival,* the Brandt Commission declared that:

> Mankind has never before had such ample technical and financial resources for coping with hunger and poverty. The immense task can be tackled once the necessary collective will is mobilized . . .Solidarity among men must go beyond national boundaries: we cannot allow it to be reduced to a meaningless phrase. International solidarity must stem both from strong mutual interests in cooperation and from compassion for the hungry. (Brandt 1980, 16)

In no domain is solidarity more urgently needed than in environmental affairs. The ecological imperative is clear and cruel: nature must be saved or we humans will die. The single greatest threat to nature comes from "development." This same "development" also perpetuates the underdevelopment of hundreds of millions of people. Therefore, the task of eliminating dehumanizing underdevelopment possesses the same urgency as the safeguard of nature. A comprehensive ethic of authentic development, of necessity, looks to sustainable resource use as well as equitable access to them. Along with this ethic, there is needed what Ignacy Sachs (1984) calls an "anthropological economics" that simultaneously serves human needs and manages nature with wisdom.

Ecology versus Development

Ecology, now a household word, presents illuminating symbolism. In its Greek etymology, *ecology* designates the science of the larger household, the total environment in which living organisms exist. Nature, the support system of all life, is the larger "economy" (household to be managed) within which the human economy—the wise stewardship of "scarce" goods—is deployed. By reinstating the ancient Greek distinction between "chrematistics" and "economics," Daly and Cobb (1989) highlight two contrasing approaches to decision-making about resource use:

> [Chrematistics] is the branch of political economy relating to the manipulation of property and wealth so as to maximize short-term monetary exchange value to the owner. Oikonomia, by contrast, is the management of the household so as to increase its use value to all members of the household over the long run. If we expand the scope of household to include the larger community of the land, of shared values, resources, biomes, institutions, language, and history, then we have a good definition of "economics for community."

Human economy, infrastructural and input goods need to be maintained and replenished. So too with natural support systems: biospheres and ecosystems must be constantly "recapitalized." Consequently, two procedures must be instituted in economic record-keeping:

> ☐ internalizing the externalities (natural support systems that are treated like other factors of production in cost-benefit calaculations); and
> ☐ measuring economic performance in ways which take account of nature (by introducing new, multi-dimensional indicators including natural depletion and replenishment).[8]

Ecology is holistic: it looks to the whole picture, the totality of relations. As a new pluridisciplinary field of study, ecology embraces four interrelated subjects: environment, demography, resource systems, and technology. Its special contribution to human knowledge is to draw a coherent portrait of how these four realms interact in patterns of vital interdependence. Ecological wisdom is the search for optimal modes and scales in which human populations are to apply technology to resource use within their environments. Both as an intellectual discipline and as a practical concern, ecology *presupposes some philosophy of nature.* Traditional human wisdoms long ago parted ways, however, in their conceptions of nature and their views as to how human beings should relate to it. All wisdoms acknowledge humans to be part of nature and subject to its laws: the common destiny of all natural beings, humans included, is generation and corruption—birth, growth, aging, death. Certain worldviews more than others, however, elevate humans above their encompassing nature and assign to them a cosmic role of domination over the very nature of which they are a part. In the interrogatory words that aptly serve as the title of a Sri Lankan publication (Samartha and DeSilva 1979), *Man in Nature: Guest or Engineer?* treating nature and human liberty as opposing poles in a dichotomy poses difficult ethical questions. Are human animals *free* to treat nature as they wish? Or must they, like other animals, submit to nature's laws, or at least to its penalties? Paradoxically, human beings are free not to respect nature, but they must do so if they are to preserve the very existential ground upon which their freedom rests. Since this is so, there can be no ultimate incompatibility between the demands of nature and the exigencies of human freedom, those of environmental sanity, of wise resource stewardship, and of technology. Problems arise whenever ecologists and resource planners fail to look at the whole picture. Looking at the whole picture also enables theorists to transcend other apparent antinomies, chief among them the alleged contradiction between anthropocentric and cosmocentric views of the universe.

The intercultural philosopher Raimundo Panikkar (1977) pleads for a radical change in our understanding of relationships between human beings and nature, "a thoroughgoing conversion which recognizes and appropriates their common destiny." Panikkar (1981, 39-45) divides history into three epochs or "kairological moments" of human consciousness: pre-historical, historical, and trans-historical. In the epoch of historical consciousness:

Man lives mainly in space . . . The World of pre-historical Man, his environment, is the *theocosmos* or *theocosm,* the divinised universe. It is not a World of Man, but it is also not the World of the Gods as a separate and superior realm hovering over the human . . . In the pre-historical mentality, it is the World that is divinised (to use historical language). The divine permeates the cosmos. The forces of nature are all divine. Nature is supernatural. Or rather, nature is that which is "natured," born, from the divine. Pre-historical Man's milieu is a cosmotheological one. *Harmony* is the supreme principle—which does not mean that it has been achieved.

In the second "kairological moment," one marked by historical consciousness, "historical time is under the spell of the future and the guidance of reason. Only the historical is real." As Panikkar explains:

> The World of historical Man, his environment, is the *anthropocosmos* or *anthropocosm,* the human world, the universe of Man. He is not interested in the evolution of the cosmos; his destiny has little to do with the fate of the stars of the phases of the moon, or even the seasons and the rivers . . . Nature has been tamed and subjugated. It has been demythicized and there is nothing "mysterious" about it. Historical Man has overcome the fear of nature. His backdrop is *cosmological.* The meaning of his life is not to be found in the cosmic cycles, but in the human sphere, the society. Justice is the supreme principle— which does not mean that it has been achieved.

Although these two degrees of consciousness, pre-historical and historical, have not disappeared from the face of the earth, Panikkar adds, "a third degree of consciousness is coming more and more to the fore." This is trans-historical consciousness, in the form of metaphysical insights and mystical experiences which have always been in the air but which nowadays gain momentum and change their character. A new emerging myth situates trans-historical Man in what Panikkar calls the *anthropocosmos.*

> "The World of trans-historical Man, his environment or ecosystem, is the cosmotheandric universe . . . The destiny of Man is not just an historical existence. It is linked with the life of the Earth and with the entire fate of reality, the divine not excluded. God or the gods are again incarnated and share in the destiny of the universe at large. We are all in the same boat, which is not just this planet Earth, but the whole mystery of Life, Consciousness, Existence. Love is the supreme principle—which, again, does not mean that it has been achieved."

The "new innocence" of which Panikkar (1977, 13-14) speaks is neither cosmocentric nor anthropocentric, but brings all together in a "consciousness lived neither naively nor by rational projection into the future." The center is "neither in God, nor in the cosmos, nor even in man. It is a moving center which is only to be found in the intersection of the three."

For ethicists who stress the integrity of nature, the highest values are the conservation of resources, the preservation of species, and the protection of nature's integrity from human depredations. Those who stress human freedom, in contrast, take as their primary values justice (which takes the form of an active assault upon human poverty, branded as the worst form of pollution) and the need to "develop" potential into actual resources. Both ethical orientations adhere to all five values listed here, but rank them differently. A "nature" emphasis locates development and the elimination of human misery below biological and resource conservation in its hierarchy of values. Conversely, a "freedom" orientation places development and the active conquest of justice in resource allocations above environmental protection or the preservation of endangered species in its scale of values. All five values enjoy parity of moral status, however. The reason is that any long-term, sustainable, equity-enhancing combat against poverty requires wisdom in the exploitation of resources. Reciprocally, the preservation of other living species cannot be persuasively held out as a priority goal if the human species itself is threatened with degrading poverty or extinction. Nature is diminished when its human members are kept "under-developed." Conversely, humans cannot become truly "developed" if they violate their supportive nature.

The only authentic form of development is that which is conducted in the mode of solidarity, binding all persons and communities to each other and to the planet they inhabit.

Conclusion: Unanswered Questions

The debate on sustainability is replete with uncertainties and unanswered (perhaps unanswerable) questions. I shall here present but two such questions.

(1) *Is "Sustainable Authentic Development" compatible with a globalized economy?*

One recent commentator on trade negotiations (GATT and NAFTA), judges that:

The philosophy inherent in these accords is directly opposed to the idea of sustainable economic development promoted in Rio . . . Neoliberal free trade policies are being pushed by a worldwide corporate elite bent on defining the environment as a trade barrier expressed in dollars. Governments have abetted this transformation by forging agreements that ensure a nation's powerlessness to defend itself against commercial activities that harm its citizens or the environment. (Stinson 1993)

Environmental sustainability may well require—not global economic integration—but a high degree of economic decentralization, this in recognition of the vast "diseconomies" attendant upon large-scale global production, distribution, and consumption.

(2) *Is Sustainable Authentic Development compatible with widening global economic disparities?*

Does it not presuppose, if not relative equality, at least the abolition of absolute poverty among the world's poor masses? What realistic prospects exist, however, either for abolishing absolute poverty or for diminishing global disparities? Aid "fatigue" in the rich has greatly reduced the volume of net resource transfers to the poor. Moreover, the world economy is growing too slowly for any "increased economic pie" to "trickle down" (assuming such "trickle-down" did occur) to spill its developmental benefits onto the world's impoverished populations. Leonard Silk (1993) sees the greatest danger as that of falling into a new worldwide depression for, contrary to euphoric expectations at the end of the Cold War, "the peace dividend only shows up in lost jobs and falling incomes." Transnational, economically driven migrations tax national and international absorptive systems beyond present capacity. Growing disparities in levels of development will but exacerbate the problem.

Environmental sustainability is but one component, among many, of authentic development. Authentic development is the only kind that is sustainable. Authentic development, however, is monumentally difficult: difficult to desire, to implement, to sustain. G. K. Chesterton (1912) once wryly observed that "the Christian ideal has not been tried and found wanting. It has been found difficult; and left untried." Sustainable development, because it is found too difficult, may likewise remain untried.

NOTES

1. For a probing analysis and critique of competing notions of wealth, see Fagard 1980.
2. On this contrast, see Leach 1993.
3. This classification is adopted from Goulet 1983 (pages 15-20).
4. This is the common thesis in all of Illich's writings. See especially Illich 1977.
5. For different comparative rankings of countries on two scales—GNP per capita and a "human development index" designed to measure the range of choices available to people to live a "fulfilled" life—see United Nations Development Programme 1993, Table 1 "Human Development Index" (pages 135-37).
6. For a detailed analysis of how the scale of technologies affects employment, see Kaplinski 1990.
7. For detailed justification and illustration, see Goulet and Kim 1989.
8. Refer to Goulet 1992.

REFERENCES

Avila, C. 1983. *Ownership: Early Christian teaching.* Orbis Books, Maryknoll, New York, USA.

Brandt, W. 1980. *North-south: A programme for survival.* MIT Press, Cambridge, Massachusetts, USA.

Chesterton, G. K. 1912. What's wrong with the world? In *Chesterton day by day.* 2d ed. Kegan Paul, London.

Daly, H. E., and J. B. Cobb, Jr. 1989. *For the common good: Redirecting the economy toward community, the environment, and a sustainable future.* Beacon, Boston.

Ekins, P. 1992. Sustainability first. In *Real-life economics,* P. Ekins and M. Max-Neef, eds. Routledge, London and New York.

Elgin, D. 1981. *Voluntary simplicity.* William Morrow, New York.

Esteva, G. 1992. Development. In *The development dictionary,* ed. W. Sachs. Zed Books, London.

Fagard, G. 1980. *La richesse, ˜essort secret de l'adventure humaine.* Le Centurion, Paris.

Fromm, E. 1976. *To have or to be?* Harper and Row, New York.

Griffin, K. 1989. *Alternative strategies for economic development.* Macmillan, London.

Goulet, D. 1992. Development indicators: A research problem, a policy problem. *Journal of Socio-Economics* 21(3): 245-60.

Goulet, D. 1983. *Mexico: Development strategies for the future.* University of Notre Dame Press, Notre Dame, Indiana, USA.

Goulet, D., and K. S. Kim. 1989. *Estrategias de desarrollo para el futuro de México.* ITESO, Guadalajara, Mexico.

Illich, I. 1977. *Toward a history of needs.* Pantheon, New York.

John Chrysostom, St. 1984. *On wealth and poverty.* St. Vladimir's Seminary Press, Crestwood, New York, USA.

Kaplinski, R. 1990. *The economies of small, appropriate technology in a changing world.* Appropriate Technology International, London.

Latouche, S. 1986. *Faut-it refuser le développement?* Presses Universitaires de France, Paris.

Leach, W. 1993. *Land of desire: Merchants, power, and the rise of a new American culture.* Pantheon, New York.

LeGuin, U. K. 1975. *The dispossessed.* Avon Books, New York.

Mumford, L. 1934. *Technics and civilization.* Harcourt Brace, New York.

Panikkar, R. 1977. The new innocence. *Cross Currents* (Spring): 7.

Panikkar, R. 1981. Is history the measure of man? Three kairological moments of human consciousness. *Teilhard Review* 16(1-2): 39-45.

Pirages, D. C., ed. 1977. *The sustainable society.* Praeger, New York.

Rifkin, J. 1980. *Entropy: A new world view.* Viking, New York.

Sachs, I. 1984. *Développer: Les champs de planification.* Université Coopérative Internationale, Paris.

Samartha, S. J., and L. DeSilva, eds. 1979. *Man in nature: Guest or engineer?* Ecumenical Institute for Study and Dialogue, Colombo, Sri Lanka.

Silk, L. 1993. Dangers of slow growth. *Foreign Affairs* 72(1): 173.

Stinson, D. 1993. Sustainable accords? Free trade and the environment. *Latinamerica Press* 25(no. 24, July): 1.

United Nations Development Programme. 1991. *Human development report.* Oxford University Press, New York.

United Nations Development Programme. 1993. *Human development report.* Oxford University Press, New York.

Sustainabilism and Twelve Other "Isms" that Threaten the Environment

ᗄᑯ

NICOLO GLIGO

Introduction

Environmental protection has become fashionable in Latin America and the Caribbean region. We see it in the newspapers and hear about it on radio and television, and it seems that each day brings with it new initiatives aimed at bettering the state of the environment. Seminars and conferences that address environmental issues are being held throughout the region. Governments are busy making innovations in institutional structure so they can better address environmental problems. New non-governmental organizations are being founded constantly, and as they identify and denounce their foes, they contribute significantly to increased awareness about the environment. The business community has declared itself in support of sustainable development, and labor unions, production cooperatives, and consumers are introducing environmental issues into their negotiations and decisions. Church leaders expound from their pulpits and demonstrate through their actions that it is necessary to reconcile human beings and nature. International organizations are reorganizing and refocusing so they can influence the implementation of Agenda 21. Development banks are establishing new conditions related to the goal of sustainable development. Protocols, conventions, and international agreements are framed in an effort to put a stop to macroecological disequilibrium, while new laws and regulations are constantly added to the books. Some consumers are demonstrating that they are unwilling to purchase products that are harmful to the environment, and this concern extends into the international trade arena as well. Finally, mothers' groups, neighborhood associations, and farmers' committees have been known to gather and discuss the state of the environment.

Despite these important and necessary efforts, however, the environmental situation in Latin America is getting worse. The marginal areas of many of the region's big cities are growing, with human settlements continually expanding into areas of low habitability, such as those subject to floods and mudslides. Water pollution, as much organic as industrial, is worsening, and it is getting more and more costly to supply the megalopolises with potable water. Urban waste is accumulating in the streams, riverbanks, and other areas peripheral to the cities. In the majority of cases, the destination of dangerous substances, whose use is increasing at high rates, is unknown. Parks and gardens are disappearing. People are breathing significant doses of dust in suspension, chemical contaminants, and heavy metals that cars and smokestacks have spewed into the air. Cadmium, lead, and other contaminants are accumulating in the soils of urban and suburban areas.

Rural areas of the region are also showing the consequences of a development approach which is decidedly at odds with the environment. Soil erosion is intensifying markedly, with many thousands of hectares of agricultural land washing out to sea each year. Deforestation, and the damage it causes to biodiversity and forest ecosystems, has been maintained at very high rates over the last several decades. Sediment is accumulating in rivers, lakes, and reservoirs, which become contaminated and, in many cases, are losing volume or have disappeared completely. Irrigated soil is suffering the effects of salinization or alkilinization. Non-forest areas of flora and fauna are disappearing as well. Farmers' incomes, meanwhile, cannot ensure an adequate quality of life, and the great majority of the region's farmers are in fact poor or indigent. Finally, processes such as the expansion of agricultural or grazing land, especially in the tropics, continue to exact a high ecological cost.

The question that immediately comes to mind is: How can we explain the contradiction between the efforts being made to improve the environment and the reality of what is happening? The answer is not simple. In Latin America and the Caribbean, the explanation must be sought in a set of factors that are the product of the predominant development approach, itself the object of much debate during the last decade (see Sunkel and Gligo 1981).

The region's predominant development style is one which makes different social actors, whether they are individuals, groups, or businesses, act counter to environmental sustainability. This occurs through people's decisions relating to production, consumption, distribution, etc., or through a philosophical mindset that can encourage the processes of environmental degradation. And while the development style that is *chosen* has an important effect on the environment, we must also deepen our understanding of the effects of spontaneous trends.

The twelve "isms" outlined in this essay can be divided into three groups according to their past, present, and future importance. The first group is comprised of traditional attitudes and positions, which most closely depend on the predominant style of development of the last few decades or on proposals made in response to the predominant style of development. Also included here are the typically traditional attitudes and positions which go beyond the predominant style and which are heirs to certain human values and anti-values. The second group is made up of positions and attitudes based in current events, which is to say that, for various circumstances, they have a strong expression in the present. They are born of current development trends in the countries of the region and, obviously, they can join the traditional group. The third group refers to the future, being understood as those positions which, although already present, will probably gain much more force in the future. It should be noted that there exist many combinations of these positions and attitudes, some openly contradictory, others neutral, but with most of them clearly enforcing anti-environmental stances.

Traditional "Isms"

Apoliticism

This is possibly the attitude that most threatens the environment in Latin America and the Caribbean. Two aspects of the political problem are pertinent to the environment: the first refers to the neutrality of politics and the second to the priorities that follow from that neutrality.

Many people claim that the subject of the environment is politically neutral since environmental deterioration affects all human beings. It is also asserted that coordinated action is necessary, but should be confined to instances where the issue is not "contaminated" politically. Such warnings tend to marginalize environmental topics from the political dialogue by making them seem less urgent. Politically "contaminating" the environment should be the basic strategy to ensure that it is in fact discussed when development decisions are made. Not to do so only encourages opponents to push environmental concerns to the margins of the debate, and to delay or excuse themselves entirely from taking action to protect the environment. At the same time, apoliticism tends to distort the issue by failing to analyze the various costs and benefits to different social groups. There is no doubt that these costs and benefits are shared inequitably across society and that it is precisely this unequal distribution that converts the subject of the environment into one of political importance.

Whenever environmental issues are raised, many politicians respond that, although they recognize the importance of the issues, their priorities are directed toward subjects of greater urgency, such as income, employment, and basic services. The absence of a conception of integrated development, in which the environment is considered an intrinsic part of development and inseparable from the problem of survival, explains the frequent use of this trap and opens up a wide field of discussion at the level of the legislative bodies of the region.

Economism

One of the most common anti-environmental mindsets is the tendency to exaggerate the importance of economics and to try to submit all decisions, without exception, to the rules of this discipline. Economism works against the environment in many ways. Frequently, decision-makers will judge policy and development strategy exclusively on the basis of economic reasoning. Under these rules, many environmental issues are categorized as "externalities" or "market imperfections," which are then ignored. Obviously, a great many environmental goods and resources lie outside the market. Economists have tried to diminish this dark side of their discipline by developing certain methodologies that, to a certain extent, simulate the market for non-market entities. This effort is important, though clearly insufficient. It is possible that some aspects of the darker side can pass into the mist, but there is no doubt that theoretical and methodological problems will persist, a matter which environmental economists are beginning to address.

Ecological economists are working on other, more sophisticated methods, and perhaps their efforts come closer to recognizing the intrinsic value of nature. But these efforts are of a much greater theoretical and methodological complexity. For many, it appears that incorporating the environmental dimension into development can only take place through an ecological economics approach, leaving behind that which cannot be worked into the model. Consequently, economism becomes a trap that is difficult to escarpe from, especially in times of economic crisis, adjustment processes, structural conversion, and market globalization, all of which tend to give an even greater weight to economic decision-makers, the great majority of whom are traditional economists.

Furthermore, economism is biased toward reductionism, the result of trying to place a value on everything. Serious confusion results from this exercise since it mixes moral, ethical, and political decisions with instrumental economic ones. For many, no environmental decision can be made without subjecting it first to an economic cost-benefit analysis. This economicist myopia reflects a lack of understanding of the significance of the environment in its relationship to society and its physical surroundings; what's more, it comes from an ignorance of the laws that govern ecosystem behavior. One need only analyze projects submitted for economic tests to realize the key limitations. In a region where present concerns take precedence over the future, economically measurable environmental factors tend to be unimportant, given that ecological processes generally mature only over the long term. As a consequence, one could justify investment in a project based on economic analysis, even on environmental economic analysis, that in reality turns out to be harmful to the environment in the long run. In this way, economism can promote environmental degradation, and yet it characterizes numerous development programs and projects.

Instrumentalism

Closely linked to the trap of economism is that of instrumentalism—that is, addressing environmental issues by means of a single instrument of environmental evaluation. The most common example is the environmental impact report (EIR). Of course, using such an evaluation instrument, in itself, does not lead to environmental degradation, since any initiative that uses the EIR to the fullest extent would be well received. The negative effect of such instruments occurs in the absence of a concept that development is intrinsically environmental. An example of instrumentalism as a negative phenomenon is where an EIR is demanded, but only after the decision to go ahead with a project or program has been made. That is to say, with project approval already granted, an EIR is ordered to give the project a positive environmental spin. The majority of the time, the scope of the EIR is limited, making the results biased and ensuring that the report's influence will be limited to negotiations at the margins of decision-making. The lack of basic, scientifically reliable information, especially with respect to ecosystem behavior, and the absence of adequate information regarding natural resources frequently creates situations that allow skillful manipulation of the EIR rather than promote its use as a tool for incorporating the environmental dimension into decision-making.

Technocratism

In light of rapid technological advances, this is one of the most commonly used approaches to solving environmental degradation. It tries to convince people that environmental problems can be solved exclusively via technology transfer. Though technology transfer is very important in Latin America and the Caribbean and can be brought to bear on some environmental problems, it must be made clear that most environmental problems in the region are not due to lack of technology, but rather derive from the socioeconomic structures of the countries and, in particular, from the predominant development style of the past few decades.

Technology will be able to eliminate some problems, but we must seek real solutions that are rooted in a profound transformation of production and measures to significantly reduce inequity. The region is familiar with a sufficient number of techniques to begin managing development in a way that is diametrically opposed to the environmentally unsustainable style now in practice. It is already clearly known how not to erode the soil, how not to deforest, how not to pollute the water, how not to catch fish beyond a harvest quota, and how not to pollute the air and the soil. It is known perfectly well how to manage river basins, how to pass regulations to protect the environment, and how to plan human settlements. And more specifically, many sound technologies and techniques have achieved widespread use in the region, including contour farming, drip irrigation, sanitary landfills, primary and secondary sewage treatment, industrial filters, catalytic converters in automobiles, natural meadows, etc. There is practically no limit to the technologies that can already be used to manage the environment significantly better than it is currently being managed. The technocratic trap consists of selling the idea that only through *additional* forms of technology can the region's environmental problems be solved.

Counterpointism

It is a common tactic in the environmental debate to take positions that are counterpoised, generally extreme, and mutually exclusive. This is a technique frequently used by people who do not understand the environment, or by those who, for various reasons, do not wish to take measures to solve environmental problems. The most prevalent example of counterpointism is the familiar development-versus-environment debate. When someone begins the well-known argument that two clear positions exist, one advocating growth without consideration for the environment and the other favoring the environment at the expense of development—and when this same person advocates an intermediate position—the discussion is sure to lead nowhere. The mere fact of proposing, at the end of the twentieth century, such a divisive argument shows that that person has ignored the permanent debate of the last several years. This discourse, sometimes apparently conciliatory, sometimes ingenuous, demonstrates how much alienation exists with respect to this topic.

Other one-sided arguments include the backward-versus-modern and the rural-versus-urban, which portray the backward and the rural as favorable to the environment, and the modern and urban as detrimental. There is nothing more dangerous than falling into this pattern of thinking. One position can be just as favorable or harmful to the environment as the other, depending on the context in which resources are developed. The environmental cause is done a disfavor when it is suggested that it take a turn back down the road toward the past or toward ruralism—and to its death. These examples of counterpointism characteristically denigrate the weak, the backward, and the rural, and allow the modern and the urban to take extreme positions that do not consider the environment.

Something similar occurs in the technology arena when people take sides between hard and soft technologies, between current and appropriate technology, or—in agriculture—between chemicals and organic inputs. For example, in the last instance, nobody is seriously suggesting eliminating agricultural chemicals altogether and replacing them with organic inputs and methods. However, chemicals should be used with respect for ecosystems.

Ecologicism

Ecologicists are people who vigorously opposes development activity of any kind because, in their view, development can be nothing but destructive to the environment. The error in this attitude consists of failing to consider that natural occurrences, too, can cause destruction. It is also a mistake to reject technologies that can improve the environment. Lack of scientific understanding allows certain NGOs to persist in this vein. Ecologicist extremism harms the environmental cause because people or groups that adopt this attitude lose credibility. It is important to note that I have referred to this extremist attitude using the term "ecologicism," and not "ecologism." The former stance lacks a serious basis, while the latter is founded on exhaustive understanding of reality.

In recent years, the ecologicist stance has led people to commit acts of ecoterrorism. This causes conflicts between the ecologicists and environmentalists who are less extremist in their words and actions. It is obvious, furthermore, that many environmental foes shield themselves with these conflicts in order to combat serious and well-founded arguments from more moderate environmentalists. For this reason, ecologicism is one of the more harmful attitudes toward the environment.

Current "Isms"

These have gained much strength in the last few years. Nevertheless, it is necessary to repeat that they do not take the place of the traditional positions and attitudes, but join them.

Institutionalism

Calling for institutional change is very much in vogue now, most notably in the public sector. This is especially true in the aftermath of the 1992 United Nations Conference on the Environment and Development. Many Latin American and Caribbean governments, in diagnosing the status of environmental protection in their countries, have focused on the absence of strong institutions that can deal with environmental problems. Often, a government's response is to create a new institution, while allowing everything else to continue as before. The only difference is that there are now more government officials, more offices, more vehicles, and more budgets.

Sometimes an environmental institution is created for the purpose of *not* doing anything for the environment. Certain governments, confronted by NGO and popular demands, have established agencies that have environmental functions, but which, in practice, are intended to trip up any environmental measure that affects the profits of large industries or restricts capital flow into the country.

A variation on creation of ineffective institutions is not providing budgets for institutional oversight or control, or saddling an organization with bureaucratic functions that divert personnel away from the environmental task at hand.

Juridicism

This "ism" is closely linked to the previous one. It is based in creating laws as a response to pressure to solve environmental problems. Currently, the countries of Latin America and the Caribbean have more than sufficient laws that, if applied, would contribute greatly to improving the environment. The reason for the inefficiency and inefficacy of these laws can be found in the fact that they are not consistent with the predominant style of development now in place.

There are always new issues that need to be dealt with through legislation. The danger lies in passing laws with no intention of doing anything or in passing a framework or general law without dictating specific regulations. Many laws in Latin America are asleep—they are not being put into effect because there are no detailed regulations to implement them. Many more are passed precisely to do the opposite of the apparent objectives, or nothing at all.

In the environmental realm, one has to be especially careful about specific policies that appear on the lawbooks. For example, a law might exempt a region from a requirement to conduct environmental impact reports (EIRs) when no basic studies of ecosystems exist. If lawmakers knew full well that no such information is available, here is obviously a position that encourages environmental degradation. Or a law that requires an EIR only when a forest project is over 500 hectares, when it is known that practically none of the projects will be above this size, also has anti-environmental effects.

Privaticism

The economic adjustment agenda that has been promoted throughout the region in recent years has unleashed intense privatization policies. Every country has in some measure initiated privatization strategies that have passed not only production, distribution, and service companies into private hands, but important public natural resources as well.

This process, if undertaken without establishing proper protective measures, conflicts with environmental concerns for the following reasons. In the first place, certain types of environmental goods are social, or public, goods; for this reason, their use should be regulated by society. The privatization process, in the majority of cases, disregards this principle. Privatization of beaches for the tourist industry is an excellent example. Here, most investment has gone into projects that are damaging to coastal ecosystems; what's more, the quality of life for local people has declined because they are often excluded from the benefits of these projects.

The second environmental problem is produced by the different time horizons used for private and social purposes. This is seen in privatization efforts that do not consider conservation since ecosystems mature on a much longer term. This happens, for example, when public lands with fragile ecosystems are passed over to private interests. It is possible to verify on these occasions that a privatized social good has become an ecosystem harvest.

A third problem is produced in many of the privatized social services when proper foresight is not exercised. Services to root out plagues, diseases, parasites, rats, etc. in many cities of the region have been privatized. Effective campaigns have been undertaken at the level of the productive unit and the individual family, but they leave a great gap at the higher level of neighborhoods and other localities that necessarily have to be dealt with in order for these to be adequate campaigns.

A fourth aspect, which has a significant anti-environmental effect as well, is associated with the privatization of processes that use only one natural resource within an ecosystem without considering secondary resources and interactive processes connected to it. A clear example comes from the numerous logging operations which harvest trees without considering the conservation of other resources such as the fauna and the herbaceous flora and the management of the forest's water supply.

In general the privatization processes in the region, in only taking into account economic objectives and not taking precautions to protect the environment, are leading to significant environmental degradation.

Future "Isms"

These refer to processes that are predicted to intensify in the future. They have already begun to appear with some force, but I see their weight continuing to increase in the future.

Worldism

The tendency to analyze and contribute resources only to the largest problems on the level of planetary destabilization often leads to neglecting the priority environmental problems of Latin America and the Caribbean. This attitude could be considered as traditional, given its frequent use over the last two decades, but it is likely that it will gain even more force in the future. People in developed countries are more occupied than are Latin Americans with problems such as global warming, the thinning of the ozone layer, the loss of biodiversity, and the pollution of international waters. These problems will surely alter the ecosystem of the earth as a whole, but they are far from having immediate harmful effects, as they will certainly have in the next fifty to hundred years. The urgencies of daily survival and the low quality of life of many Latin Americans cause them to dismiss long-term problems and focus exclusively on the short-term ones. Consequently, regional environmental priorities—such as erosion, the disappearance of topsoil, management of urban waste, the inhabitability of marginal urban areas, deforestation, water pollution, etc.—are totally different from those of the industrialized world.

The fundamental conflict arises over assignment of resources. It was clear at the United Nations Conference on Environment and Development in 1992 that the position of the northern countries was going to prevail. Agreements to channel international aid through the Global Environment Facility consolidated the position of the developed countries in opposition to that of the less developed countries. As a result, scarce international resources will not be assigned to solve environmental problems of priority to Latin America and the Caribbean, except in cases where the projects undertaken are of concern to everyone, such as biodiversity.

The situation is complicated by the fact that many researchers in science and technology have shifted their priorities from the national to the international arena in order to attract funds, thus abandoning national environmental priorities. For this reason, there is not enough research being done on such important topics as the physical make-up of national natural resources, the advance of soil erosion, behavior and attributes of diverse ecosystems, urban environment, destruction of forest ecosystems, and expansion of grazing lands.

NGOism

In many countries—both developed and less developed— civil society is not incorporated into environmental decision-making. This has led to increased participation on the part of non-governmental organizations (NGOs) in environmental debates. Furthermore, pressure for more debate has increased with proliferation of environmental groups, umbrella organizations, and networks.

The proliferation of these organizations is associated with increased numbers of international meetings, some of which can present a dilemma for participating countries. That is, what direction will be imposed upon those countries through control of financial resources? The trend is toward creating a kind of clientelism that puts limits on their independence.

In another area, there is a trend toward transferring responsibility for environmental activities from government agencies to NGOs. Many of these transfers take place without adequately evaluating the effectiveness of the NGO in question. This becomes an anti-environmental trap when responsibilities delegated to a poorly chosen NGO destroy the credibility of a project that could have been handled perfectly well by a better qualified group.

Bilateralism

After drastic periods of economic adjustment, many countries in the region are now trying to create bilateral free trade agreements with the United States. The North American Free Trade Agreement (NAFTA) and agreements with Chile, as well as contacts initiated by Argentina, show clear advances in this direction.

All of these agreements need to include clauses dealing with the environment. The clauses should cover such issues as border problems; management of shared river basins and protected areas; research into common environmental problems; consumer protection as it relates to traded products, particularly food products; and dumping and similar practices that result from overuse of natural resources.

While these bilateral agreements have potential to provide many benefits, it is possible that negative aspects that are difficult to manage will also arise. The first relates to the fact that United States environmental priorities differ somewhat from those of its neighbors to the south. The United States is primarily concerned with pollution, while Latin America and the Caribbean view the conservation of natural resources as a more relevant problem.

This leads to a second issue that free trade agreements could provoke: Some North American products made with the latest technology and large economies of scale will interrupt Latin American markets as they displace locally made products. This process could be harmful to maintaining biodiversity because it could lead to elimination of local crops containing great genetic differentiation.

The third problem, which is already in evidence, is that the United States is pressuring other countries to adopt pro-environmental measures based on U.S. models of institution-building and law-making. These models are not necessarily suited to solving the problems of Latin America and the Caribbean; instead, they could distract public attention or replace other, more effective measures.

Sustainabilism

This approach to the problem of environmental degradation will tend to take on much more force in the future due to the increasingly frequent and overly casual use of the term *sustainable development.*

That the term was coined with a generalized ignorance of what it means has allowed many social actors to adopt a cosmetic approach to development projects that does not assure substantial changes in their treatment of environmental problems. Everyone subscribes to sustainable development, and many claim to practice it. The force of the environmental movement can be neutralized by the apparent efforts of everyone to follow the path of sustainable development. But to declare one's support for sustainable development is not the same as actually practicing it. Herein lies the confusion or—in many cases—the manipulation. The panacea of sustainable development is brandished as a new standard by those who do not really want to change the current pattern of development. They declare that through sustainable development they are seeking equity and environmental sustainability, all the while adhering to a program of unequal and environmentally unsustainable development.

This approach could channel needed support away from serious environmental measures. It is well known that the transition to an environmentally sustainable pattern of development requires more than cosmetic or marginal measures. And yet, there is a danger that just such a superficial approach may be taken in implementing Agenda 21. If misused or misinterpreted, the concept of sustainable development—instead of contributing positively to the environment—will become yet another factor in worldwide environmental degradation.

NOTE

This article was translated, with changes, from the Spanish version, "Posiciones y Actitudes de Involución Ambiental en América Latina y el Caribe."

REFERENCES

Sunkel, O., and N. Gligo. 1981. Estilos de desarrollo y medio ambiente en América Latina [Styles of development and the environment in Latin America]. In Fondo de Cultura Económica, Lecture Series 36, vol. 2. Mexico City.

PART II

Measuring Progress

Monitoring for Sustainability

CR

ERIC RODENBURG

Information is the essential raw material of policy formulation and decision-making. To achieve sustainable development, policy-makers will need to know where they are starting from; where it is they want to go; and when or whether they have diverged from their planned path between the two points.

Setting sustainability goals, assessing the current state of the environment, and monitoring the conditions and trends of relevant environmental sectors are information-hungry activities. What is more, these activities are poorly fed by existing national and international institutions. There are no global programs that adequately monitor the conditions and trends of any environmental sector, and such programs rarely exist at regional or national scales. Yet, the quality of policies to achieve sustainable development depends on just that type of basic information. Unfortunately, when it comes to the environment and natural resources, the information base is often of poor quality.

Monitoring

By 2020, the earth's human population will have grown from 5.3 billion to more than 8 billion people. The implications of this growth for the environment and natural resource base are sobering. For instance, the rate of loss of tropical forests, which accelerated by fifty percent during the 1980s, could continue to speed up, threatening their existence. Soil fertility, already severely compromised by erosion and overgrazing, could decline further due to the proliferation of unsustainable agricultural practices. Coastal oceans, already under severe pressure, will have to bear further insults from expanded fisheries and pollution.

In light of these and other challenges, responsible planetary management will not be easy. National, regional, and global environmental and resource problems resist facile solutions and may require unprecedented international cooperation. To manage the planet's environment rationally, we need a sound understanding of earth system processes, an accurate measure of the baseline conditions of the earth's resources, and an efficient system for monitoring and reporting on changes in resource condition or quality. Decision-makers need these three kinds of information at a local and national level to manage local resources and allocate scarce human and financial resources. At the global level, the information is needed to do the same for the global commons in the context of the international community.

The subject of environmental monitoring and the development of environmental indicators has been a special interest of the Resource and Environmental Information Program (REIP) of the World Resources Institute (WRI). This emphasis has grown out of REIP's experience gathering information and data for the *World Resources* report series and a series of *Environmental Almanacs,* contributing to the United Nations Environment Programme's *Environmental Data Report,* creating an electronic environmental database, delving into the available scientific and international data sets, and documenting the need for global environmental monitoring in the WRI whitepaper *Eyeless in Gaia* (Rodenburg 1992). These activities have taught us that there is surprisingly little quality data with which to assess the conditions and trends of important environmental sectors. At the same time, we have become convinced that there is incredible demand for high-quality data with which to inform policy-makers, decision-makers, and resource managers. It has also convinced us of the need to develop indicators that can communicate complex findings on the conditions, trends, and impacts in important environmental sectors to policy-makers, as well as to the public, so that they can act or demand action. We have in place projects that aim to promote the creation or reordering of institutions that could fund and carry out data collection, analysis, and information dissemination in support of environmental monitoring. A further aim is to develop indicators to communicate the results of that monitoring to decision-makers so they can pursue sustainability.

Information is the essential raw material of policy formulation and decision-making. The scope and accuracy of information available to those who make decisions determines to a great degree the quality of their policies and decisions. Moreover, in the absence of information, mistaken decisions will be made or the question of necessary decisions may not even arise. With the exception of the World Weather Watch (which successfully informs decision-makers at all scales) and the possible exception of the Global Atmosphere Watch, there are few programs that successfully monitor environmentally relevant questions on a global scale. Indeed, much of what we call monitoring is in reality just a one-time assessment, at best an inventory, of an important resource. The Food and Agriculture Organization's 1990 tropical forest assessment (published only just in 1993) is a case in point.

What is monitoring? As used here, monitoring has a policy orientation. While it is scientific, monitoring is not science. Science is research into process—how an ecosystem works, for example. Monitoring looks into state and changes in that state: What is the state of a given ecosystem, and how is it changing over time? Science, generally, is original research with a conclusion; monitoring is ongoing. Finally, results of science are published leisurely in peer-reviewed journals; results of monitoring, on the other hand, are dispatched and used immediately.

Monitoring is the institutionalized and ongoing observation of the conditions and trends in a target sector to answer the specific information needs of a policy-maker, policy-shaper, or resource manager.

Monitoring for sustainability requires the creation of an *information* system. In its ideal form, such a system includes: identified users; a problem focus based on the user's information needs; the collection of data at a temporal and spatial scale appropriate to the problem; a framework for analysis appropriate to the problem; data availability; reporting requirements; and a reporting function to the users, who in turn respond to the reports and fine tune their information needs.

Without each of these parts, explicitly denoted where possible, an information system will fail to meet the information needs of the actors

---

Figure 1

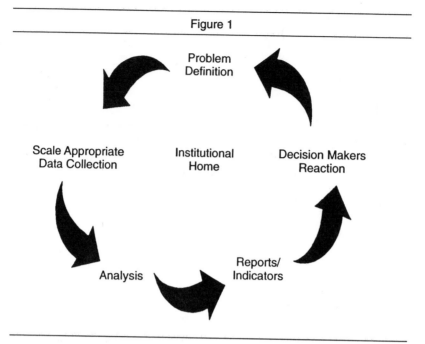

---

on the environmental stage. While all of the functions of an information system need not be centralized in some institutional home, someone must be paying attention and reporting on a regular basis to identified users if it is to be a monitoring system. The primary requirement is that paying attention—analyzing and reporting—be part of an institution's mandate, so that the monitoring function will continue beyond any individual and have a lifetime as long as the institution's.

An example of an effective monitoring system is the Famine Early Warning System (FEWS) of the U.S. Agency for International Development. FEWS has now been in place for eight years and another five-year plan is in development. FEWS pays attention to the potential for food emergencies in various African countries, using a variety of physical and socioeconomic data. The personnel of FEWS come and go, but the institutional mandate to pay attention remains.

On the other hand, various proposed and implemented coastal monitoring systems in Europe have had operational lifetimes of less than a decade, as original researchers, resources, and enthusiasm move on. In the United States only one of the National Oceanic and Atmospheric Administration's coastal monitoring programs (the Mussel Watch) has reached the ten-year mark; it may continue.

Problem Definition

A surprising number of information activities have no defined audience, except to serve otherwise-undefined "decision-makers." This is a technique scientists use to make their work appear relevant and therefore attractive for funding purposes. Several large U.S. government activities fall into this category, as does UNEP's Global Environment Monitoring System—Air Quality (GEMS-AIR).

In contrast, the Dutch environmental information system explicitly serves parliamentarians. Local air quality monitoring systems might serve public health officials, elected leaders, or the public.

Whatever the audience, its members' needs must define the entire system. They must define the problem, data collection and analysis, and reporting. This is extremely rare. The handful of examples includes FEWS, FAO's Global Information and Early Warning System, and the World Conservation Monitoring Centre. The latter is noteworthy for having assembled reports from members of the Convention on International Trade in Endangered Species of Wild Flora and Fauna (CITES) in order to observe and adjust the flow of protected species.

Users' information needs must sometimes be recast for greater precision or to reflect real-world constraints (financial or personnel limits) and real-world problems of data acquisition. A question such as, "Where are endangered species threatened?" might be more realistically pursued in the form of a surrogate question, "Where is potential habitat threatened?" Furthermore, the problem and its desired solution must be phrased in terms that are concrete enough to act upon; they should not dissolve into vague mists of "sustainable" or "healthy." Specific targets and goals (which might, in fact, have political origins) are the best means for making a problem operational. Examples of specific questions are: How far is a nation away from protecting at least ten percent of each of its biomes? How much land remains in each biome? What is its rate of conversion?

Having accepted that the type of information gathered should be determined by the end-user's needs leaves one question unanswered, however: If decision-makers receive this custom-fit information, does it in fact make a difference? In other words, does monitoring do any good? In the case of FEWS, decision-makers are forced to consider and act on FEWS information. If they ignore the information and a food emergency occurs, they will be held responsible and perhaps lose their jobs. The existence of information can therefore force a response—

even if that response is to deny the relevance of the information. The existence of information allows outsiders to second guess the actions of decision-makers, a guarantee that information will be used.

Figure 2

Problem Definition

- Who is the audience?
- What do they want to know?
- What can a monitoring system tell them?
- Why do they want to know?/Can they react?

Scale-Appropriate Data Collection

Data collection must have a fine-enough spatial resolution to capture the problem being investigated. A country's agricultural production might be increasing, for example, at the same time that locust infestations are creating a food emergency in particular districts. Flooding might threaten certain narrow riverine ecosystems while larger grassland areas flourish. On the other hand, it is possible to miss the greater meaning of local change by failing to cast a wide-enough net. Meaning can be lost in the "invisible place." Too small a scale of data collection could result in failure to put local coral reef bleaching into the context of a global problem. New disease outbreaks might not be seen in their regional ecological context, or the disappearance of frogs might not be seen as a global problem related to increased ultraviolet radiation.

Data collection must also have a fine-enough temporal resolution. An example of inappropriate temporal scale would be an annual survey that misses migratory species in its counts. Data collection must also be reiterative and long-term if trends are not to be lost in the "invisible present." Had Charles Keeling not begun the continuing monitoring of carbon dioxide concentrations in 1959, we might still be arguing about whether increases in the atmosphere have actually occurred.[1]

Data collection must also be cost-effective relative to the problem. Regardless of its humanitarian purposes, the FEWS system was invented to save the United States government money. The system permitted food to be pre-positioned using slow, inexpensive transport; in this way, crises were avoided and, also important, so was the need to use expensive transport such as helicopters. An appropriate level of funding is something less than the cost of not doing monitoring at all.

Finally, the technological scale must be appropriate to the problem. Why use satellite remote sensing if aerial surveys will do? Why use a dedicated technical staff for reporting on reef conditions if volunteers such as scuba tour operators can report as accurately? While computerized geographic information systems are attractive, a particular problem might be just as effectively addressed using mylar overlays on paper maps, at a great savings in financial and human resources.

Figure 3

Scale Appropriate Data Collection

• What is the appropriate spatial scale?
• What is the appropriate temporal scale?
• What are the costs of collecting information and the costs of not collecting information?
• What is the appropriate level of technology?

Analysis

Developing a conceptual framework for analyzing and reporting on the data is difficult and sometimes more art than science. The result of any analysis must be reported in a way that makes sense to decision-makers. Thus, it would do little good to analyze geographically referenced data using an apolitical or an a-ecological grid system since decision-makers must deal with real borders, both artificial (e.g., districts, counties, states, and nations) and natural (e.g., watersheds, wetlands, forests, and estuaries). Analysis must include those variables that not only measure a problem, but can be controlled by users. Measurements of disappearing fish populations are irrelevant to a policy-maker who needs to control land use and the conversion of wetlands.

In the ideal world, both data and analysis should be transparent and open for criticism. If it is to be believed, analysis must be replicable. Mere assertions of the existence or nonexistence of a problem are not politically viable; nor are they intellectually honest. By extension, in the ideal world analysis should be seen to be politically neutral— independent of established interests. The real world is not always so. The U.S. Forest Service assessments of its own resources and management strategies, for example, have been widely doubted. Intelligence agencies would not make good monitoring institutions because, culturally, they are unable to be open or transparent and they are not perceived to be politically neutral.

Figure 4

Analysis

• Is there a framework for analysis?

• Is it transparent in data and method?

• Is it independent?

Reports and Indicators

The reporting function is the heart of any monitoring system. How can people act on analysis of the conditions and trends of a resource unless they are told? Yet there are many information systems that either do not report their findings or report them so late as to be irrelevant. In its first phase, GEMS/WATER, for example, was always four or five years behind in reporting its information on water quality. No decision-maker can be served by that kind of delay. The failure to report is a result of the failure to have a defined target audience with time-sensitive and operational information needs.

Reports must be accessible to users. Maps of areas vulnerable to food emergencies is one of the report forms of FEWS. The organization publishes a bulletin every ten days to keep decision-makers up-to-date on agricultural progress. A year-end "Harvest Assessment" provides both an overview of the situation and a possible evaluation of FEWS performance.

Indexes and indicators are a form of presenting data that policy-makers can make relevant through use. For example, for all its failings, the GNP figure is an indicator that policy-makers and the public use to measure national economic performance.

Figure 5

Reports and Indicators

• How will results be disseminated?

• How will complex relationships be made accessible to the target audience?

• How will technical results be made policy relevant?

Indicators

Indicators are special data sets or transformed data that become essential information for policy-makers, policy-shapers, and the public. Indicators are an area of considerable ongoing research as developers attempt to provide the minimum information that will tell a complex technical story to a non-technical audience. The obvious use and success of economic indicators has led to a call for environmental and sustainability indicators. There are essentially two kinds of indicators: rhetorical indicators that are meant to gain attention, and policy-relevant indicators intended for management purposes. For monitoring systems, only the latter is important.

Even though they are scientifically based, policy-relevant indicators must communicate essential information to non-scientific audiences. WRI's Greenhouse Gas Index, for instance, assembles information on the national emissions of several greenhouse gases and puts them all into common terms, weighted by their greenhouse-heating effect. Users of this index learn of the relative national and per capita responsibilities for future climate change, as well as the relative importance of the different greenhouse gases.

Indicators are effective because they facilitate comparisons, either implicitly or explicitly. The greenhouse index provides a comparison between countries. The Dutch government sets explicit goals and targets (which are mileposts on the way to a goal) for their indices. This allows for assessments of policy performance. Indicators facilitate action because the comparison between a baseline figure and some threshold measure, goal, or target provides a direction for policy.

Figure 6

Indicators

- Reliable statistical measure.

- Measurable in a comparable fashion over time and space.

- Its changes can be assessed against a scientifically valid norm, standard, or baseline.

- It bears a clearly defined social goal (that might be a particular vision of sustainability).

The Target Audience

Identifying who will use the results of a monitoring system defines the system. Such a system must serve people with real responsibilities, who need the information the system supplies to do their jobs better, and who can redefine their needs, and the system, as the problem changes.

This identification returns the circle to problem definition and reemphasizes the integrated nature of a monitoring system. Such a system cannot be an empty data-collection exercise or scientific research into process, although these might inform the analytical process and even be the source of data for analysis and reporting. While environmental monitoring systems are still rare, without them and the information they generate, decision-makers will continue to fly blindly, guessing at a sustainable path through complex environmental terrain.

Figure 7

The Target Audience

• Do they have operational or policy shaping/making responsibilities?

• What can they do with monitoring results?

• How can they redefine the problem?

NOTES

1. Charles Keeling of the Scripps Institution of Oceanography, University of California, La Jolla, California 92093, USA, has been monitoring and reporting CO_2 concentrations at Mauna Loa, Hawaii continuously since 1959. This is the longest of modern concentration records. See WRI/UNDP/UNEP 1994, p.366 for the annual concentrations, 1965-1992.

REFERENCES

Rodenburg, E. 1992. *Eyeless in Gaia*. World Resources Institute, Resources and Environmental Information Program White Paper. WRI, Washington, D.C.

United Nations Environment Programme. 1993. *Environmental data report: 1993-94*. Blackwell, Oxford.

World Resources Institute. 1993. *The 1994 information please environmental almanac*. Houghton Mifflin, Boston.

WRI/UNDP/UNEP. 1994. *World resources 1994-95: A guide to the global environment*. Oxford University Press, New York.

Toward Environmentally Sustainable Development: Measuring Progress

cg

JOHN C. O'CONNOR

Introduction

The World Bank is considering producing an annual report on global progress toward environmentally sustainable development (ESD).[1] The report's empirical base will be the many strands of indicator work in progress at the Bank and elsewhere, including a slowly growing body of studies on natural resource accounting and exploratory work on monitoring land quality, biodiversity indicators, etc. The options for presenting such information range from non-controversial tabulations for the separate strands to syntheses that can be controversial.

The World Resources Institute's *World Resources Report* is an admirable example of what can be done with an encyclopedic approach. With modest resources and relatively little controversy, the World Bank could imitate the WRI *Report*. The difference between the Bank's version and the WRI *Report* would be the way the Bank recasts information to make it more meaningful to non-experts. Examples of such refinements by the Bank are the air and water quality graphs in the 1992 *World Development Report; The World Bank Atlas* (which now has

separate sections on the economy, the people, and the environment);
and the *Environmental Data Book,* which targets secondary school students in particular.

With a modest increase in resources but more risk of controversy,
the World Bank's ESD report could press the limits of current thinking
by cobbling initiatives on indicators, methodologies, and concepts into
a tentative, loosely analytical "report card." At a minimum, this form of
the report would yield broad-gauge, baseline estimates for major country groupings (e.g., separate estimates for low, middle, and high income
economies) and suggest which indicators are robust enough to be reported at the national level. This would help flag priorities for further
data work, across topics and with due regard to decision-makers' interest in summary, performance-oriented measures.

It should be emphasized that this effort to synthesize the available
information in no way signals a lessening of World Bank support for
topic- and country-specific studies; nor is the Bank losing interest in international efforts to devise guidelines for environmental and sustainable development indicators. Indeed, as discussed in Section 1, below,
this new task should complement those two areas of interest by improving feedback between those working on international guidelines and
those working on databases tailored to meet country needs.

Section 2 suggests a possible framework for the report card, which
was created by cobbling together existing initiatives. Table 1 gives a
tentative example of the report card that could be available by the
World Bank's Second Annual Conference on ESD, in September 1994.
Further iterations will surely be required, and only a limited number of
entries are discussed in much detail below. Section 3 considers how
the report card approach could help communication between those trying to complete various parts of the whole and those more concerned
with broad goals and knowing whether actions are being taken to attain
those goals. Section 4 notes practical considerations, including the key
question of what can realistically be expected from the first set of ESD
indicators.

1. Recent Developments in Indicator Work

A separate paper by the author, *Accounting for the Environment* (World
Bank 1993) catalogs topic- and country-specific studies expected to
provide the empirical base for the Bank's first ESD report. That cata-

loguing process revealed that there has been a surge in basic monitoring work in recent years. Although some areas have been neglected, and certainly many others could benefit from more detailed work, the main problem now seems to be information overload, rather than a lack of basic data. Despite this overload, decisions about the choice of what to do, and where, may not be as haphazard as it sometimes seems. Monitoring patterns are beginning to emerge, although they do not always conform with the expectations inherent in initial work on international guidelines for environmental and sustainable development indicators.

This discrepancy between expectations and observed monitoring patterns has led to a subtle but profound change in the type of documents that emerge from international meetings of statistical experts concerned with monitoring the environment and sustainable development. In the past, experts produced ever-expanding lists of items to be monitored and then worked on organizing these lists into accounting schemes. Now attention has shifted toward analytical clustering of items around issues, which entail using models of natural processes and how humans impinge on them. While there are many interesting variations on the theme, the consensus now seems to favor "work from the most general to the specific—from the whole to its components and back again"(Hodge 1993, 32).

This change in emphasis can be explained in part by recognition of "the need to understand development of environmental statistics largely as a task involving coordination of a variety of data sources that exist outside statistical agencies"(European Conference of Statisticians 1993, paragraph 11). The new emphasis is explained also by the increasingly complex problems of spatial referencing since "different scale levels may be considered ranging from global to drainage basins to cities"(van der Born and others 1993, 81). Finally, more explicit attention is being given to the need to help today's decision-makers. As Eurostat (1993, 2) put it, "The conflict between the various goals of society, such as a better environment, employment for all, and material well-being, must be solved in a rational and democratic way. This requires detailed information on the *costs and benefits of policy options.*"

When policy relevance becomes the touchstone for developing indicators, new ways of clustering statistics into indicators emerge. A particular indicator (that is, a particular grouping of statistics) may prove better suited to a given policy situation than another. It matters, for example, if one is at the problem identification stage, the policy development stage (identifying solutions), or the monitoring implementation stage (problem control). Different indicators may be required for different countries, since it is difficult to compare a single indicator across nations that are at markedly different points along the policy continuum described above (UNEP 1993). Furthermore, "we have to recognize that an environmental *problem* consists of a physical phenomena *plus* an evaluation of this phenomena by society."(Eurostat 1993, 4). Distinct indicators are therefore needed for monitoring sources of environmental pressure, the state of the environment, and human responses. This is known as the pressure-state-response (PSR) approach.

On a more practical level, countries will also differ in terms of the measurable proxy indicators that are available today, regardless of consensus on first-choice indicators. And, looking ahead to the special problems of spatial acuity, there can be pronounced differences within, as well as among, nations in terms of how much refinement any specific indicator really needs. The result is more a cascade than catalog of indicators.

However, according to experts (Eurostat 1993, 4), "the formulation of a rational policy will not be possible if we remain on the level of several hundred *physical* indicators, such as SO_2 emissions or household water waste volumes." They conclude that to "evaluate the benefits of measures, the reduction of pressures must be given in a common unit." Others voice a related concern that "a conceptual model is needed as a framework for designing environmental and sustainable development indicators"(UNEP 1993). Organizations such as the World Resources Institute that have been working on indicators for many years are finding that "essential insight came from grouping potential environmental measures into categories reflecting the context (political, economic, and environmental) in which they might be used and realizing that each group of measures could be combined to form a comprehensive environmental indicator"(WRI 1993).

Finding a common unit is not simple, but consensus seems to be emerging, among experts, on three alternative branches of composition. Most experts favor preparing results according to each branch, where possible; in this way, official statistics need not be based entirely on one particular school of thought. One branch may be called *monetization,* which would use values such as market prices, willingness-to-pay, and remediation costs to determine the weighting of specific items. The second is *expert assessments,* where scientists are asked to devise technical weighting schemes, such as reducing phosphates and nitrates to eutrophication equivalents (see, for example, Adriaanse 1993, 41-45) or default back to preference for monitoring a single item (e.g., phosphates), which is tantamount to a weighting scheme that gives a zero value to all but one item. The third branch is *compliance with official policy goals,* with initial work tending to give equal weight to each issue (combining them based on "distance-to-goal"), although alternative weighting schemes can be tested. This is much like the comparison of alternative monetization schemes.

Against this background, the recent meeting of the UNEP/UNSTAT Consultative Expert Group concluded:

> The indicators should reflect the interface between social, economic, and environmental issues. More attention needed to be given to the symbiosis between statistics and models. Statistics alone are not enough for decision-making and must be supplemented by textual and geographically referenced information...
>
> The role of indicators as signals for action was stressed. The usefulness of models for indicator development, interpretation, for exploration of future implications, and as a means for estimating missing data was noted. (Eurostat 1993)

A similar reaction emerged when an early draft of this paper was discussed by the World Bank's external Advisory Group on Environmentally Sustainable Development, which met in October 1993. While not in favor of distilling all ESD concerns into a few "magic numbers," the Group considered aggregation to be desirable in principle, no matter how hard it may be in practice. Its members therefore generally favored moving toward so-called composite indicators, while not losing sight of the power of one or two "gripping" indicators.

The Advisory Group suggested some conceptual limits to the aggregation process. First, composite indicators are plausible for components of a whole, like the summation of production activities across a given economic sector such as agriculture, but they are not plausible for causally linked items. An example of linked items are production and the pollution it may generate. In this case, a model might give the appropriate mathematical expression of the pollution. Second, distinct measures might be required for studying sensitivity (i.e., how a natural process reacts to a particular pressure) and stability (i.e., when and why a system leaves equilibrium). It was agreed that the World Bank's work on composite indicators would not only take these points into account but also develop and document a more complete explanation of the limits to such compilations.

II. Devising a Tentative "Sustainability Matrix"

For practical reasons, the World Bank's initial work on the empirical base for the ESD Report uses the pressure-state-response (PSR) approach to descriptive environmental indicators developed by the Organisation for Economic Co-operation and Development. As summarized in a recent synthesis report (OECD 1993), the PSR approach offers conceptual guidance on how to describe relationships between *pressures* of human activities (in areas of energy, transport, industry, and agriculture), the *state* of the environment (air, water, land, and natural resources), and *responses* by economic and environmental agents (administrations, households, enterprises, and the international community). OECD has gone further and used the approach to organize indicators that are widely available at present and then apply them to fourteen issue categories: climate change, ozone layer depletion, eutrophication, acidification, toxic contamination, urban environmental quality, biodiversity and landscape, waste, water resources, forest resources, fish resources, soil degradation, and general (which includes population growth, structure of energy supply, and industrial and agricultural production). The organization has also suggested and documented a systematic approach to statistical improvements for each issue area.

World Bank experts on each issue are being asked to adapt these issue categories to their understanding of what is feasible for developing countries. In some areas covered by OECD, e.g., urban environmental quality, the Bank may be able to provide a more articulate statement. Also, the Bank will have to consider additional items of special importance to developing economies, notably, subsoil minerals. And while OECD takes some aspects of the global commons such as climate change into account, the World Bank may also need to consider this category more generally (e.g., adding oceans). But first, given the interdisciplinary nature of ESD, the applicability of the PSR framework to economic and social indicators deserves attention.

Incorporating Economic and Social Concerns

The World Bank publishes volumes of economic and social indicators. Some volumes focus on particular topics, with *Social Indicators of Development* and *World Population Projections* being the most relevant to the ESD theme. Others, like the *Atlas, World Development Indicators,* and *World Tables,* are limited only by the broad interests of the Bank and give subsets of economic, social, and environmental indicators elaborated elsewhere. However, subsets tend to be chosen by specialists using essentially the criteria applied for topical publications of what is most important for the individual field of study. Something more is needed for the ESD report.

Ideally, a harmonized scheme of economic, social, and environmental issues would guide selection of indicators. In practice, this is a long-term endeavor, with problems in each field compounded by those of interdisciplinary efforts, as experts in each field grope toward a shared sense of standards for areas of common interest. Some, notably economists, exchange information through highly structured conventions; for them, something like the United Nations' System of Economic and Environmental Accounts (SEEA) represents a significant outreach to other fields. However, such a system may seem like "topical imperialism" to experts in other fields, who are accustomed to conveying empirical work with more contextual documentation and less reliance on formal conventions.

In this sense, the PSR framework may be seen as an outreach by those who prefer contextual reporting to those who want tabulated data backed by rigorous conventions. The approach is more a typology of indicators than it is a description or model of environmental processes. The approach is neutral about how any ecological process works or what the consequences of human interactions will be. The framework just says that the state we observe is subject to pressures and elicits societal responses designed to reduce pressures and improve the state. At this level of abstraction, the same typology ought to apply to economic or sociological processes as well as to environmental processes. Recasting all indicators to fit the PSR framework is thus a means of reaching those who approach ESD along the environmental path, who may be more comfortable with the PSR than with the SEEA framework.

The task of recasting economic and social indicators to fit the PSR framework raises some questions that only appear to be simple. For example, how many issues need to be added to the framework? OECD has reduced the ecological domain, with the least articulate conventions, to about a dozen issues; the other domains should be more compact still. For the sake of argument, let us assume that we need the same number of socioeconomic indicators as we have ecological indicators—that is, twelve. The economics aspect, which has been articulated extensively elsewhere, should require the least space in the tentative ESD sustainability matrix. Therefore, we might assign four economics-related issues (leaving eight for the social domain); three of which might be those dealt with in national accounts (production, expenditure, and income), with labor being the fourth.

Even with these simplifying assumptions, it is not obvious which measure should represent the state of production in a PSR framework. Presumably, a "green" national accounting aggregate, similar to the Environmentally Adjusted Product that SEEA is working on, should be the centerpiece of the ESD sustainability matrix. However, it will be years before many developing countries can provide such measures according to the SEEA framework, and the existing system of national accounts is not well-suited to the purpose.

Thus, while continuing to support medium-term efforts to arrive at a "green" national accounting aggregate, the World Bank is experimenting with shortcut methods that make two adjustments to the aggregate it reports most frequently—namely, the Gross National Product per capita.[2] The first adjustment involves accounting for consumption of capital by reporting Net National Product (NNP) instead of GNP. Comparable estimates of depreciation of produced assets have been generated for most countries. Moving from principle to practice for the well-established concept of allowance for consumption of capital— that is, making the switch from GNP to NNP—seems to be a prerequisite for broadening the concept further to encompass degradation and depletion of natural resources (say, from NNP to NNP'). The second adjustment involves giving *in situ* natural resources some non-zero value, whether as another allowance for capital consumption or to reflect more accurately their role as intermediate inputs. The results are tentatively called NNP' to distinguish them from the more rigorous SEEA efforts to estimate Environmentally Adjusted Product.

Much can be done to refine these shortcut methods and to develop similar methods for other issues—notably, for so-called defensive expenditures, such as expenditures on air and water clean-up. However, it is not clear that such refinements will make a big difference. Preliminary results suggest that if NNP' were to be used in place of GNP, countries' positions relative to each other for levels and trends would not be altered as significantly as one might have imagined—even when a rather high value is assigned to *in situ* natural resources. This does not lessen the case for showing NNP' in the ESD report, but it does suggest that the aggregate is so broad that it is fairly insensitive to specific ESD concerns like depletion of natural resources.

Finally, it is not certain that income is the best variable to study in the first place. The latest theoretical results are suggesting that an adjusted concept of saving may in fact be more relevant for such purposes. In effect, drawing down the stock of natural resources can be likened to borrowing from abroad; it is a means of closing the gap between genuine domestic saving and investment (which might be interpreted more broadly to include investment in the stock of knowledge via education). The analogy to foreign borrowing, and the relevance for analyzing saving, may help environmentalists understand economists' preoccupation with what can be expressed in monetary terms (discount premiums are an example). Priorities for further work on national accounts might need to be reconsidered if it were agreed that saving, rather than income, is the key variable. To summarize, the NNP' could potentially serve as the pivot-point of the economic section of the ESD report card, but there are theoretical questions to be worked out first.

In addition to determining an appropriate representation for the state, we need to consider what to qualify as pressures on production and where to look for society's responses. One line of reasoning, pursued in Table 1, depicts pressure as the demand for inputs. An economic response to this pressure would be improved production efficiency. In this example, then, environmental pressure can be monitored by looking at input-output ratio(s), and societal response would be evaluated by the productivity of produced assets.[3]

Even such tentative answers to questions about applying the PSR framework are likely to suggest ways in which conventional economic and social indicators might be refined or recast. The idea is to have indicators that make more sense in an issues-oriented PSR framework. Something like OECD's plan for environmental indicators (see as an example OECD 1994) might prove equally useful for proposing improvements in these domains over the short-, medium-, and long-term. For example, if we could gauge the value of produced assets on hand (what economists usually call capital stock), would this be the preferred indicator for monitoring the state of production or some other economic issue?[4] Since there are schools of economists who assign a high priority

Table 1

Initial Indicators for a "Sustainability Matrix" on Environmentally Sustainable Development

This template begins with the OECD framework for environmental indicators (see OECD 1994, Table 1, p.12), adding key socioeconomic indicators and clustering environmental issues. Where models have fostered consensus about main issues (e.g., economics), more aggregated indicators suffice; where underlying dynamics are poorly understood (e.g., ecology), more indicators are needed. Initially, separate Report Cards are envisaged only for the world as a whole and broad country groups (low, middle, high income); country report cards would require greater precision of indicators and documentation than is currently feasible. Indicator work in each category will need to be made explicit by World Bank experts; ideally, each cell would show a performance indicator (the ration of a baseline estimate to a goal). In practice, qualitative "grades" may have to be devised.

Issue	#	A. Pressure	B. State	C. Response
I. Economic				
Production	1	Intermediate Inputs (I) as % GNP	Value Added Per Capita (NNP')	Efficiency of Produced Assets (NNP'/Capital Stock)
Expenditure	2	Inflation	Gross National Expenditure (GNP)	Saving (Adjusted)/ GNP
Income	3	Population (growth rate)	Distributional Inequality	Safety Nets
Labor	4	Wages, etc. (share in GNP)	Human Capital (Educational Attainment)	% EDP Spent on Education
II. Social				
Urbanization	5		Population in Urban Areas (% total)	
Housing	6	Population Density (persons per sq. km.)		% EDP Spent on Housing
Water Quality	7	Energy Demand	Dissolved Oxygen	
Air Quality	8	Burden of Disease (DALYs per 1000 persons)	Concentration of particulates, SO_2, etc.	
Health	9		Life Expectancy at Birth	% EDP Spent on Health, Vaccination
Nutrition	10	Prevalence of Underweight Children	Dietary Energy Supply	
Transport	11		% of Total Produced Assets	
Women's Status, Caring Capacity	12	Maternal Mortality Rate	Total Fertility Rate	Females per 100 Males in Secondary School
III. Ecological				
Global Commons Climate Change	13	Emissions of CO_2	Atmospheric Concentration of Greenhouse Gases	Energy Efficiency of EDP

Initial Indicators for a "Sustainability Matrix" on Environmentally Sustainable Development, *continued*

Issue	#	A. Pressure	B. State	C. Response
III. Ecological *(continued)*				
Stratospheric Ozone	14	Apparent Consumption of CFCs	Atmospheric Concentration of CFCs	% Coverage of International Protocols and Conventions
Oceans[1]	15	—	—	—
Marine Resources	16	Contaminants, Demand for Fish as Food	Stock of Marine Species	—
National Trusts Biodiversity	17	Land Use Changes	Threatened, Extinct Species (% total)	Protected Areas as % Threatened
Water	18	Intensity of Use	Accessibility to Population (weighted % total)	Water Efficiency Measures
Marketable Assets Gas, Oil, and Coal	19	Extraction Rate(s)	Proven Reserves	Reserve Energy Subsidies
Metals and Minerals	20	Extraction Rate(s)	Proven Reserves	Input/Output Ratios, Main Users; Recycling Rates
Forest Resources	21	Land Use Changes, Inputs for EDP	Area, Volumes, Distribution; Value of Forests	Input/Output Ratios, Main Users; Recycling Rates
Land (Soil Quality)[2] Carrying Capacity	22	Human-Induced Soil Degradation	Climatic Classes and Soil Constraints	
Eutrophication	23	Use of Phosphates (P), Nitrates (N)	Biological Oxygen Demand, P, N in Rivers	% Population with Waste Treatment
Acidification	24	Emissions of SOx, NOx	Concentration of pH, SOx, NOx in Precipitation	Expenditure on Pollution Abatement
Toxic Contaminants	25	Generation of Hazardous Waste	Concentration of Lead, Cadmium, etc. in Rivers	% Petrol Unleaded
Waste	26	Generation of Industrial, Municipal Waste	Accumulation To Date	Expenditure on Collection and Treatment; Recycling Rates
General Indicators[3]	27	—	Opinion Polls on Environment, etc.	Expenditure on Pollution Control, Abatement

[1] For monitoring options, see Sheram and Solow 1992.
[2] Available measures focus on nature as a "pollution sink"; more work is needed on the absorptive and processing role of nature.
[3] Legal and institutional aspects might be included here.

to estimating such stocks, the incremental support from environmentalists could have an impact.

The PSR approach should also underscore the shared view that no one domain, let alone a single indicator, can cover the ESD theme. Modifications may be made in each domain, but analysts will still relate indicators from different disciplines. The Dutch have provided a glimpse of this in their approach to monitoring *both* environmental pressure and economic activity (see Adriaanse 1993).

The items listed in Table 1 for the economic and social domains are either well-established time series' or refinements (including composites within issues) where the World Bank has reasonable expectations of providing preliminary results in time for the ESD Report. Only the example of NNP' has been detailed, above, since the choice of indicators is still open for discussion. The immediate question is to what degree analysts, in and outside the Bank, would find useful a recasting of socioeconomic indicators to fit a framework originally designed for environmental issues.

Composing Indicators for Ecological Issues

The PSR framework implies that there are limits to the way statistics can be combined, meaningfully, into indicators. These limits are being made explicit for Bank purposes, although they will remain in the form of guidelines rather than rules. By considering the relevance and strength of subordinate statistical series', the guidelines winnow a plethora of potentially interesting statistics down to a few that can be handled; provide a statement of expectations about when composites can (and cannot) be compiled; and suggest the kind of documentation users can expect when composites are not available.

Relevance. Each issue requires separate composites to evaluate pressure, state, and response. This means that indicators cannot be combined across those three columns without blurring the processes that explain how pressures alter states, how altered states elicit responses, and how responses alter pressures. It also suggests that detailed statistics underlying analytical indicators must relate not only to an issue but to a specific column in the PSR framework. Statistics whose relevance is low or ambiguous across the PSR framework would not be Bank priorities for collection and processing of data.

Weighting. The common unit for an issue need not be applicable beyond a specific column, for a specific issue. Within a single cell, however, it must provide a defensible basis for weighting or aggregating subordinate series, meaning that they are equivalent in terms of that unit, in the context of the issue and column selected. For example, phosphates and nitrates might be expressed as Eutrophication Pressure Equivalents based on a technical consideration like the ratio of these two found in living organisms; that would not necessarily be the common unit for monitoring the state of eutrophication. Expressing details in terms of issue-column equivalencies provides a second compilation filter: priorities for work on basic statistics should be higher for series' given more weight; series' with less than some minimum weight should be disregarded.

Hierarchy among columns. The proposed sustainability matrix rearranges the fourteen issues from the OECD framework into four clusters.[5] This intermediate tier, between individual issues and the whole domain, provides a hierarchy within columns for summarizing indicators, as and when composite indicators appear for specific issues. Such a hierarchy emphasizes that one should not attempt to combine indicators for fairly disparate issues until agreement is reached on how to do so for more similar ones.

Composition of Table 1. The clusters shown in Table 1 are based on a somewhat arbitrary mix of conceptual and practical concerns. Conceptually, they focus on similarities in responses, rather than pressure or state aspects of the PSR framework. Practically, they reflect the way composites are most likely to arise with similar or distinct aggregation procedures.

The term Global Commons is used to cluster issues that are global in scope and not just globally recurrent. These involve natural resources that are unpriced in the UN's SEEA *and* that depend on responses by international protocols and conventions, which means that collective action is required of national governments. Protocols and conventions tend to provide statements of goals which can be developed into common units as discussed above.

Two issues, management of biodiversity and water resources, are categorized as National Trusts. They are generally viewed as part of the national patrimony even though they are not priced in the UN's SEEA, and mitigating pressure probably requires individual governments to respond as if the resources were marketed. Composite indicators for biodiversity and water resources are unlikely to emerge from either a distance-to-goal approach (since this could be quite different across nations) or the kind of market pricing techniques accepted for the UN's SEEA.

The determination of a market price is technically easy for the next group, Marketed Assets. What is less clear is whether the application of market prices is the best choice when conditions seem far from equilibrium and market imperfections abound. Alternative valuations, possibly even some based on technical or policy considerations, might provide a better indication of how relative prices would weight items if ideal economic conditions applied.

Finally, there are pollution-load issues clustered under Carrying Capacity. This grouping is suggested not because the associated indicators measure nature's ability to carry the load, although that would be preferable; it is just not feasible at present. Rather, response indicators in this cluster are about what national accountants call "defensive expenditures." A more positive set of responses should emerge once indicators of technological innovation can be devised.

A key question remains just beneath the surface of this discussion. If it is too difficult to assign a specific value to certain natural resources, would it be better to accept some non-monetary weighting scheme? Implicit in recent developments in indicator work (see Section 1, above) is the view that monetization is a special case of valuation, and current prices represent a special case of monetization. Hence, while there are good reasons to continue exploring various monetization techniques, this need not limit efforts to value essentially all natural resources, with careful documentation of the rules-of-thumb used for this purpose. This is particularly true when the objective is policy- or goal-oriented indicators.

3. Relating Baseline Estimates to Goals

At whatever level of aggregation one prefers, indicators need to be related to goals before they become meaningful. Frequently, people disagree on which of several goals should receive highest priority—that is, they differ in the value they attribute to attaining each goal. This occurs even when the issues in question can be expressed in monetary terms. In this sense, measuring progress towards ESD implies the need for a non-monetary weighting scheme. Statisticians may shy away from this sort of valuation problem,[7] but it must be addressed openly if one is to set realistic expectations for what can be achieved with more and more careful monitoring, data collection, etc. Additional basic data work can only be a placebo when end-users of the data have not acknowledged existing conflicts about substantive goals and policy priorities.

A goals-oriented approach requires indicators that are themselves ratios of descriptive indicators to target values—where targets are defined either technically or by policies. Guidelines are needed for promoting consensus about the "right" targets. At least for a first iteration, the World Bank is exploring the possibilities of weaving work by Dutch environmentalists and Sen's thoughts on monitoring economic regress into performance indicators; this process is described directly below. Attention is also being given to the ways in which a goals-oriented approach can streamline indicator work (described in the following section on "optimally inaccurate" indicators.)

Developing Performance Indicators

OECD (1993, 6) observes that an indicator must have "significance extending beyond that directly associated with a parameter value." Adriaanse, a key architect of the Dutch approach, has elaborated the idea of indicators as fractions designed for evaluation; they compare a quantity (numerator) with a scientifically or arbitrarily chosen measure (denominator) which serves as a norm or reference value (Adriaanse 1993). For descriptive indicators, such as those envisaged by the OECD study, the denominator is usually unspecified or implicit; for performance indicators, it must be made explicit. For example, descriptive indicators of air quality are usually expressed in micrograms per cubic meter. Relating these to World Health Organization guidelines (which was done implicitly in Figure 1) yields performance indicators (which are more easily understood, across pollutants, because they express distance to goals).

If the ESD report is to monitor global progress, it must seek performance indicators while recognizing that initial results may do little more than set priorities for further data work. In effect, goals for action and for better monitoring are coevolutionary. OECD countries are experimenting with performance indicators using goals that are politically set targets as well as expert judgments about sustainability levels.

The 1987 Montreal Protocol on Substances that Deplete the Ozone Layer is an example of this method.

The key, for Bank purposes, is to select criteria by which success or failure—indeed, the importance of monitoring conditions—could be judged. As a start, the ESD report will use four criteria suggested by Sen (1993) in another performance context:

> *Focal variable.* In terms of what variable should progress or regress be judged? Should we talk of real income or real product (such as GDP or GNP per head) or some other indicator of quality of life (such as longevity or good health)?

> *Time stretch.* Are we to identify setbacks with a declining long-run trend line or with short-run phenomenon of a sharp decline? The issues raised by a slow [but] lasting downward trend can be quite different from that of a temporary but severe deterioration (as, for example, in a famine).

> *Relativity.* Is regress to be understood as setback in absolute terms or only as falling behind other communities or groups (relative to their progress)? This question can be asked in each space, that is, in the context of each variable (income, product, quality of life, etc.), and also each segment of time (short or long runs).

> *Units.* Are countries the right units for assessing regress? Are we mainly concerned with the average situation within a country or the predicament of particular groups (for example, the worst-off)? (pp. 2-3)

Given a coevolutionary view of goals for action and monitoring, these criteria help avoid the conundrums that have traditionally prevented aggregation of basic data up to the point where they can serve interdisciplinary purposes like an ESD report. By clarifying conditions for use of data, they should promote consensus about use of single indicators in specific contexts, including the contentious underlying issue of how far one can go in composing indicators from distinct pieces of basic information. This should bridge the gap between advocates of highly composite indicators like the UNDP's Human Development Index and traditional statisticians. It may also help to generate rules-of-thumb for relating social, economic, and environmental variables which, in turn, could spark new thinking about global ESD modeling.

At the same time, World Bank experts will have to approach each issue on a case-by-case basis to decide whether to focus on a single performance indicator or devise some clustering method. The Dutch approach (see Adriaanse 1993) could serve as a default option. Over time, the sustainability matrix should include more issues, appearing in more aggregated forms.

The Case for "Optimally Inaccurate" Indicators

Pass/Fail indicators. Policy-makers are often content to know that a specific issue is or is not relevant in *their* present situation. This level of information need corresponds to a very simple, binary reporting system—i.e., an issue receives a 1 or a 0 to indicate whether it is "relevant" or "not relevant" to the policy-maker. If it were always that simple, one could measure progress by looking at a pattern of "hotspots" or 0's where one would hope for 1's, in something like Table 1. This would not prevent people from interpreting a given pattern differently, based on the importance they attach to attaining one or another goal, however.

When empirical results are ambiguous, however, measuring progress toward ESD requires more than a binary, pass/fail scheme, even with agreed goals. The ambiguity tends to be about results near the borderline between pass and fail, when the range of uncertainty about the empirical work is enough to argue for either side of the borderline, depending on whether one takes the high or low side of the plausible range. Narrowing the range of uncertainty would be ideal, but there will always be some observations that do not clearly signal pass or fail. Allowance for an intermediate zone between pass and fail is thus unavoidable in practice.

The 1-to-5 scale. The intermediate zone may itself need to be subdivided when the number of observations falling into it becomes large. The process of expanding categories could be open-ended, but for practical reasons it will be limited to a threesome for the ESD Report. Taken together with the categories for "clear-pass" and "clear-fail," the plan is to report performance indicators on a scale of 1 (clearly cool) to 5 (clearly hot).

For most policy-oriented purposes, there is little reason to know more than a categorical ranking for indicators in categories 1 and 5. In category 1, the problem is not worth acting upon; in category 5, resources should be spent on mitigation rather than monitoring and evaluation. People may disagree on the importance of pursuing more precise information in the intermediate zone (categories 2 through 4); this usually reflects priorities about the importance of attaining one or another goal. Hence, expressing performance indicators on a 1-to-5 scale is a way of matching policy-makers' concerns about issues with compilers' uncertainties about the underlying empirical evidence.

It should be emphasized that the intention of the ESD report is to report performance indicators in this way, without affecting the presentation of descriptive indicators. It may take presentation of two versions of Table 1, one for descriptive and one for performance indicators, to make this point. However, the task in moving from descriptive to performance indicators is not inherently different from the compression of indicators into ranges for maps in *The World Bank Atlas*. Not coincidentally, *Atlas* maps use five colors. By equating category numbers to colors, one could in fact "colorize" descriptive indicators as a way to convey their categorization as performance indicators. Hence, the numbers shown in Table 1 might relate to descriptive indicators, while the color of each cell might denote its range as the related performance indicator. The color pattern of the table as a whole would give a semi-digested assessment of progress toward ESD goals.

Going beyond the 1-to-5 scale. It is arguable that any indicator of interest to a policy-maker must be reducible to something like a five-point scale, based on distance to a prescribed goal.[8] That would be equally true for the numerous indicators that might be relevant to making decisions on a specific sector or for a specific locality within a country. If indicators that are relevant to local, sectoral decision-makers were reduced to a five-point scale, policy-makers with wider purview would presumably be interested in knowing how many localities or sectors reported clear-fail marks, near-fail marks, etc., even before going into specifics. They might also wish to have some aggregate measures that are not so driven by problem-identification, but these, too, would probably be more digestible if policy-makers could also see them on a five-point scale before going into specifics.

That is the essence of what are here called "optimally inaccurate" indicators. This involves more than a notion that policy-makers make due with less accuracy since they only care about "hotspots"—that is, issues that are highly relevant to their situation. The implication of that, alone, would be that the purpose at hand justifies a lower standard for data quality than technicians require. No such double standard is intended here. While that will sometimes be true, technicians are equally likely to "over-engineer" information systems—and possibly ignore important points. For example, traditional statistical methods, however unintentionally, tend to loose sight of hotspots within a generally sound whole, in ways that optimally inaccurate indicators would not.

Practical Considerations[9]

There is a risk in producing composite indicators for an ESD report in a short amount of time, as has been proposed here. Subsequent work might show decision-makers that their attention was directed at the wrong indicator or indicators, and this might discredit empirical work in general. The alternative to making some attempt now, however, is tantamount to discrediting empirical processes now and would imply that the best scientific minds are no more able to point out the likely direction of change than are busy politicians concerned primarily with other matters.

The case in favor of proceeding rather than waiting is that a summary, analytical approach would increase the visibility of ESD concerns. A parallel can be drawn to UNDP's Human Development Index, which drew high-level attention to the issue of human capital.

The Bank is mindful of the gain from greater visibility that comes with more synthetic indicators. It is not, however, in favor of going as far as distilling all ESD concerns into a few "magic numbers" for each nation. The trick is to be sure the effort yields more than an aggregation of "pity, sorrow, and rage" by continuing to assign priority to work on details while adding something on top of all that. The sustainability matrix is designed to be consistent with this approach, although the most that can be done in the short run may prove to be a renewed striving toward an index of human welfare, development, or both. Nor will the Bank lose sight of the power of one or two "gripping" indicators. The more synthetic the indicator, the less likely it is to capture the imagination of the general public and key decision-makers.

The following sections outline some of the practical problems associated with data collection and presentation and suggest ways of dealing with those problems.

Empty Cells in the Sustainability Matrix

At this point, Table 1 is far from complete. Initial indicators have not been suggested for about a fifth of the cells. Furthermore, given the magnitude of computational work involved in delivering composites for all the items in the cells of Table 1, it may not be possible to complete the task in time for the first ESD report. Progress on filling in the cells of Table 1 depends heavily on the extent to which topical experts, from outside the Bank as well as from within, contribute to the process. It is expected that the ESD report will include brief sections elaborating on the summary measures given in the sustainability matrix. In these sections topical experts would disaggregate, qualify, and analyze a given issue and describe efforts to provide more robust indicators in the future. While this form of presentation may be unfamiliar in the beginning, it is hoped that topical experts will want to work with it, having recognized its potential for alerting policy-makers to their efforts and priorities.

In the case where topical experts have difficulty filling in a cell with an indicator—even an optimally inaccurate indicator—it is probable that those experts are not clear about their goals or about the monitoring and evaluation processes to be used. The brief issues sections mentioned above could therefore focus on plans to improve the empirical base; for without empirical evidence, resources are unlikely to be obtained. In many areas, progress beyond single indicators may depend on modelling, whether a simple mental model like a child's high temperature as a warning signal of illness, more formal mathematical models, or intermediate positions like multi-criteria analyses. This is because traditional statistical techniques, when confronted with novel problems of data quality (see below), "require many strengthening assumptions about the data for their applications to be legitimate." The ESD report could describe any strengthening processes that are underway, particularly where the cells of Table 1 are empty.

Spatial Acuity

Most of the data that are available today are national in coverage; unfortunately, nations are a particularly poor unit for representing ecosystems. A more disaggregated, or subnational, approach to data collection is needed, therefore, before we can significantly improve the empirical base for ESD indicators. This approach is currently possible in some nations, and the ESD report may choose to use one or two of those nations as case studies. These studies could show how using a finer grain of information (i.e., collected at the subnational rather than national level) to represent links among social, economic, and environmental factors improves the accuracy and relevance of indicators. The studies could also explore potential contributions from innovative information sources, notably, geographic information systems (GIS) and World Bank projects.

A predicament arises when we consider the spatial aspect of ESD indicators. That is to say that although ESD indicators are inherently location-specific, they are usually available only at the national scale, which is less precise. Moreover, the first efforts to disseminate indicators, such as the ESD report, may be on an even less-precise, regional scale. One solution to the predicament is to base indicator work on, say, village-level data. It is at this level that one could detect what needs to be measured and what data collection and processing is responsive. An alternative solution is to employ an ecosystem approach, or at least to seek a better understanding of inter-relationships within and between ecosystems.

Spatial aggregation can be as tricky as combining statistics that deal with attributes of the same issue or summing observations over time. There is an ill-defined scale below which a finer grain of spatial information is unlikely to improve analysis, but above which there is a high risk of "mixing apples and oranges." An illustration from Table 1 is the potential value of information on land use changes in monitoring pressure on biodiversity. The underlying functional relationship concerns habitat; the problem is that nation-level indicators for countries with substantial landmass are likely to average conditions over many distinct habitats.

This reinforces the case for using optimally inaccurate indicators. It also suggests why national indicators can be misleading unless they are developed with due regard to possible heterogeneity in the items being added, averaged, etc. This, in turn, explains much of the reason for compiling the ESD report only for supranational units, for the present.

Problems with Data Quality

Even for OECD nations, and within the range of indicators that they have explored actively in their framework for environmental indicators, the empirical base is admittedly weak. For the near term, therefore, perhaps it would be best to focus efforts on agreeing what indicators are appropriate and how they can be compiled. This is focus is all the more appropriate for the Bank in its efforts to extend the framework to countries with weaker statistical systems. While stressing the need to strengthen such systems, and indicating Bank efforts in this regard, the ESD report will have to recognize another aspect of data quality—that is, the difficulties associated with obtaining comprehensive data.

Given the multiplicity of issues, each with many attributes to monitor, potentially in a massive number of locations; it is not realistic to expect data collection procedures to be comprehensive, as this term has been used in traditional statistical systems.[10] Relative to the complexities under study, empirical evidence will be sparse and coarse. Nor can one expect the evidence to be collected according to established statistical norms, which were designed to deal with random variability and presuppose that data are numerous and of good quality.

To complicate matters, much of the key empirical evidence will be collected precisely where systems are assumed to be vulnerable, whether in a socioeconomic context (e.g., monitoring the living conditions of the poor) or an ecological one (e.g., monitoring water quality in places where humans exert the most pressure on rivers). In terms of methods designed to deal with random variability, these situations would be considered biased samples. And the more intensively one monitors vulnerable elements, the more biased the sample becomes— and the less relevant the sample is for gauging the whole system. (This is another way of concluding that data collection will tend to be mainly in the intermediate zones discussed in the section on "optimally inaccurate" indicators, above.)

Moreover, statistical methods have not yet been devised to cope with the complexities involved in systems of living organisms that interact, sometimes cooperatively and sometimes competitively. What some call the emerging science at the edge of chaos (Waldrop 1993), complexity theory may provide a justification for what appears to be biased sampling according to conventional standards. There are "phase transitions" at certain points in complex processes, which might be expressed as nonlinearities in models if they could be properly studied; it is around these points that more empirical evidence is needed. Quite possibly, standard statistical methods could still work if they were applied to observations properly restricted to the area around phase transitions.

This helps explain the importance of distinguishing between precision and accuracy of empirical evidence. The example used by Costanza, Funtowicz, and Ravetz (1992) is:

> A marksman shooting at a target will produce a pattern of shots. They may all cluster tightly, in which case we speak of high precision, but we are also concerned with how closely they come to the bull's-eye, which we describe in terms of accuracy. If the sighting apparatus is defective, the marksman's shots may well have a high precision and low accuracy.

Precision can be measured by instruments; accuracy is known only indirectly, by judging outcomes relative to expectations. Also, accuracy cannot be gauged without some sense of where the bull's-eye is, which returns the discussion to the need for a goals-oriented approach.

These forms of uncertainty often swamp random variability in empirical evidence. They can also outweigh problems of faulty monitoring equipment or human error in using equipment, if only because conventional statistical methods can more easily cope with such problems. However, until some means is found of distinguishing random variability from other forms of uncertainty that are inherent in most empirical evidence, genuine problems of inadequate equipment and training will be indistinguishable from those where more expenditure along these lines will produce little analytical gain.

With this in mind, the Bank is considering a novel form of documentation, building on the "NUSAP" approach of Costanza, Funtowicz, and Ravetz (1992). The acronym for this notational system refers to the "numeral" and "unit" that denote a balance between three elements, namely, "spread," "assessment," and "pedigree." The main purpose is to place indicators in a "pedigree framework" designed to clarify three key aspects of the underlying numbers: theoretical (quality of models), empirical (quality of data), and social (degree of acceptance of the process used). Apart from the usual form of textual documentation of sources and methods, this approach leads to numeric expressions of data quality that adjust with the level of aggregation.

A full exposition of the NUSAP approach is beyond the scope of this paper. However, it should be noted that its notational system includes an arithmetic formula for describing data quality. It promises to help all users of the the approach make roughly comparable evaluations of the empirical evidence they present; it also allows various forms of uncertainty to be tracked through progress computational stages. Specifically for Table 1, it could translate uncertainties about subordinate series into a data quality "grade" at the cell level.

The decision to publish or drop a particular indicator for the ESD report can then be made on the basis of its data quality grade, which provides a structured guess about the range of uncertainty surrounding the estimate. The NUSAP notation system also enables users to trace uncertainty back to its components, which should help target areas which should receive the most attention and eventually help us to improve the reliability of the composite indicator. Areas targeted for more work might be modeling, data collection, or peer review (as a means of raising social acceptability of results); it would not necessarily mean more data collection.

Inventory of Goals

The near-term priority is to organize available information to provide baselines or at least identify analytically significant omissions so as to highlight gaps of greatest importance to agreeing on goals—and ways of monitoring progress towards such goals. However, it will soon be necessary to prepare an inventory of goals, paralleling the inventory of databases that one takes for granted as a prerequisite for an exercise of this kind.

The term *goals* will be used loosely in preparing the inventory. For example, the Bank's graduation line (the per capita income level above which countries are not expected to borrow from the Bank) implies a goal—that all countries should be above that level. A demographic goal is implied by the concept of an assumed year of reaching a net reproduction rate of 1 (see, for example, Table 27 of the Bank's 1993 *World Development Indicators*).

Some other international agencies offer explicit as well as implicit goals that may prove useful. For example, UNICEF advocates a target, for the year 2000, of a fifty percent reduction in the prevalence of underweight children (UNICEF 1993,17). Other targets are proposed that are relevant to Table 1, notably, a halving of maternal mortality rates and completion of a basic education by at least eighty percent of children. As noted under Global Commons, international protocols can also provide relevant goals. However, even an expansive approach to an inventory of goals is likely to reveal a number of areas within Table 1 for which there is lack of clarity about goals. Little can be done in terms of measuring progress until there is consensus at least about some rough goals, such as those described above. What is more, the argument for further basic data collection is difficult to support where there is not a reasonable expectation of measuring progress.

Directions for Further Work

The emphasis in this paper has been on baseline estimates and goals. Once these are established, it will of course be necessary to collect empirical evidence over time, to measure progress. In many cases time series' already exist—at least in principle. Many important social statistics are collected so infrequently, however, and rely so heavily on models for filling in gaps in the data, that it is not always possible to tell how much empirical evidence is actually being conveyed by the time series. Documenting these through the NUSAP system should help and at least shed some light on the relative force of data quality problems across the ESD domains. At the other extreme, some variables such as air quality reports and inflation measures are available with such high temporal frequency (if low spatial acuity) that outlying data points can complicate efforts to express the evidence in terms of longer time segments (e.g., years).

Apart from giving some attention to these ubiquitous problems of temporal aggregation, interpolation, etc., more thought needs to be given to the relationship between frequency of measurement and rapidity of change that we expect to see. In effect, there is little point in high-frequency monitoring of a phenomenon that is likely to change only gradually. These practical aspects of temporal scaling might also need to be related to Sen's concept of "time stretch" as a selection criterion for more work on basic data.

Particularly as the time stretch lengthens, it is not enough to add composites to a continuing effort on accepted topics like pollution loads. More attention is needed to data work that explores the mathematics of natural functions and human effects on them. For example, the illustrative report card reduced the eutrophication issue to pollution loads; but such figures mean little without an understanding of how natural processes cope with such pressures. At least in the medium- or long-term, the sustainability matrix should go beyond the OECD framework and the few empirical studies currently available to support performance indicators in this area.

Institutional and legal mechanisms should also figure in the eventual report card. Some ideas along this line were included in a proposal (Moldan 1993) to a recent UNEP/UNSTAT meeting on environmental and sustainable development indicators. Progress on such mechanisms certainly merits attention; the technical problem is to find meaningful indicators for what is often a qualitative judgment. For example, it is easy and inexpensive to treat the signing of a convention as an indicator, but the meaning may depend on an evaluation of institutional capacity to implement the substance of the agreement or even on monitoring compliance.

Given the extensive amount of new information, the Bank is considering releasing a more technical document as a companion to the ESD report. Tentatively entitled *Global Approach to Environmental Analyses (GAEA)*, the technical document would be geared more toward nation-level information (text and indicators), dissemination of more experimental indicators (including efforts at the subnational level), and basic statistical issues.

Ideally, an overall "grade" would appear on the sustainability matrix each year. In practice, this is unlikely until far more insight has been gained into how ecosystems prosper and perish, and how human interventions affect those processes. At the same time, gaining such insights will be difficult without a bold effort to squeeze more policy-relevance from the data that exist and are currently being collected, which is the objective of the framework proposed here.

NOTES

1. This paper describes a Bank effort in its formative stage. The views expressed are those of the author and not necessarily those of the World Bank. For an update on this effort through early 1995, see World Bank 1995.
2. This process has been described more fully in technical reports by the author.
3. While measures of the stock of produced assets are generally not available, the Bank has generated preliminary estimates for some ninety countries as part of the study that generated estimates of depreciation, discussed below. These, too, might be available for the ESD report.
4. This is more than a hypothetical issue. The Bank has prepared a very tentative time series on the value of produced assets for about ninety countries, using a perpetual inventory model and on human capital based on educational attainment. While the time series is still too crude for use in country-level analyses, consideration is being given to reporting results at the regional level in the ESD report, if similarly crude composites can be devised for natural resources.

5. See Proops and Atkinson 1993 and Hamilton. These studies elaborate practical methods of calculation for the "weak" sustainability criterion, which permits trade-offs within the broadly defined capital stock (comprised of produced assets, natural resources, and the stock of knowledge).

6. It also treats urbanization issues as part of the social, rather than ecological, domain. This has been done mainly for practical reasons. Concerns like housing (quantity as well as quality) figure prominently in Bank monitoring of urbanization; monitoring of water and air quality is in practice mainly concerned with human health, a point that can be made by locating them near health indicators.

7. Some experts prefer to use the term "evaluation" rather than broaden the definition of "valuation." Either way, the challenge arises in the next step—that is, in relating description indicators to goals.

8. While beyond the scope of this paper, distance-to-goal can be measured in terms of time (years) required to reach a desired category, presuming continuation of past trends or policy-induced changes. The time-distance measurement pioneered by Pavle Sicherl overcomes one form of arbitrariness of most goals-oriented composites, which assign equal weight to each issue in an indefinite future when all goals are attained. Time-distance would allow goals to refer to definite but distinct years in the future and record the expected number of years in the appropriate cell of Table 1, e.g., x years for pressure on issue A, y years on issue B. Averaging these years would be a quick, if still rather arbitrary, way to find a common unit to form higher-level composites.

9. This section, particularly the discussion on problems with data quality, draws heavily on Costanza, Funtowicz, and Ravetz 1992.

10. This is becoming true even for economics. For example, Joseph Duncan, Chief Economist for Dun & Bradstreet has argued (references on request) that the relevance of comprehensiveness is fading for merchandise trade; that trade promotion, etc., require the kind of information that can only be obtained by detailed questionnaires, of the type that can only be obtained by survey.

REFERENCES

Adriaanse, A. 1993. *Environmental policy performance indicators: A study on the development of indicators for environmental policy in the Netherlands.* Netherlands Ministry of Housing, Physical Planning, and Environment. The Hague, The Netherlands.

Costanza, R., S. Funtowicz, and J. Ravetz. 1992. Assessing and communicating data quality in policy-relevant research. *Environmental Management* 16(1).

European Conference of Statisticians. Secretariat. 1993. *Specific methodological issues in environmental statistics.* CES/794.

Eurostat. 1993. Submission to UNEP/UNSTAT Consultative Group Meeting on Environmental and Sustainable Development Indicators, 6-8 December, Geneva.

Hamilton, K. n.d. Modifying the Human Development Index for environmental concerns. Report to the United Nations Development Programme.

Hodge, R. A. Reporting on sustainable and equitable development: Conceptual approach. 1993. Project paper no. 1. IDRC, Ottawa, Canada.

Moldan, B. 1993. Discussion paper.

OECD. 1993. Indicators for environmental performance reviews: Progress report by the Group on the State of the Environment. OECD, Paris.

OECD. 1994. *Environmental indicators: OECD core set.* OECD, Paris.

Proops, and Atkinson. 1993. A practical sustainability criterion when there is international trade. Manuscript.

Sen, A. 1993. Economic regress: Concepts and features. Paper presented at The World Bank Annual Conference on Development Economics, May.

Sheram, and Solow. 1992. The changing states and health of a large marine ecosystem. Prepared for International Council for the Exploration of the Sea.

Thomas, W. A., ed. 1972. *Indicators of Environmental Quality.* Plenum, New York.

UNEP/RIVM/University of Cambridge. 1993. An overview of environmental indicators: State of the art and perspectives, by van der Born and others. December draft.

UNICEF. 1993. *The progress of nations.* UNICEF, New York.

Waldrop, M. 1992. *Complexity: The emerging science at the edge of order and chaos.* Simon and Schuster, New York.

World Bank. annual. *The World Bank atlas.* World Bank, Washington, D.C.

World Bank. 1992. *Development and the environment: World development report.* Oxford University Press, New York.

World Bank. 1993a. Accounting for the environment. Environment Department, World Bank, Washington, D.C. August draft.

World Bank. 1993b. *Environmental indicators and accounting.* World Bank internal working paper, no. F3. Washington, D.C.

World Bank. 1993c. *World development indicators.* World Bank, Washington, D.C.

World Bank. 1995. Monitoring environmental progress: A report on work in progress. Environment Department, World Bank, Washington, D.C. March draft.

WRI. 1993. Global environmental indicators. World Resources Institue, Washington, D.C.

The European Sustainability Index Project

cଓ

TJEERD DEELSTRA

Introduction

The Sustainability Index Project is a European project, coordinated by The International Institute for the Urban Environment, which involves twelve European cities: Aalborg (Denmark), Amsterdam (The Netherlands), Angers (France), Breda (The Netherlands), Brussels (Belgium), Den Haag (The Hague) (The Netherlands), Freiburg (Germany), Hannover (Germany), Leicester (United Kingdom), Leipzig (Germany), Terni (Italy), and Valencia (Spain). The project is co-funded by the European Com-mission, Directorate General XI. The aim of the project was to develop a system of indicators which can be measured in cities throughout Europe. The twelve participating cities were selected based on their proven experience in working with indicators or developing indexes. An attempt was made to select cities that were representative of all of Europe. Some of the cities or organizations involved had established cooperative efforts with the Institute prior to this project.

The Sustainability Index is an empirical model of reality (or a part thereof); it describes the situation in view of the development of the city—or its region, or an area within the city—by means of a number of representative elements and compares this with the situation in previous years. Indicators are instruments to bring the efforts toward sustainability to light, simplifying the complexity of the city, without taking it out of context.

An important part of the project was the European Workshop on Sustainability Indicators, where participants discussed a questionnaire that project cities had completed prior to the workshop and that would be used to compose the Sustainability Index. The questionnaire consisted of twenty-six items, or indicators, to be collected for 1985 and 1990. The setup of the Index was open for discussion and could be modified. The workshop was also intended to provide participating cities and contributing experts an opportunity to share experiences.

In many European cities efforts have already begun, as there is increased awareness of the need to change policies, behavior, and local visions. Most of the cities involved in this project are aware of the rapid progress made over the past few years in the area of monitoring and are familiar with newly developed observation and registration systems. Still, there is still a long way to go before new models of sustainable development are implemented.

It is important to realize that *measuring* progress is only one step toward *making* progress; the latter requires an evolving local policy process, in which indicators can play an important role. The intention of the European Sustainability Index Project is threefold:

☐ to provide cities with a method to make a Local Sustainability Index,
☐ to make an inventory or assess the "state of the environment" in the participating cities, and
☐ to compare the cities and report the progress made toward local sustainability.

Requirements for a European Sustainability Index

Every community will have its own conception of sustainability and its own set of environmental problems; for each city and town there are reasons to concentrate on particular aspects of sustainability and not others. Many municipalities in Europe and elsewhere are involved in indicators work and are starting to incorporate indicators into the policy-making process. However, local indicators will refer to very different elements of the environment.

Put another way, municipalities' aims and requirements—not forgetting the variety of cultural, socioeconomic, climatic, and landscape circumstances—can differ greatly across regions and countries. This makes a uniform, all-encompassing set of indicators covering all local dimensions of Europe impossible to develop.

The European Sustainability Index Project therefore offers a compact index that is flexible and adjustable, intended for general application at the local level and for comparisons at the international level.

The set of indicators developed for the European Index can help to stimulate elaboration of additional area-specific indicators at the local level in Europe or enable the further development and connection of existing local methods and observation techniques in cities that already use an indicator system.

The Sustainability Index Project encompassed the following objectives and criteria.

(1) A compact set of indicators should be made available for international application, with a competitive aspect, in order to give credit to nations where progress toward local sustainability is occurring.

(2) The reference framework, or areas of concern, covered by the Sustainability Index must be recognizable for each city and must not lead to a monitoring system focusing on completely different elements.

(3) The indicators must apply to a specified geographical area.

(4) The Sustainability Index must form a basis for the elaboration of advanced local policies and/or be well connected to local (strategic or municipal) plans.

(5) Indicators should be easily and directly measurable, designed to use available figures and data whenever possible.

(6) Cities should provide a detailed explanation of the values to be measured. They should make an effort to explain trends, which can lead to a better understanding of causes and effects, as well as observable compensation.

(7) The Index must be connected to a local system providing continuous evaluation, to enable observation of improvement (or deterioration) and allow the incorporation of certain trends over a period of time.

The evolving process of the development, use, evaluation, and adaptation of indicators can be reflected systematically: designing, measurements, analysis of measurements, evaluation, formulation of new action, testing the implementation, and adaptation of the indicator.

(8) Data contained in the Index must fulfill a public information function; that is, data must be understandable and considered relevant by politicians, experts, and the public-at-large, including citizens, businesses, and industry.

(9) The European Sustainability Index should incorporate available expert knowledge on local sustainability indicators.

(10)The Sustainability Index should be compatible with methods already in use in European municipalities and not require developing completely new local monitoring systems.

The ABC-Indicator Model®

Many cities develop their own indicators that are specific to local issues and problems. A complete set of indicators that synthesizes the methods used by all participating cities would result in an impractical volume of indicators, making the set irrelevant for the majority of cities in Europe.

Therefore, The International Institute for the Urban Environment developed the ABC-indicator model® to set up the Sustainability Index (see Figure 1). The model consists of *Area*-specific, *Basis*, and *Core* indicators:

☐ *Area-specific indicators.* Developed by local organizations or authorities to measure development, these indicators are attuned to the specific problems, conditions, or features of the area. Area-specific indicators can be developed independently from the indicators of the Sustainability Index, or supplementary to the Index and more specific to the basis indicators.

☐ *Basis indicators.* These support the Sustainability Index's core indicators by providing additional details about core indicator results. A set of basis indicators was provided by The International Institute for the Urban Environment at the start of the project. The set can (and should), however, be expanded by local organizations or authorities since basis indicators often represent only a small part of a complex situation. In the case of air quality, for example, the Index requires measuring only the concentration of sulphur dioxide, whereas the concerned area might suffer severely from high levels of carbon monoxide caused by incomplete combustion from traffic or space heating. Therefore the city could expand the Index, in this case by including the area-specific indicator, "concentration of carbon monoxide."

☐ *Core indicators.* These are the main indicators that form the European Sustainability Index and provide minimal information for measuring local sustainability. A set of core indicators was initially developed by The International Institute for the Urban Environment and elaborated in this project in cooperation with the participating cities. The set consists of themes related to sustainability (initially there were six, later evolving into a set of ten); each theme is represented by a core indicator.

At the start of this project the International Institute for the Urban Environment formulated the six themes, or "container issues," (which roughly reflect the image of a "sustainable city") and translated these into a proposed set of core indicators. A *container issue* is defined here as an aspect of sustainability which is related to a compilation of concrete, measurable data. It is comparable to a box which contains various items that can be defined under the heading of the container.

The issues (not stated in order of importance) were: healthy air, safe streets, good housing, greenery, environmental compliance, and sustainable resource use.

It is clear that there is a relation between A, B, and C indicators, and there is sometimes considerable overlap, even within the sets of indicators. The complexity of relations is illustrative for the role of indicators in the evolving process toward sustainability.

The ABC-indicator model® makes it possible to create a simple, generally applicable Local Index, consisting of a number of core indicators and a certain number of basis indicators. The core indicators should always be easily recognizable and provide sufficient stimulus for cities and towns to apply the full set of basis indicators. Cities and towns can add existing or new area-specific indicators to the core and basis indicators as they wish. The International Institute for the Urban

Figure 1

The ABC-indicator model®.

B (Basis indicator) and C (Core indicator) represent the Local Sustainability Index as part of the European Sustainability Index. A (Area-specific indicator) represents the indicators developed by the municipality.

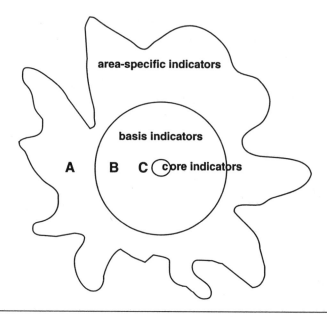

Environment highly recommends completing the system with area-specific indicators.

Applying the ABC-indicator model®, and therefore working with the Index, is an evolving process. It needs continuous evaluation, analysis, testing, adaptation, and creative handling.

The set of core indicators developed in this project is not intended to be complete or to cover all aspects of sustainability in full detail; instead, it is intended to give a basic impression of sustainability to be further elaborated and developed by the cities and towns using the Local Sustainability Index. The ABC-indicator model® offers the possibility to do so. Area-specific indicators measure specific local issues, while basis indicators amplify the core indicators, some of which are determined locally. Core indicators, on the other hand, are to be measured in each participating city and can provide a manageable set of information on local sustainability for comparison across Europe.

State of the Urban Environment in Europe

Collecting Data

The International Institute for the Urban Environment prepared a questionnaire to facilitate data collection. Ten of the twelve participating cities completed the questionnaire, which consisted of eleven items of background information and a total of twenty-six core and basis indicators, for both 1985 and 1990. Terni (Italy) and Angers (France) were not able to return the questionnaire within the allotted time.

A number of figures, based on the information gathered through the questionnaire, show comparisons of the project cities. Figure 2 shows

---

Figure 2

Percentage of data collected for each city

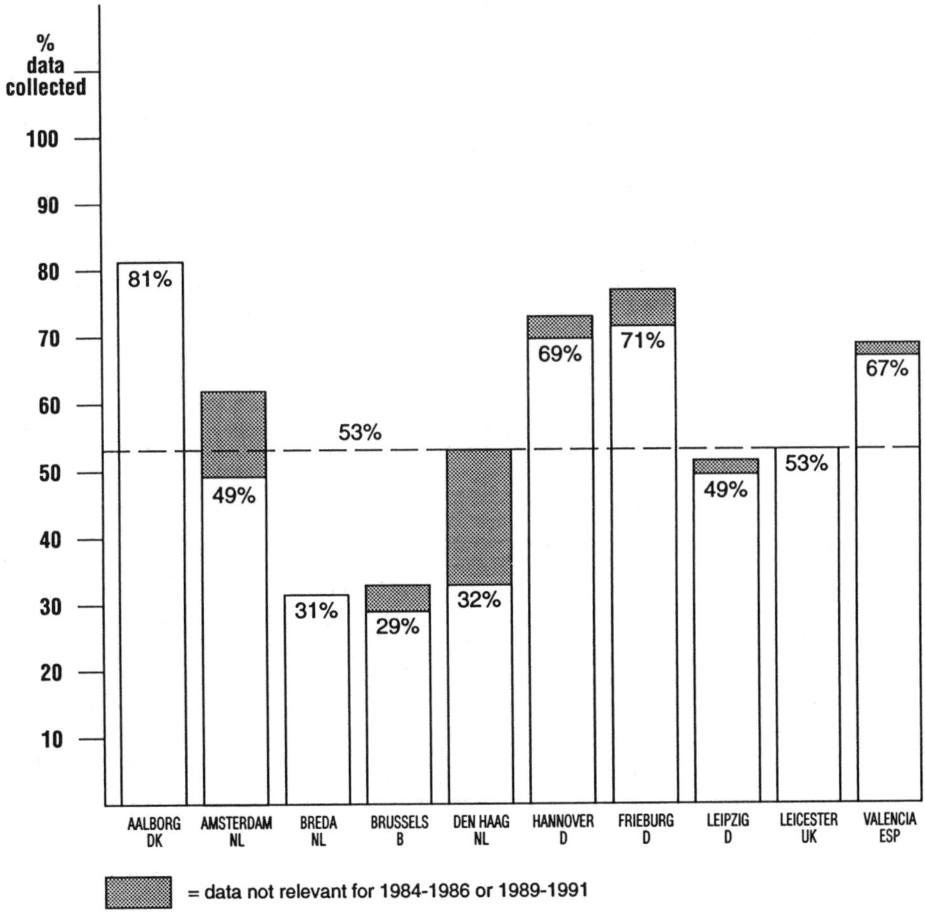

= data not relevant for 1984-1986 or 1989-1991

that an average of 53% of the data were collected by the cities. The background information was easy to collect: Cities were able to supply almost 80% of the requested data.

Since cities found it difficult to provide the data for the precise years of 1985 and 1990, a margin of one year plus or minus was permitted. The difference of data in the respective years is depicted by two columns per city: the left (white) column for 1984-1986, the right (shaded) column for 1989-1991. Unfortunately, some of the cities supplied information that was not relevant for either time span. This information therefore does not appear in the figures. The city of Den Haag was affected most by the limitation on the time span in relation to the data it supplied.

It is assumed that the twelve cities involved in this project are representative of European cities as a whole. Therefore, some of the histograms show a "European" average for each time period (represented by a dotted horizontal line). It is not a weighted average; it is based solely on the data that were collected by the project cities. The average could only be calculated when both the data for 1985 and 1990 were available. Cities missing data for either one of the two years are not calculated into the average.

Some of the data represent the national level and are assumed to be applicable at the local level, too. This variation is not mentioned in the charts.

The city of Leipzig had difficulties collecting data for 1985, since data sources from former East Germany are considered unreliable. The data situation improved with German unification in November 1989. In some cases the data for Leipzig are estimates based on current knowledge, in some cases official data are used.

It is important to note that measurement methods and interpretation of terms vary from city to city, which may cause results to differ from what is regarded or experienced as reality. Data presented in the pages that follow require more extensive explanation than is possible here. Conclusions are therefore based on the data that were submitted, without comparisons of circumstances under which they were collected. Furthermore, the data refer to geographical units that are dissimilar. For example, comparing the number of inhabitants in one city to another might lead to the conclusion that the first is more populated, whereas the total surface of the two cities may differ greatly. For this reason, figures have been provided when appropriate to show relative progress or decline and aid comparison among the cities.

Background Information on Project Cities

Participating cities were asked to choose a geographical unit to work on in this project. Regardless of neighborhood, district, or city chosen as geographical unit, the character of the selected area had to be described according to certain specifications. This essential background information is also necessary for comparing results between cities that differ in character and size. The International Institute for the Urban Environment proposed describing the following aspects of each of the chosen areas:

(a) The total surface space of the specific area to be dealt with in the Sustainability Index;
(b) The total number of inhabitants in the area;
(c) The total number of cars owned by residents and businesses;
(d) The average housing occupancy;
(e) The average net income per head of population per year;
(f) The inflation index; and
(g) The number of registered companies.

The cities were also asked to provide information that would indicate changes in awareness and behavior. This was registered through the following descriptors:

(h) The number of environmental education or information centers;
(i) The number of grocery shops stocking only natural products;
(j) The number of environmental organizations or organizations which produce or distribute periodicals concentrating on the improvement of the quality of life; and
(k) A map or aerial photograph of the area.

For each indicator defined in the questionnaire, the following additional aspects were also taken into consideration: the origin of data (sources); relevant standards (maximum, minimum, and, if necessary, the target year set by the organization that formulated the standards); and interpretation and evaluation of data, with critical comments by the organization or person completing the questionnaire.

It can be useful for a participating city to link certain data with other details, thereby upgrading the environmental picture of the geographical unit and showing relations between indicators and trends.

Results of the Background Survey

(a) Total surface space of the specific area.

The questionnaire was applied to specific geographical areas. Some of the participating cities applied it to a part of the surface within the municipal boundaries, others chose the entire municipality. Aalborg, for example, chose to define the surface of the municipality as the city, the surrounding land, and various non-urban settlements. Brussels applied the questionnaire to only a part of the total municipal surface. Overall, city surface areas changed little between 1985 and 1990 (see Figure 3).

Figure 3

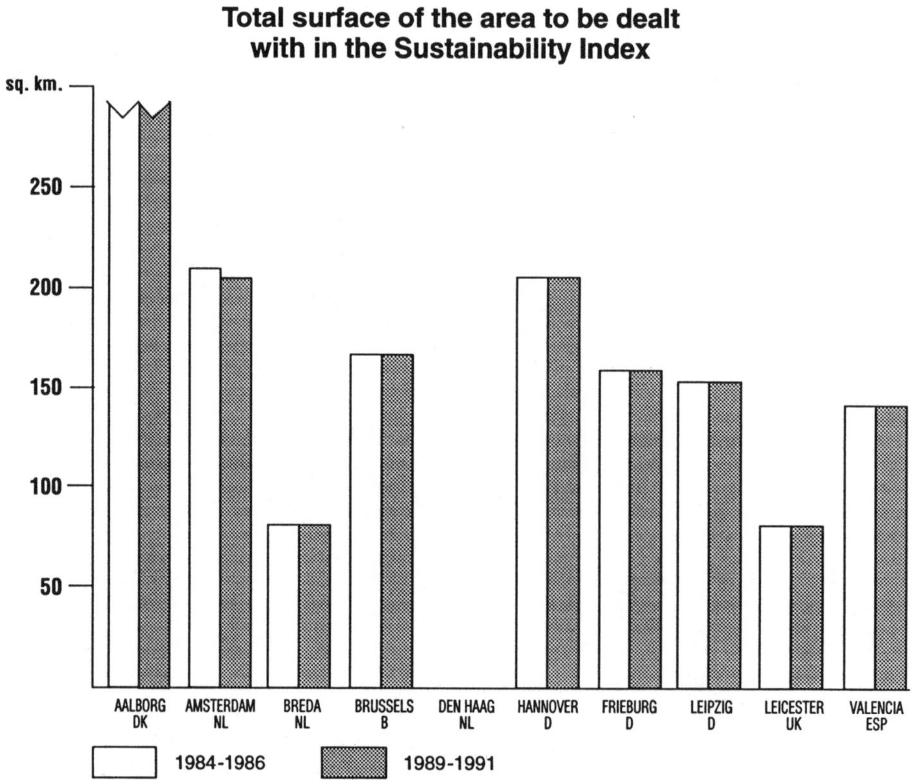

Total surface of the area to be dealt with in the Sustainability Index

1984-1986   1989-1991

(b) Total number of inhabitants (residents, as registered at "home address").

Note that the number of inhabitants only concerns those who are registered within the specific area at "home address." These data do not include people who work or visit the area but live elsewhere. The total number of inhabitants hardly changed over the five years in question (see Figure 4). Compared to the city surface (the black columns), it is obvious that the population density is highest in Brussels and lowest in Aalborg. This is however not a very representative figure, since the surface of the municipality of Aalborg is comprised of large pieces of land and non-urban settlements, whereas the percentage of open space in the

---

Figure 4

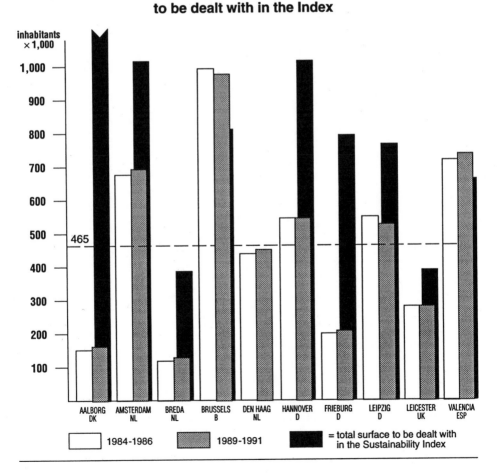

**Total number of inhabitants in the area
to be dealt with in the Index**

urbanized area of Brussels is relatively low. Therefore the data do not supply information on the urban patterns (structure of the city) and the ratio between built-up and open space.

(c) Total number of cars owned by residents and businesses.

According to the data in Figure 5, overall car ownership in the project cities increased by a dramatic 19%. The increase in Leipzig since the union of Germany is explicable: Inhabitants of the former socialist republic regarded the automobile as a symbol of regained freedom and liberty, since car ownership had been restricted prior to reunification.

The figures shown here do not accurately portray the total number of cars within a city as a whole, since this indicator was limited to cars owned by residents and businesses in the specified area (and registered there). Therefore, the number of cars of visitors or through traffic is not included in calculations (which could change the picture drastically).

Table 1

What is the ratio between the number of cars and the number of inhabitants?

	1985 **# of** **inhabitants** **per car**	**1990** **# of** **inhabitants** **per car**	**Decrease**
Leicester	4.97	3.87	22%
Valencia	3.16	2.93	7%
Aalborg	3.14	2.76	12%
Leipzig	2.92	1.92	34%
Amsterdam	2.87	2.78	3%
Breda	2.78	2.40	21%
Freiburg	2.72	2.40	12%
Hannover	2.72	2.35	14%
Brussels	2.68	2.33	13%

The percentage decreases seen in Table 1 do not exactly match the Figure 5 percentages showing increased number of cars; this could be explained by the fact that the number of cars is related to all registered vehicles (including company cars), whereas the data supplied by the cities on the number of inhabitants refer to people registered at home addresses and do not include companies or their employees.

Figure 5

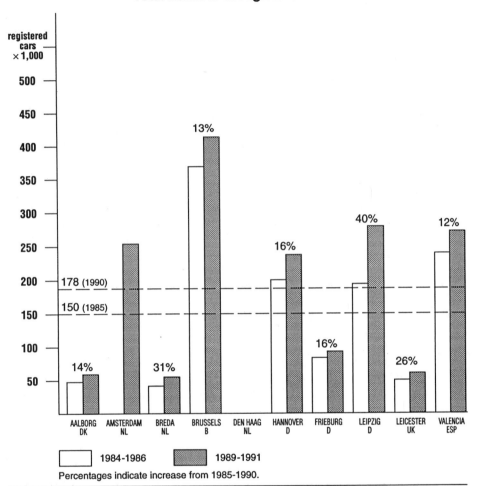

Total number of registered cars

(d) Average housing occupancy.

Figure 6 reveals a slight difference between the housing occupancy in northern and southern Europe. More significant is the general decrease in the number of persons per household, namely, from 2.29 to 2.18—a 5% drop. This is related to the increasing number of one-person households (result of an ageing population as well as the trend for young people to start their own households earlier and stay single longer).

Figure 6

Average housing occupancy

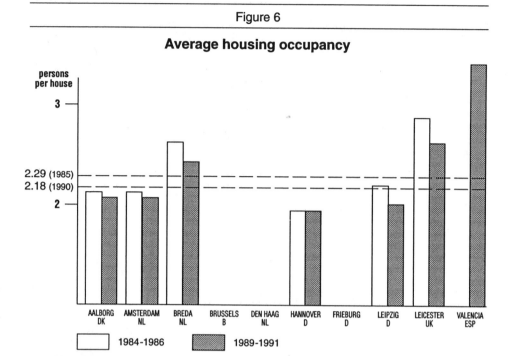

(e) Average net income (in ECUs) per head of population per year.

It was impossible to compare the data on this indicator across cities since the exchange rates cities used to convert national currency into ECU were not reliable and, more importantly, because the interpretation of what should be included in (or excluded from) net income varied greatly (the definition was too vague in this respect).

(f) The inflation index.

The influence of the national economic situation is reflected in the figures on inflation indexes. Denmark, The Netherlands, and Spain show a considerable decrease in inflation (77% to 45%), whereas Germany, influenced by reunification, had an increase of about 40%. The United Kingdom suffered the most, with an increase of 90%.

(g) Number of registered companies.

Increase in the number of companies can be explained by the fact that many relatively small businesses were established between 1985 and 1990. Industries and larger businesses moved out of the city (for environmental reasons, for reasons of accessibility, or because of limited space for expansion) but stayed registered in the same place. Only "registered companies" were included in this indicator.

Another European trend is the development of industrial areas or business parks outside the cities, but close to main highways or railways. Limited accessibility within cities is one reason for this trend. Unfortunately, the new industrial areas often result in increased automobile traffic because inadequate public transport and long distances between work and residential areas force employees to travel by car (see also indicator 5.4).

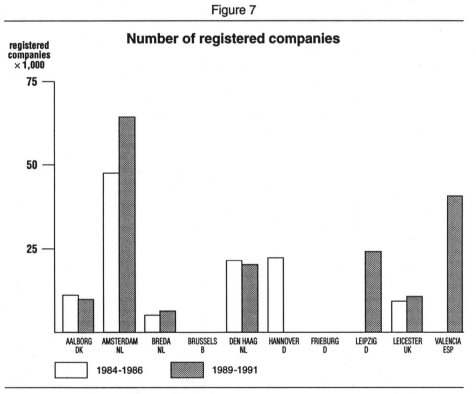

Figure 7

(h) Number of environment education or information centers.

(i) Number of grocery shops stocking only natural products.

(j) Number of environment organizations or organizations which produce/distribute periodicals concentrating on the improvement of the quality of life.

Data from the background indicators (h), (i), and (j) are combined in Figure 8 because they all relate to changes in citizens' awareness and behavior on aspects of sustainability. The high number of "grocery shops stocking natural products only" in Valencia (Spain)is striking. This is caused not by a unique interpretation of the terms in the question, but is due to the fact that people in southern European countries are used to consuming natural, seasonal products from the region, sold by local producers. Climate is a factor in this traditional consumer pattern.

The total number of environmental education or information centers (not including school programs) in the participating cities has tripled between 1985 and 1990. Amsterdam established eight centers in this period (there was no center in 1985), and the number of centers in Freiburg and Hannover increased considerably.

Figure 8

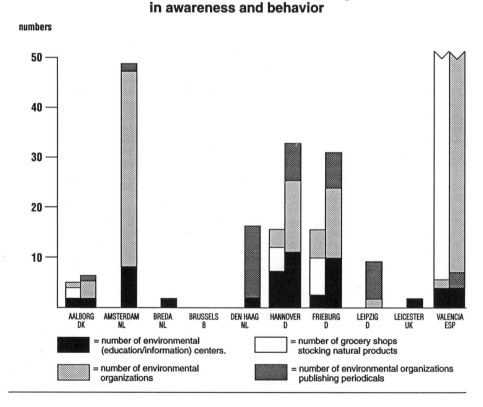

Information which can indicate changes in awareness and behavior

The figures of Hannover and Freiburg are more or less representative for the other cities: the number of environmental centers increased, as did the number of grocery shops which only stock natural products, and the number of environmental organizations (significant increase since 1990). The majority of cities involved in this project state that the total number of (non-governmental) environmental groups is far higher than the number of environmental organizations who publish periodicals. Many of the environmental groups are incorporated into coordinating organizations.

Table 2

How many citizens were supplied with environmental information by one center in 1990?

Freiburg	1 center per 19,000 citizens
Hannover	1 center per 49,000 citizens
Amsterdam	1 center per 87,000 citizens
Breda	1 center per 123,000 citizens
Aalborg	1 center per 155,000 citizens
Valencia	1 center per 250,000 citizens
Leicester	1 center per 278,000 citizens
Den Haag	1 center per 440,000 citizens

(k) A map or aerial photograph of the area in which the questionnaire is to be applied.

The majority of the project cities supplied colored maps of the area to which questionnaire data were related.

Initial Core- and Basis-Indicator Results

Having supplied background and descriptive information, project cities were then asked to provide data that would make up the initial round of core and basis indicators.

Healthy Air

1.0. The number of days per year that the (local) standard for air quality is exceeded.

The data on what was intended to be the core indicator of one of the container issues of aspects related to sustainability was apparently very difficult to collect. Most certainly the complexity of the indicator, representing a whole range of aspects, required too much study and interpretation to supply data. The definition of this rather broad aspect was regarded as too vague: the cities were not able to fully identify with the requested data. The same difficulties occurred with the other core indicators. Only the indicator for "Greenery—access to outdoor space within a certain distance" was identified by some of the participating cities (see Figure 14).

Only the city of Valencia (Spain) supplied data on this indicator. The number of unhealthy days have been reduced in the respective time span by 18%, although it is still above the locally applied standard. The situation has changed considerably since 1990, when through traffic was diverted out of the city.

1.1. The average annual concentration of aerosols (dust) (g/m^3).

1.2. The average annual concentration of sulphur dioxide (SO_2) (g/m^3).

Although the majority of cities involved in this project were able to supply data on these indicators, comparison is not possible because there was some confusion about the definitions of terms. Concentrations of dust and sulphur dioxide are measured in 50, 95, or 98 percentiles.

There is, however, a European trend which can be inferred from the supplied data. The concentration of aerosols was reduced over the five-year period by an average of 35%. This reduction is influenced by the switch from coal and oil to natural gas for heating, the reduction of lead content in fuel, and the use of catalytic converters in cars.

The concentration of sulphur dioxide was even reduced by an average of 42% (and by nearly 60% in Hannover!). This is due to energy-saving measures and alternative systems for generating heat, the reduction of sulphur content in fuel, more efficient combustion, and the increased use of natural gas for heating.

1.3. Number of days of summer and winter smog per year.

The definition of summer and winter smog was apparently interpreted in different ways. Some of the cities reported the number of days that a smog warning was given. These warnings are based on the maximum concentration of various substances during a certain time span and without expected decrease on short notice. Such data are highly influenced by climate conditions in the city. The majority of cities relied on the World Health Organization Air Quality Guidelines, some of them also used the EEC directives (however, mostly from 1992 onwards).

Aalborg is the only city that reported no smog warning since 1988 (see Figure 9). The average number of summer smog days doubled between 1985 and 1990, whereas the average number of winter smog days has declined by 45%. Whether this is related to global climate change is not known.

Figure 9

Number of days of summer and winter smog per year

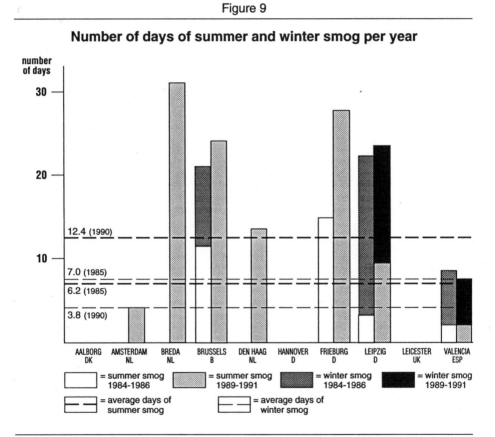

Safe Streets

2.0. The number of meters of street space that has been adapted to reduce car traffic, and percentage (which is a comparison to the total number of kilometers of streets).

Again the complexity of the indicator and the general definition that does not entirely match with the practical interpretations, resulted in insufficient information being collected for comparison.

Worthwhile mentioning are efforts by some cities to achieve a large number of "pedestrian-friendly streets" within a certain time span. The city of Leicester aims to calm 100% of residential streets. The city of Aalborg has already provided 35% of the total street length with cycle paths. The number of meters of street space adapted to reduce car traffic in Valencia increased four times in the 1985-1990 period, although the total number is still modest.

2.1. Percentage of the total number of people affected by traffic noise that exceeds the level of 50dB(A) during the night (22.00 -07.00 hrs).

There was insufficient information to compare the participating cities on this indicator. Studies such as traffic noise maps or reports on traffic noise were not available in the majority of the participating cities. Some mentioned they had recently begun research on this topic, which represents one of the main complaints by citizens about their living conditions. Traffic noise has been shown to affect significantly peoples' feelings of well-being and their perceived quality of life.

2.2. Annual total of reported deaths and injuries in traffic accidents.

The data for this indicator was supplied—in most cases—by the municipal traffic departments or from national or local statistics (see Figure 10). According to some cities, the average increase in the number of reported deaths and injuries is influenced by an increase in traffic level (which is confirmed by background indicator (c) Number of vehicles owned by residents and businesses).

The city of Hannover ascribes the reduced number of reported deaths and injuries in their city to special awareness programs run by local authorities and non-governmental organizations. The number of streets adapted to better accomodate cyclists and pedestrians also contribute to this reduction, which is therefore exactly in accordance with the meaning of the container issue, "Safe Streets," presented in the questionnaire.

The city of Leipzig ascribes the increased number of deaths and injuries to the enormous increase in the number of vehicles since 1989, seen in background indicator (c).

In 1985, car traffic was most dangerous in Leicester, while Leipzig was the safest city in this category. In 1990, Leicester was still the least

---

Table 3

What is the number of traffic-related deaths and injuries per 1,000 inhabitants?

	1985	1990	Increase/ Decrease
Leicester	9.54	11.73	+23%
Hannover	7.70	6.57	-15%
Frieburg	6.87	5.94	-14%
Amsterdam	5.35	5.42	+1%
Brussels	4.63	4.67	_1%
Breda	4.35	4.56	+5%
Aalborg	3.45	2.50	-28%
Leipzig	3.19	4.53	+42%

safe city, while Aalborg was the safest. The increase in "unsafety" over the five-year period was the highest in Leipzig (although the 1985 figures were probably artificially low). Amsterdam, Brussels, and Breda stayed stable, and a considerable decrease was achieved in Aalborg.

Figure 10

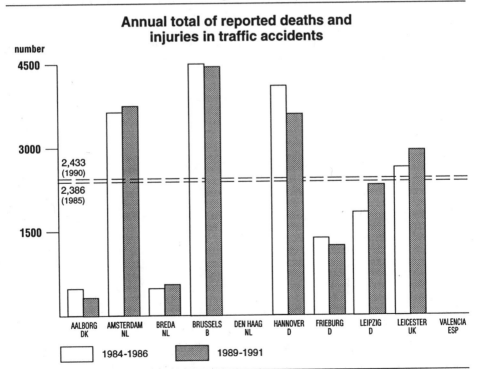

Annual total of reported deaths and injuries in traffic accidents

2.3. Average number of trips per year by means of public transport per inhabitant.

Data were insufficient here for comparing the project cities. In terms of percentage, the number of trips by public transport hardly changed between 1985 and 1990 in Amsterdam, Hannover, and Brussels. An increase of 30% was achieved in Freiburg, due to the banishment of cars from the city center and improvement of the quality and frequency of public transport, without considerable increase of costs.

Good Housing

3.0. The average duration of occupancy of housing units.

It was not possible to compare all of the participating cities due to insufficient information. The comparison of the figures for Valencia to those of Amsterdam, Hannover, and Freiburg, however, is striking: the average duration of occupancy in the Spanish city is considerably longer than in the other cities, and even increased by 45% from 1985 to 1990.

3.1. Percentage of the total number of inhabitants registered unemployed for longer than one year.

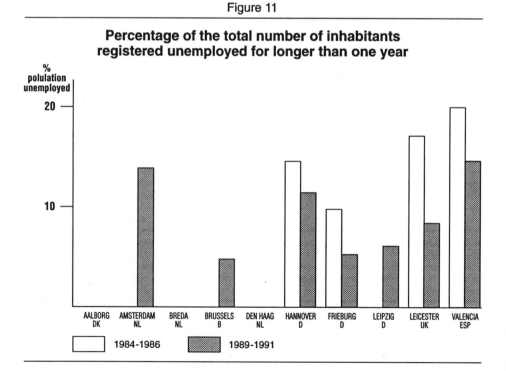

Figure 11

Percentage of the total number of inhabitants registered unemployed for longer than one year

According to the averages shown in Figure 11, the economic situation in the project cities improved between 1985 and 1990, and unemployment rates went down by 23%. The majority of cities, however, mentioned that there had been a change in the way governments statistics were collected between 1985 and 1990, and this affected the figures they supplied. According to the East German government, there was no unemployment in Leipzig in 1985. The city of Hannover regards the long-lasting percentage of unemployment as too high for a city like Hannover, even taking into account the 19% decrease between 1985 and 1990.

Although the city of Leicester shows a reduction of 47% (and therefore an apparent decline in long-term unemployment), these figures were collected according to different methods, and therefore are not comparable.

3.2. Number of reported violent crimes and burglaries per year.

This indicator is strongly related to citizens' satisfaction with the quality of their lives and living environments. The data for this indicator were mainly supplied by local police statistics. The extremely high

Figure 12

Number of reported violent crimes
and burglaries per year

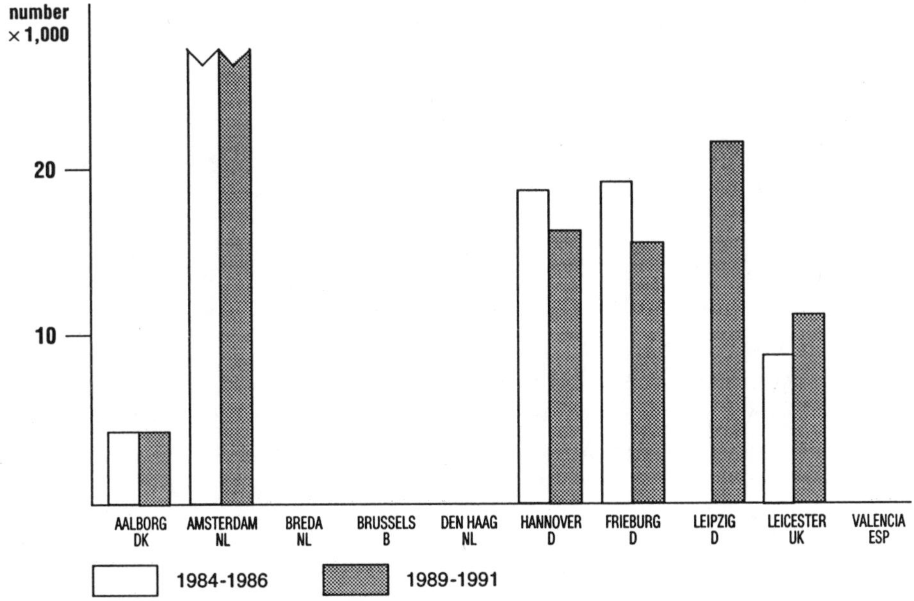

number of reported crimes and burglaries in Amsterdam seen in Figure 12 is due to the kind of crimes that were included in that city's reported data: Amsterdam's was the most comprehensive data supplied for this indicator. The reduction in crimes and burglary figures is highly influenced by a change in registration method between 1985 and 1990, and therefore not representative. Some cities ascribe the reduction of crimes and burglaries to special awareness campaigns on television and in newspapers.

In 1985, Amsterdam was the most dangerous city to live in and visit (96% crimes of the total figure), while Aalborg was the safest city with respect to violent crimes and burglaries. In 1990, Aalborg was still the "safest" and Amsterdam the most "unsafe" city (87% "crimes agains property"), despite the change in measurement method and a considerable overall decrease of 21%. The increase in "unsafety" over the five-year period was the highest in Leicester.

Table 4

What is the number of violent crimes and burglaries per 1,000 inhabitants?

	1985	1990	Increase/ Decrease
Aalborg	29.73	29.67	—
Leicester	31.36	39.51	+26%
Hannover	34.39	31.09	-10%
Leipzig	n.a.	42.13	—
Freiburg	101.82	81.82	-20%
Amsterdam	194.78	153.47	-21%

3.3. (Average) percentagr of electorate voting in local elections or in referenda for local affairs, in the respective year.

The figures presented in Figure 13 relate to local council elections. If this indicator is an accurate reflection of public participation in local policies, then the 11% average decrease would seem to confirm the rumor heard among local authorities that citizens' interest in local policy is on the decline. On the other hand, public awareness is increasing in practice, and citizens want a say in how their city is managed. At the very least, they want to know is what is going on in their city and how their tax money is spent. Analysis of the supplied data cannot, however, confirm these interpretations.

Voting is obligatory in Brussels and therefore participation statistics similar to those used in other cities were not available. Furthermore, there were no elections in Brussels in the years included in the Index. The percentage of electorate voting in Leipzig was officially reported to be "almost 100%," as the statistic had been used by the former socialist government to demonstrate citizens' commitment to policies.

Figure 13

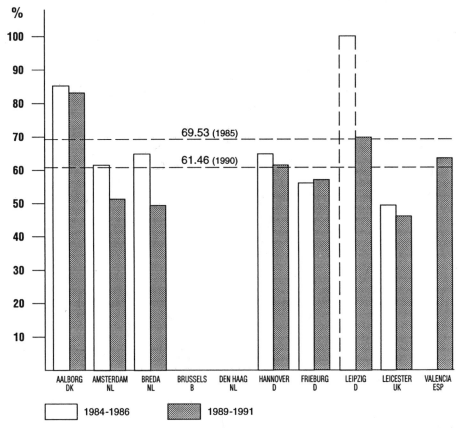

(Average) percentage of electorate voting in local elections or in referenda for local affairs.

3.4. Percentage of the total number of inhabitants living within 400 meters of a food supply center (grocery store, supermarket, etc.).

Again, data were insufficient here for comparing the project cities. According to a majority of the project cities, food supply centers are within reach for all inhabitants. They therefore do not regard this indicator to be important for local sustainability.

Greenery

4.0. The number of people having access to outdoor space with private and/or public recreational greenery within 400 meters walking distance of their home, in percentage to the total population.

According to Figure 14, European cities are relatively "green" since the majority of their inhabitants seem to have access to outdoor green space (defined in the background information) within walking distance of

---

Figure 14

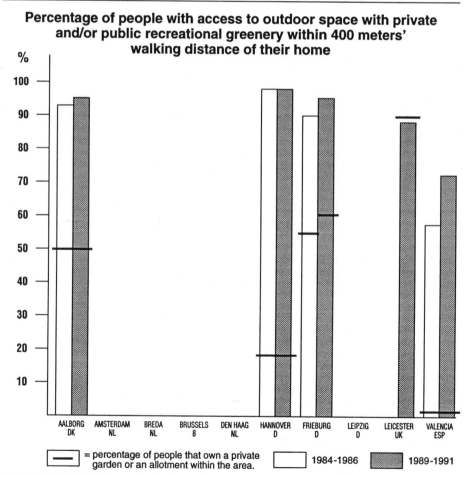

Percentage of people with access to outdoor space with private and/or public recreational greenery within 400 meters' walking distance of their home

their homes. The information presented by Valencia is probably the most reliable, as the questionnaire was completed by the Head of the Green Plan Bureau.

The figures for this indicator are combined with those of indicator 4.2 on "private gardens and allotments," which shows that the percentage of "private green" has not changed considerably between 1985 and 1990. The increase in access to public green space is therefore related to the planting of additional public trees and the layout of more urban greenery.

4.1. Total number of plant species.

Data were insufficient for comparing the project cities. Apparently the information on this indicator is not available through municipal departments. Some of the project cities noted that monitoring on this subject is often the domain of local environmental organizations. Figures and results in this category seem to be difficult to obtain, although some cities also stated that new efforts to monitor the number of plant and animal species and the number of trees began in the early nineties.

4.2. Percentage of the total number of inhabitants which have use of a private garden or an allotment within the area measured.

See Figure 14 and the explanation under indicator 4.0.

Environmental Compliance

5.0. The number of housing units and office or industrial buildings that comply with local environment standards, in percentage to the total.

There was a lack of or insufficient information available to compare the participating cities. It appears that local environmental standards hardly existed before 1990 in the cities involved in this project. Some of the cities explained that they had only begun developing local standards within the past few years, in most cases, in response to requests from newly formed environmental departments.

5.1. Percentage of the total number of registered companies following a recycling scheme and/or an environmental management system, strategy, or plan.

Data were insufficient here for comparing the project cities. See also the explanation under indicator 5.0. An exception should be made for the city of Freiburg, which encourages companies to follow an environmentally sound management strategy. According to the figures reported in the questionnaire, their achievements are very successful.

5.2. Percentage of the total number of municipal buildings that have been constructed or reconstructed in the given year according to a reduced-energy consumption standard (the reduced energy standard is presumed to lead to at least 20% less energy consumption per office-user/dweller).

There was lack of or insufficient information available to compare the participating cities. See also under indicators 5.0 and 5.1. ·

5.3. Percentage of the total number of building projects realized in the respective year in the area in which construction and/or demolition waste has been collected separately for reuse, in accordance with municipal building/demolition permits.

Insufficient information was available to compare the participating cities. See also under 5.0, 5.1, and 5.2.

5.4. Number of licenses or permits issued for construction of public buildings and/or offices meeting municipal criteria for short walking distances to public transport.

Information was insufficient for to comparing the participating cities. Some cities involved in this project state that their public transport system is so highly condensed, that all public buildings are within short walking distance to public transport. The Netherlands has a standard system of assessing building locations in relation to accessibility by means of transport. There is, however, no legislation that regulates the construction of buildings depending on the walking distance to public transport.

The data for this indicator are impossible to collect, since this aspect is not yet defined through licenses or permits.

5.5. Percentage of the total number of housing units with a dual piping system for drinking water and grey water.

Only the city of Freiburg experiments with installing dual piping systems, and this experiment is on a very small scale. The majority of the project cities ascribed their response of "0%" for this indicator to the high standards for hygiene that are applied and which do not yet allow the development of dual piping systems.

Sustainable Resource Use

6.0. Average yearly amount (in ECUs) that households spend on energy, water, and waste processing.

It was impossible to compare the data on this indicator, since the exchange rates that cities used to convert national currency into ECU were not reliable and, more important, because the definition was not applicable in some cities and the requested information was not available.

6.1. Average use of drinking-quality water per person per day in liters.

Figure 15 shows an average increase of water consumption of almost 5% in the between 1985 and 1990; only Freiburg, Hannover, and Leipzig report reductions. Again, it is not entirely possible to compare the data, since the interpretation of the indicator definition varies greatly. Moreover, cities supplied data based on available figures that

Figure 15

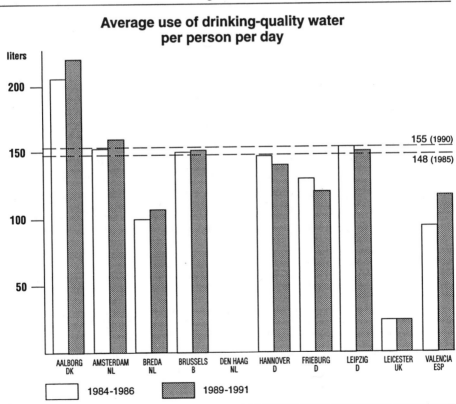

were not completely in accordance with the definition. Some cities deal with various water companies and can therefore not supply complete data. Other cities give the total use of drinking water per capita in their city (and not per household), which also includes the use of drinking water by companies and assessed leakage quantity.

6.2. Percentage of the total number of buildings using solar energy by photo-voltaic cells or devices.

Some project cities are in an early experimental or research phase on the use of photo-voltaic cells, though still on a very small scale. The majority of cities responded with an answer of "practically 0%" for this indicator. The commonly cited reason was the high price of extracting solar energy compared to the low costs of energy resources used at present.

6.3. Percentage of the total number of households practicing separation of organic waste for composting purposes.

While some of the project cities had programs encouraging the practice of separating organic waste for composting purposes, many of these programs began in 1990 or later. In The Netherlands, organic waste is now collected separately from other wastes in many parts of the country, excluding the city centers.

Workshop on Sustainability Indicators

A European workshop was held within the framework of the European Sustainability Indicators Project from 5-8 October 1994, in The Netherlands. Participants came from each of the European project cities; in most cases two officials from environmental departments of the city's municipal office attended. The questionnaire completed by the participating cities formed the basis for the Workshop on Sustainability Indicators.

Evaluation of the Questionnaire

The questionnaire had to be completed within a relatively short time by the participating cities. What conclusions did the cities come to about this questionnaire, concerning the manner in which it was presented and the value of the information requested?

The participants felt that indicators should flow from the vision of a sustainable community. This requires a local discussion on the definition of sustainability in a broader sense. In this way, the definition of the indicators is related to local standards and it is almost impossible to create a uniform version for all participating cities.

Although it is difficult to measure sustainability, the approach must always be practical—understandable for environmentalists as well as for politicians, businesses, and the public-at-large.

The underlying message of the reference framework should be communicated to localities and depicted as relevant for local sustainable development. The cities agreed that the main intention of the Index should be to highlight trends and not to compare data.

Although a surprisingly high number of indicators were filled in by the city representatives in the questionnaire (within the short time available), they all regarded the background information that accompanied the form to be insufficiently detailed and the data difficult to gather. The meaning of the questionnaire and the choice of the years 1985 and 1990 (and the time span of five years) were not completely clear. However, the general opinion was that the questionnaire brought to light various new aspects of measuring sustainability.

Some cities regarded the range of issues for data collection to be too broad; they initially asserted that a compact set of 4 to 6 core indicators would suffice (and be less costly to measure), but in the course of the workshop all agreed on a set of ten core indicators.

Selection of Relevant Indicators

The workshop included an exercise on the selection of indicators in which the participants were divided into three working parties. Each party received twenty-six cards stating the Index core and basis indicators and five additional blank cards. The assignment was to select (and adjust when necessary) the given indicators. Although each indicator has its own practical advantages and disadvantages, its relevance for the measuring of sustainability plays an important role. Not all twenty-six indicators need be used. If the group found some to be totally irrelevant, those indicators could be left out. A maximum of five new cards (representing indicators) per working party could be added.

Surprisingly, the option to formulate new indicators was hardly used by the working parties. They fully agreed on several indicators, especially on those to measure air quality (expressed in concentrations or compared to locally used standards), access to green within certain distance, and the number of trees and plant and animal species. Some of the indicators were redefined. It was suggested that the "total street lengths adapted to reduce car traffic" be changed to "the usage of space by cars." Also the "passenger kilometers traveled by mode per annum/per capita" was regarded to be part of the basic meaning of mobility or accessibility. The flows of energy, water, materials, and waste were specified in indicators such as "the total amount of waste for final disposal in tons per annum/by sector" and "the energy consumption per annum/per sector." Public participation and human well-being were regarded as important, but were not defined by indicators.

Container Issues Covering Sustainability

Regarding indicators selected by the working parties which were supposed to act as core-indicators, a consensus was reached on a first list of container issues:

☐ Air quality
☐ Greenery
☐ Resources
☐ Mobility
☐ Public participation

This list was compared to a list of those indicators in the questionnaire for which more than fifty percent of the participating cities were able to supply data. The availability of data matched significantly with this list. Almost every city was able to give data on air quality, the number of plant species, the access to green (both indicators for "greenery") and the average use of water ("resources"). The percentage of electorate voting gave easy insight into "public participation," as did the percentage of people unemployed for socioeconomic aspects. The number of reported deaths/injuries and violent crimes (both indicators for "safety") are not referred to in the list of container issues.

Once the five container issues were agreed upon, the participants felt the need to check whether all aspects of sustainability were covered. It appeared that many aspects were indeed already covered.

"Social justice," "Well-being," "Green economy," "Built environment," and "Vitality" were added. "Air quality" was changed into "Healthy environment" and "Mobility" into "Accessibility." There was also a discussion on the need to reword the container issues in a more positive sense, as the process toward sustainability is generally regarded as connected to positive thinking, to improvement and change of behavior.

Participants agreed on a list of ten container issues to be incorporated in the European Sustainability Index (see Table 5). Since the availability of data on the urban environment is the result of policies that started ten to fifteen years ago, it could well take some time before the data that the cities find relevant for measuring sustainability is available through measuring programs. This sets new goals for the future!

Finding Consensus on a Set of Core Indicators

Once a consensus was reached on the container issues, discussion (in plenary and in working parties) turned to defining the core indicators. Keeping in mind the indicators that were already mentioned in an earlier stage of the workshop, the city representatives were asked individually whether they were able to supply the data for their city and if they regarded the indicator to be relevant for measuring sustainability at the local level. Both discussions are incorporated in the following summary.

There was an undiscussed consensus about the core indicator for "healthy environment." The indicator for the "number of days that the locally applied standards for air quality are exceeded" is very difficult to measure directly, however. It needs supportive data, such as the concentration of dust, ozone, and benzene. These figures could be supplied by basis or area-specific indicators. It also implies that the core indicator needs to be further defined at the local level. The given or directly measurable indicators related to air quality are locally determined.

An interesting discussion started on the role of traffic and transport. It is often heard that restricting cars from cities can contribute a great deal to urban sustainability. Some of the participants regard this idea to be an obsession among its proponents. They stated that the number of "calm streets" does not necessarily lead to more sustainability and that lower car density does not necessarily lead to safer streets (with fewer deaths, injuries, and violent crimes) nor does it directly contribute to the

---

Table 5

The European Sustainability Index: Container Issues and Core Indicators

Healthy Environment
Number of days per year that local standards for air quality are not exceeded.

Green Space
Percentage of people with access to green within a certain distance.

Efficient Use of Resources
Total energy and water consumption and production of waste for final disposal per capita per annum.
Ratio of renewable to non-renewable energy sources.

Quality of the Built Environment
Ratio of open space to the area used by cars.

Accessibility
Kilometers traveled by mode of transport (car, bicycle, public transport, etc.) per capita per annum.

Green Economy
Percentage of companies that have joined Eco-Management and Audit Schemes (EMAS) or similar schemes.

Vitality
Number of social and cultural activities or facilities (add list).

Community Involvement
Number of voluntary organizations or groups per 1,000 inhabitants (and an educated guess about the number of members).

Social Justice
Percentage of people living below the poverty line.

Well-being
Survey of citizens' satisfaction of the "Quality of Life" (contents of survey to be determined locally).

---

quality of life. Furthermore, it appears to be very difficult to measure things like "adapted street length" and "kilometers traveled" at the local level, since the necessary data are difficult to gather. Traffic and transport at the local level is often strongly influenced by the economic features of the city. Some cities attract many cars because of the high number of offices, others "suffer" from transit routes going through their city. There are data available from on-the-street surveys of car owners, but the participants finally agreed that the "number of kilometers traveled by mode of transport per annum/per capita" is the most sensible indicator for accessibility (and mobility).

The participants agreed that the container issues and the core-indicators presented in the workshop gave sufficient information to calculate results to measure sustainability. The core indicators could be completed with a set of basic-indicators. There is however a third (large) group of indicators—the area-specific indicators—which have been left out in the Institute's general indicator system on purpose. These were also not a subject of the workshop, since the ABC-indicator model® provides the opportunity to add Area-specific indicators, and in doing so to complete and attune the European core and basis indicator system making it a useful local policy tool.

Core indicators for each container issue as agreed upon in conclusion of the project are highlighted in Table 5.

Wording of Container Issues and the Indicators

The workshop resulted in a consensus on the indicators representing the container issues. After discussing various indicators, the participants concluded that most of these could also be regarded as "area-specific" indicators, and therefore needed local definitions. This once again stressed the meaning and importance of completing the Sustainability Index on the local level with locally defined indicators. By leaving the definition and reference framework to be filled in by the city applying the Index, it could become something of their own, and not defined from the top down.

This can be illustrated with the indicators for "community involvement" and "social justice." Some representatives regarded the "percentage of electorate voting" as more relevant for community involvement than "the number of voluntary organizations/groups per 1,000 inhabitants." Others found the "percentage of people living below the poverty line" to be most important to indicate "social justice; but some were not entirely happy with this indicator. Debate arose over the issue of "greenery" which, according to some of the participants, should be considered with respect to natural habitats. When discussing "efficient use of resources," some found it more important to measure flows of energy, water, materials, and waste from a point of view of consumption patterns, while others preferred to concentrate on the proportion of renewable and non-renewable resources in the area.

Some of the participants felt that "biodiversity" and "ecosystems" were missing as "container issues" or should be brought in as indicators under one of the headings now chosen. But it was agreed that these could be expressed or defined in area-specific indicators.

Conclusion

The development of the European Sustainability Index has proven to be a most useful and necessary tool to continue the accelerating process and progress toward sustainability of (European) cities.

One of the aims of the project was to enable comparison of cities. However, comparison on the basis of the data collected by means of the questionnaire, was not possible because the interpretation of definitions varied so greatly from place to place. Furthermore, measurement methods in Europe are still far from being fine-tuned. Solving the problem of comparison would require an unpractical volume of explanations and definitions which is incompatible with the goal of simplicity in using iindicators. The twelve participating cities, which are representative for Europe, represent an early step in a process toward sustainability. As stated in the conclusion of the project workshop: "We are not there yet."

Looking at the available data that the participating cities have managed to collect, the conclusion *could* be drawn that we are already able to measure quite a number of aspects concerning the process toward sustainability. On the other hand, it should not be forgotten that many of the data that were easy to collect relate to policies that were established ten to fifteen years ago. Although much experience with environmental policies has been gained, it obviously takes time before data are available to measure the effects of more recent policies and, unfortunately, time is running out. Fast-moving political aims are needed: more simplicity, observable effects, and direct measurability. Sustainability requires setting new political goals and activities for the near-future. This means that rather drastic changes in environmental policies—in comparison to the former way of implementing and monitoring—should take place soon. In this respect, the required data for the (still rather complicated) core indicators of the Index that were agreed upon by the conclusion of this project could be collected. The majority of the cities involved mentioned the rapid progress achieved over the past few years, and were aware that this was partly due to newly developed monitoring systems now in existence. They were therefore more anxious to show the data from, say, 1993 and compare it with the 1990 situation in order to evaluate and analyze their recent achievements. They regarded the period from 1985 to 1990 not only to be less relevant, but also to be too long; in their opinion, a three-year period would be more representative of their efforts.

The Index, based on the ten core indicators shown in Table 5, is the result of a creative and evolving process in which the twelve European project cities formed conclusions on a uniform and compact set of indicators that cover a wide range of sustainability aspects. However, the European Sustainability Index does need further elaboration, particulary for the cities that are going to use it in day-to-day practice. A reference framework for the Sustainability Index can not be defined in a uniform way for all cities. It is strongly related to the experience, knowledge, and the vision that local communities have developed. Formulating a reference framework which can be identified by them is one of the most important aspects to stimulate working with an Index.

In this respect the participating cities in this project regard the European Sustainability Index to be a valuable leitmotiv for the development, analyses, adjustment, and improvement of local policies. Cities that choose to use the Index in the future will have to formulate their own message and vision behind the Index, make it recognizable, and add their own area-specific indicators—indicators that represent the features of their cities and data with which they can identify. The Index can thus also play an important role in the development of local agendas and a sustainable vision of the future.

Assessing Progress toward Sustainability: A New Approach

CƷ

The IUCN/IDRC Project on Monitoring and Assessing
Progress Toward Sustainability: Approach, Methods, Tools,
Progress

IUCN INTERNATIONAL ASSESSMENT TEAM

Preface

In 1992, strategy practitioners from Asia, Africa, and Latin America
asked the Strategies for Sustainability Programme of IUCN to provide
assistance in monitoring and evaluating strategies. Since there was no
"off-the-shelf" method of assessing strategies, the Programme set out
to develop one with the assistance of the Canadian International Development Agency (CIDA) and the International Development Research
Centre (IDRC).

In December 1993, IUCN and the Delhi-based NGO, Development
Alternatives, organized a workshop in India on monitoring and evaluating strategies for sustainability. Three days were spent discussing indicators of sustainability. Yet the more material we assembled, the less
headway we made. We felt as if we were sinking in an ocean of indicators with no sense of direction or context.

Meanwhile, IDRC had undertaken a comprehensive review of
the topic and concluded that people first had to agree on a conceptual framework and on the process of assessment before addressing

indicators. It had published a conceptual approach to assessing sustainability (Hodge 1993), which it was interested in testing and developing further.

Thus IUCN and IDRC came together with a common interest in assessing sustainability and scepticism about focusing on indicators. Both were also convinced of the necessity of tying theory to practice by closely combining research, development, and field-testing.

With the support of IDRC, IUCN assembled an international assessment team to develop and test a practical method of assessing progress toward sustainability. The team consists of people experienced in participatory development and communications, state-of-the-environment reporting, monitoring and evaluation, and strategy formulation.

We began to focus on the process of assessment and the context in which indicators are used. Issues were tackled like "sustainability for whom?", differing value and decision-making systems, and how to motivate people to take action in response to assessments.

From this debate has emerged the approach to assessing sustainability that is summarized in this document. A set of methods and tools is being tested, adapted, and refined in Asia, Africa, and Latin America by local strategy teams:

☐ Asia. The Development Alternatives team working with district level planning officials in Tumkur district, Karnataka State, India: George C. Varughese, Vijay Pillai, C. Ashok Kumar, and Sriparna Sanyal.

☐ Africa. The District Environmental Action Plan teams in Zimbabwe: Elliott Makha, Sam Chimbuya, and Carmel Lue-Mbizvo.

☐ Latin America. The monitoring team of the Fundación Pro-Sierra Nevada de Santa Marta: Natalia Ortíz, and Hernando Sanchez.

The members of the international team are:

☐ Ashoke Chatterjee, National Institute of Design, India
☐ Eric Dudley, development consultant, UK
☐ Tony Hodge, consultant, Canada
☐ Alejandro Imbach, CATIE, Costa Rica
☐ Diana Lee-Smith, Mazingira Institute, Kenya
☐ Adil Najam, Massachusetts Institute of Technology, USA
☐ Robert Prescott-Allen, PADATA, Canada

Although particular products have been attributed to the individuals directly responsible for their development, all members of the international and national teams have contributed essential ideas and feedback. In addition, we owe a particular debt to the villagers with whom we have worked, for their patience, candor, hospitality, humor, and insights.

NANCY MACPHERSON
Coordinator, Programme on Strategies for Sustainability
IUCN - The World Conservation Union

This report has been produced by IUCN with assistance from the International Development Research Centre (IDRC), Canada.

Purpose and Approach

Purpose

The purpose of this project is to develop and test a practical method of assessing progress toward sustainability. The aim is for the method to be useful and usable in a range of contexts at local, regional, and national levels. To achieve this purpose, IUCN has formed an international team and linked it to national teams working on local strategies for sustainability in Colombia, India, and Zimbabwe.

Approach: Systemic User-driven Sustainability Assessment (SUSA)

The project is developing and testing an approach to assessment, together with a set of methods, tools, and training materials. We call the approach Systemic User-driven Sustainability Assessment (SUSA), to emphasize its distinguishing features:

Systemic
　□ *Systemic*—providing a sense of the overall system (the human subsystem within the ecosystem), not just of the parts.
　□ *Goal-directed*—focusing assessment on improving the condition of people and the ecosystem.
　□ *Hierarchical*—grouping indicators into sets and arranging them from the particular and local to the more general and universal. The hierarchy enables indicators to be aggregated (nec-

essary for a sense of whether the overall system is getting better or worse). It also permits the use of locally relevant indicators while allowing comparisons at a higher level of generalization.

☐ *Hypothesis-led*—formulating assessments and proposed actions as hypotheses so that users may learn from them and improve their actions.

User-driven

☐ *User-driven*—reflecting the conditions, needs, and priorities of the people using the assessment, and allowing users to choose their own indicators.

☐ *Consensus-based*—incorporating widely accepted elements of other conceptual frameworks and approaches to assessment.

☐ *Visually immediate*—so that people can quickly grasp where they are and where they are going.

☐ *Transparent and accessible*—making values and judgments clear, and presenting data in such a way that others may explore alternative interpretations.

The model of the system is shown in Figure 1. Human societies form a subsystem within the ecosystem, just as the yolk of an egg is within the white. For an egg to be good, both the yolk and the white have to be good. Likewise, a society is sustainable only if *both* the human condition and the condition of the ecosystem are satisfactory or improving. People and ecosystem are equally important. If the condition of *either* is unsatisfactory or worsening, the society is unsustainable.

Figure 1

The Egg of Sustainability (Prescott-Allen 1995)

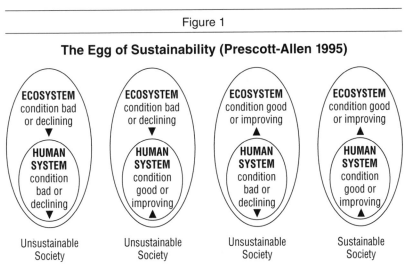

Recognizing that people are an integral part of the ecosystem, a logical goal for every society is *to improve and maintain the well-being of people* and *the ecosystem*. To assess progress toward this goal an assessment needs to ask the five questions below. These questions provide the assessment framework (Figure 2).

☐ What is the condition of the ecosystem, how is it changing and why?
☐ What is the condition of people, how is it changing and why?
☐ What are the main interactions between people and the ecosystem?
☐ What conclusions can be drawn about progress toward the goal? (synthesis)
☐ What needs to be done to make progress toward the goal? (strategy)

Figure 2

Assessment Framework (based on Hodge 1993, 1995)

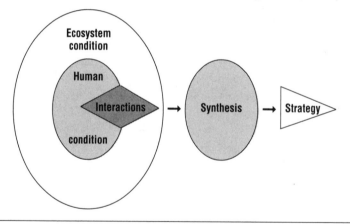

Distinguishing features of the SUSA approach include:

☐ *SUSA treats people and the ecosystem together as one system.* Many other approaches divide the system into three components: economy, society, and environment. Such a division is misleading because it: (a) puts people outside the ecosystem; (b) demotes the ecosystem to one of three factors; (c) splits economic and social aspects of the human subsystem, although they are intertwined (and differently defined by different disciplines); and (d) sets human and ecosystem well-being against each other when the need now is to improve and maintain both.

☐ *SUSA assesses the whole system as well as the parts.* Most other approaches lack a method of combining the parts to show the big picture.

☐ *SUSA treats people and the ecosystem as equally important.* Most other approaches have a bias toward one or the other.

☐ *SUSA allows each issue to be analyzed with the most appropriate method.* Most other approaches are either economic (for example, modified national accounts or the Index of Sustainable Economic Welfare) or environmental (for example, pressure-state-response), and distort analysis of issues for which they were not designed.

☐ *SUSA lets users choose their own indicators.* Most other approaches choose the indicators in advance.

Methods

The project has helped to develop and test four methods:

 ☐ *Barometer of Sustainability*—a method of assessing human and ecosystem well-being, and a tool for synthesizing and portraying the results in an index of sustainability (or overall well-being);
 ☐ *Rapid Assessment Mapping for Sustainability (RAMS)*—a method of quickly obtaining a broad understanding of a system and of identifying priority areas for action;
 ☐ *Assessing and Planning Rural Sustainability*—a step-by-step method for strategy teams working with villagers; and
 ☐ *Asking Questions of Survival*—a method of helping institutions to assess and manage people-ecosystem interactions.

(1) Barometer of Sustainability

The Barometer of Sustainability provides a systematic way of organizing and combining indicators so that users can draw conclusions about the conditions of people and the ecosystem and the effects of people-ecosystem interactions. It presents those conclusions visually, providing anyone—from villager to head of state—with an immediate picture of where they are and where they are going.

The Barometer combines indices of ecosystem well-being and human well-being into an index of sustainability without trading one off against the other. It may be used at any level: local, provincial, national, or international.

Figure 3

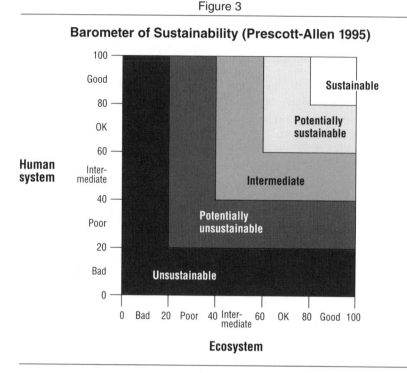

Barometer of Sustainability (Prescott-Allen 1995)

Aggregating indicators to indices is done via the hierarchy:

SUBSYSTEM	ECOSYSTEM	PEOPLE
Dimension	e.g., ecosystem quality	e.g., knowledge
indicative issue	e.g., land quality	e.g., education
indicator	e.g., eroded land as	e.g., adult
	percentage of land area	literacy rate

Dimensions are universal. The four ecosystem dimensions build on the components of ecosystem conservation of the *World Conservation Strategy* (IUCN/UNEP/WWF 1980) and *Caring for the Earth* (IUCN/ UNEP/WWF 1991). They are:

☐ *Naturalness or conversion.* Gives a sense of the scale and rate of a society's overall impact on the ecosystem, both within and beyond its territory. The proportions of the territory that are natural, modified, cultivated, or built suggest how much of the planetary support system the society has taken for its own immediate use, and how much it has left both for other people and for the rest of life.

☐ *Ecosystem quality.* Deals with the general condition of air, water, and land, including use of the ecosystem as a sink for wastes. Covers productivity, pollution, and degradation.

☐ *Biodiversity.* Looks at whether we are maintaining or reducing the diversity of ecological communities, wild species, and genetic variants such as crop varieties, livestock breeds, and wild populations.

☐ *Resource use.* Covers use of the ecosystem as a source of goods, both renewable (timber, fisheries, forage, wildlife, soil, water) and nonrenewable (minerals, oil, gas, coal).

Similarly, the four human dimensions build on the indicators of human development of the *Human Development Report* (UNDP 1990 and following years). They are:

☐ *Health and population.* Comprises fertility, mortality, disease, food and nutrition, health practices, and health services. A long and healthy life increases the opportunity for a person to pursue goals and develop abilities.

☐ *Wealth and livelihood.* Considers income, employment, housing, transport, infrastructure, technology, and other goods that enable people to survive or that expand opportunities and provide means to exploit them.

☐ *Knowledge.* Includes formal and informal education, research, and communication. Knowledge equips individuals, organizations, and society to fulfil their potential, improve understanding of the ecosystem and human system, and develop the information and skills required to live sustainably.

☐ *Behavior and institutions.* Covers social behavior and institutions in their widest sense—the values, customs, laws, incentives, and organizations that enable societies to manage people's relationships with each other and the ecosystem.

Indicative issues are widely but not always applicable. Examples of indicative issues include water quality, species diversity, employment, and conflicts and violence. The choice of issues will depend on which ones reveal the dimension most clearly, what issues most concern people (recognizing also that different issues matter more or less to different interest groups), and for what issues can indicators be developed.

Indicators are context-specific and chosen by users. Examples of indicators include fecal coliform levels, number of threatened species, unemployment rate, and homicides per 100,000 people. The choice of indicators will depend on which ones reveal the issue most clearly and for which data can be obtained. The more indicators there are per issue, the more they will neutralize each other. As a rule of thumb, the maximum number of indicators is four per issue. Often one or two per issue will be enough. These suggestions apply only to indicators that are used to calculate the Barometer's indices of human well-being and ecosystem well-being. Additional indicators may be compiled to improve analysis of the issues.

Transforming many different indicators into one big picture requires combining or aggregating the indicators up the hierarchy: from indicators to indicative issues; from indicative issues to dimensions; and from dimensions to systems. Prescott-Allen (1995) describes a way of doing this and explains the method in more detail, discussing its uses and potential misuses.

A simplified Barometer has been translated into Shona and Ndebele as part of the method of assessing rural sustainability in Zimbabwe (see below). Simplification involves using the qualitative scale only. When drawn on the spot (rather than prepared in advance) and explained as it is drawn, it is easy for villagers to grasp. The next step is to move from a qualitative to a quantitative version as part of the assessment of action plans. The Barometer has also been adapted for use in Rapid Assessment Mapping for Sustainability (RAMS) in the Sierra Nevada de Santa Marta, Colombia.

The method is being promoted for use nationally and internationally, as well as locally. The project has tested the Barometer at the national level in Zimbabwe to see how easy it was to use in countries where data on a wide range of indicative issues are unavailable or difficult to obtain. The experiment was successful. It is hoped that Zimbabwe and other countries will develop their own Barometers.

(2) Rapid Assessment Mapping for Sustainability (RAMS)

Rapid Assessment Mapping for Sustainability allows planners, field workers, and researchers to get a broad understanding of a system from an early stage and provides a method for identifying priority areas for action and research. It has emerged from the approach described in

"Asking Questions of Survival" (Dudley and Imbach 1995) and is designed to make use of Map Maker software (both described below). RAMS can be used to assess any spatial region, from a continent to a village. The method stresses four points:

☐ *Expert groups.* A participatory approach in which expert groups (e.g., scientists, field workers, long-distance truck drivers, village women) are the key sources of data.

☐ *Integrated analysis.* The integration of ecological and social issues into a single framework of analysis which considers both the state of the environment and the characteristics of human values and power that influence it.

☐ *A spatial hierarchy.* The use of a hierarchy of spatial levels in which each level is divided into cells which are themselves the next level down, e.g., region, province, landscape, village, and farm.

☐ *Simple maps.* The use of simple maps as tools for analysis, discussion, consensus, communication, and project documentation.

The method involves six stages:

☐ *Level.* Identify the area or region (the level of complexity) to be assessed, which could be anything from a continent to a village.

☐ *Cells.* Identify the spatial cells of analysis. These should typically be one level down from the overall area to be assessed. In other words, a continent would normally be divided into cells corresponding to countries, whereas a village is divided into farms. If the cell is too small relative to the area, the grain becomes too fine and the overall picture cannot be grasped.

☐ *Actors.* Identify the social agents or "stakeholders" involved in the area being examined.

☐ *Measure.* For each cell, assess both the state and the tendencies of the various dimensions being assessed. The nature of the measurement will vary, but for the purposes of rapid mapping, two key techniques are used: the desk study of existing data and the expert group meeting. The expert group may be specialist scientists, long-distance truck drivers, or village women, depending on the issue being analyzed (it is structured gossip).

☐ *Map.* Map the results, showing both aggregated results and individual variables. Where appropriate, average (or sample) data for cells should be used to generate continuous "data surfaces" so that values for areas without hard data may be interpolated. The RAMS method is predicated on always having a "best guess" for the values of the variables at any point in the area of interest. In this way, composite data surfaces may be created from disparate data sets for different variables, some detailed, some crude.

☐ *Prioritize.* Use the maps to help identify and prioritize action to bring about change and research to fill key data gaps. In making priorities, it is often necessary to work back from data surfaces to extract average values for a cell, since the cell of analysis should also be the grain at which actions are taken.

This cycle of analysis may reveal that one or more of the cells is particularly interesting or problematic. The RAMS method can then be applied to that one cell—breaking it down in turn into a finer grain of cells.

The RAMS method may be used to analyze any kind of continuously varying data with any kind of underlying model. It is described in a draft document in English and Spanish (Imbach and Dudley 1995) and has been presented to meetings of IUCN members in Central America, Ethiopia, and Switzerland.

(3) Assessing and Planning Rural Sustainability

This is a participatory method of assessing rural sustainability and planning action. The method is divided into two stages:

☐ Assessing rural sustainability. Exploring the conditions of the ecosystem and people and preparing for action planning. This stage is intended to help villagers and the strategy team arrive at a common understanding of ecosystem well-being, human well-being, the need to improve both together, and the need for action to be based on villagers' own commitments.

☐ Planning action for rural sustainability. This stage has two phases. First, the villagers prepare a preliminary action plan. This identifies a few priority issues, the actions the villagers will take to tackle these issues, the additional actions they could take with help (such as training, tools or equipment, seed money), the help that is needed, and the outside support that is required. Then the strategy team returns to conduct a joint assessment with the villagers of the practicality of the plan and the villagers' commitment. At the same time, the villagers and team clarify the hypotheses underlying the plan and develop indicators to assess them and the progress and effectiveness of the plan.

Assessing rural sustainability consists of four steps before going into the field and twenty-one steps in the field. The latter can be covered in three meetings of about four to five hours each (a total of twelve to fifteen hours). The steps include a variety of tools used in participatory rural assessment. Some are standard—games, mapping, and dialogue (semi-structured interviewing)—and some have been developed for the project: the Egg of Sustainability; a simplified Barometer of Sustainability; and the Pyramid of Action (described below).

The team first sets the scene. A game is played to show that sustainable development depends on people learning to do things for themselves. The team explains the project and then uses the Pyramid of Action to reinforce the need for the community's strategy to be founded on the villagers' own actions. The team introduces the Egg of Sustainability to get across the idea that people are a part of the ecosystem and that the well-being of both people and the ecosystem need to be improved. Next, the team facilitator draws the Barometer of Sustainability, which reinforces this idea and provides the community with a tool for measuring human and ecosystem well-being. The villagers define the sectors of each scale (from bad to good) using their own terms. Afterwards, they discuss where they are on each scale (an initial reading of the Barometer) and list the factors that contribute to human well-being and ecosystem well-being.

In the next series of steps, the community explores the condition of the ecosystem. Villagers define components of their ecosystem (forests, rivers, wetlands, grazing lands, croplands, settlements) and divide into groups to draw past and present maps. On the maps and in diagrams, they analyze and show changes in each component: area, condition, diversity of plants and animals, and products and services. Group findings are discussed by the meeting as a whole to try to reach consensus or (failing that) record differences.

This leads to the exploration of the condition of people. The villagers again divide into groups to examine and portray concepts, status and trends of food, income, wealth and poverty, infrastructure, health and population, knowledge, and institutions. As with the ecosystem exploration, group findings are discussed by the meeting as a whole to try to reach consensus or record differences.

The final series of steps prepares the community to work on its own action plan. The meeting revisits the Barometer to see if people want to reassess their positions on the human and ecosystem scales, in light of their assessment of their own condition and the ecosystem condition. They discuss improvement of both conditions. The team then asks the community to prepare a preliminary action plan to move it in the desired direction.

Planning action for rural sustainability also suggests preparatory steps, followed by steps in the field. The first series of steps covers a joint assessment by the villagers and team of the practicality of the plan and the villagers' commitment. Part of the purpose of this is for the community to examine whether the solutions it proposes are likely to solve the problems (for example, a proposed dam will not work unless land use practices are changed to reduce erosion). This may require further discussion about the causes of problems, how problems are connected, and what the villagers can do about them. It certainly calls for clarification of the hypotheses underlying the plan. The remaining steps deal with the selection and development of indicators to assess the hypotheses and the plan's progress and results.

"Assessing Rural Sustainability" is available as a draft booklet, and a booklet is being prepared on planning action for rural sustainability (Lee-Smith and others 1995). The method is being tested in Zimbabwe by the national and district teams working on District Environmental Action Plans. The booklets will then provide a method of assessing and planning rural sustainability that we hope will be generally applicable to rural sub-Saharan Africa. Adaptation of the method to other regions or to urban areas would require testing and development in a follow up project.

(4) Asking Questions of Survival

"Questions of Survival" is a resource booklet for workshops. It is designed primarily for use with community groups and local field workers, although the questions are more widely applicable. The questions are intended to act as a starting point for a problem-solving approach in which the participants are encouraged to examine their own situation and take on the search for answers as their own task. The draft booklet was produced in mid-1994 and has been translated from the original English into Spanish, Hindi, and Gujurati. In response to feedback, a new version is being prepared, consisting of six questions:

☐ *Change.* In what way is your environment changing? What is the state and what are the tendencies in the environment? What are the problems?
☐ *Victim.* How is your environment being affected by others in ways which seem out of your control?
☐ *Culprit.* How are you adversely affecting other peoples' lives?
☐ *Knowledge.* Who knows what about your environment?
☐ *Community.* Who else shares your problems or has similar ones?
☐ *Values.* What are your aspirations? What kind of society are you trying to build? What are you prepared to lose to gain what you want?

The original "Questions of Survival" was also summarized in a draft black and white poster as a means of keeping it in the minds of field workers. This poster is being updated.

The "Questions of Survival" booklet was the first of a series of draft booklets produced and tested as part of the project. Others include "Reflective Institutions"; "What are Strategies for Sustainability?"; "Principles of Evaluation"; and "Mapping Sustainability." "Asking Questions of Survival" (Dudley and Imbach 1995) draws on these booklets. It is aimed at the institutions—the interveners—that are trying to conserve or improve the environment. The document acts as a guide not only to using "Questions of Survival," but also to developing a people-focused approach to sustainable development. Specifically it provides:

☐ The fundamental questions that need to be asked before we can recognize whether development is sustainable or not;
☐ Guidance on how the "Questions of Survival" booklet can help both to explore these questions and stimulate action;
☐ Guidance on institutional structures that can best make use of the findings; and
☐ Practical techniques for communicating and sharing the findings in ways designed to lead to action.

Two contentions underlie the method. First, *We don't know what we are doing*. Nobody has the answers for how to do sustainable development. We need to adopt a humble approach in which we explicitly recognize our own ignorance and regard all our actions as experiments to test ideas and learn a little more. Second, *The arena for action is in influencing human behavior*. Environmental problems are generally caused by human actions. Our task is to understand the interaction between people and the environment and influence human behavior to improve that relationship.

The environment and the institutions that wish to conserve or improve it are at either end of a chain of influence. The intervening institutions need to influence the stakeholders in the environment who in turn have an impact on it. In this chain of influence there are four questions which assessments need to answer:

☐ *What are the environmental problems?* The state of the environment. Are there any environmental problems? How are things changing for good or bad?

☐ *What human behaviors are causing the problems?* A human impact analysis. What aspects of the interaction between people and the environment do we think are causing the environmental problems? The problems may result from either action or inaction.

☐ *What human characteristics are behind the behavior?* The sociological analysis. With regards to the problematic behavior, why are people doing what they are doing or not doing what they are not doing?

☐ *What openings are there for influencing that behavior?* The institutional capacity for social change. What, realistically, are the areas where the institution concerned may have the chance to influence people's values and the distribution and exercise of power?

The "Questions of Survival" booklet uses simple language to explore these more fundamental questions indirectly and to suggest possible avenues for action. "Asking Questions of Survival" (Dudley and Imbach 1995) suggests that traditional institutions are often poorly equipped to ask the necessary questions and respond constructively to the answers. It suggests that sustainable development needs a new breed of "reflective institutions" which can learn through doing. Although there is no blueprint for such institutions, it is suggested that they have these characteristics:

☐ *Feedback.* Experience of action informs and changes policy.

☐ *Hypothesis-led planning.* Projects are designed to test and improve hypotheses.

☐ *Strong horizontal linkages.* Communication among disciplines, departments, and institutions is encouraged.

☐ *Explicit vision of past, present, and future.* Institutional memory, understanding, and objectives are shared and debated.

☐ *A tendency to breed reflective institutions.* Beneficiaries and participants are encouraged to take control of their own projects.

☐ *The constructive identification of failure.* Errors and failures are seen as important resources for learning.

For institutions, individual professionals, and communities to reflect on their knowledge and ignorance, there is a need to present data in a way that can be shared and readily understood. While there are many analytical and communication tools available, it is suggested that simple maps should be a common and powerful theme. To be useful, maps should be:

☐ *Appropriately complex.* A map should not have superfluous detail but nor should it be over simplified. Its divisions should conform to the divisions that people actually use.

☐ *Comprehensive and transparent.* There should be a best guess for each variable for each point on the map but its level of certainty should be explicit.

☐ *Modifiable by the users.* Maps should be made by the people that need to use them. They should be readily modifiable and reproducible.

The general approach to using maps discussed in "Asking Questions of Survival" leads to the detailed "Rapid Assessment Mapping for Sustainability (RAMS)," described above.

The answers to the questions and the analysis encapsulated in the maps need to be turned into action. The arena for action for long-term impact is in influencing human behavior. "Asking Questions of Survival" identifies three basic motivators for problematic human behavior which can be translated into three basic strategic approaches:

☐ *Ignorance—Aim for self-repairing systems.* Repair and improve the processes of feedback between the components of society.

☐ *Desperation—Offer practical choices.* Wherever possible, rather than criticizing behavior, present people with realistic alternatives.

☐ *Greed—Encourage equitable development.* Develop a political commitment to protecting society and the environment from individual greed.

It suggests that the responses to these three problems are different. For example, there is little point having a program of education if ignorance is not the problem.

Tools and Training Materials

Map Maker

Map Maker is a Windows™-based application for making maps and displaying data on maps. It has been designed to be used by non-experts while still having a sophisticated capacity for complex analyses of varied data. Map Maker was designed specifically for development projects and includes support for carrying out field surveys. The author of the software is making it available for free to non-profit institutions, students, and academics through Internet, mail order, and courses. It is currently in use in 40 countries. The project is using the Map Maker software in its field trials, is helping to make it available through the IUCN network of members, and is assisting in the production of training materials in English, Spanish, and French.

Booklets

Draft booklets have been prepared as training and workshop materials on: "Questions of Survival"; "Barometer of Sustainability: what it's for and how to use it"; "What are Strategies for Sustainability?"; "Characteristics of Reflective Institutions"; "Mapping Sustainability"; "Monitoring and Assessment of Local Strategies for Sustainability";

"Community-based Indicators"; and "Assessing Rural Sustainability: 25 steps."

The first two will be issued separately. The next three will be merged into "Asking Questions of Survival." The last three will be incorporated in the pair, "Assessing Rural Sustainability" and "Planning Action for Rural Sustainability."

Visual Aids

The Barometer of Sustainability, the Egg of Sustainability, and the Pyramid of Action (Figure 4) are visual aids to communicating key ideas for a common understanding of sustainability. The Pyramid of Action is designed to start people thinking about what they can do for themselves and to reduce expectations of assistance from external agencies and governments.

Figure 4

Pyramid of Action

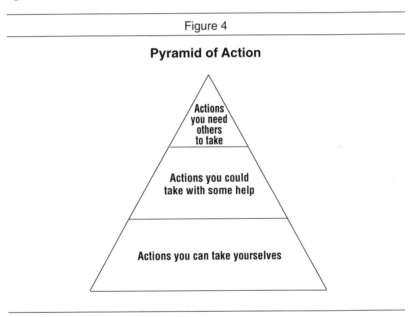

Tools for Community Participation

Tools for community participation have been extensively developed and described in manuals for primary health care, agricultural research, and others. There are many publications on participatory techniques. *Tools for Community Participation* (Srinivasan 1990) is one of the best.

Field testing

Sierra Nevada de Santa Marta, Colombia

The Sierra Nevada de Santa Marta, on the Caribbean coast of Colombia, is a complex region of outstanding ecological interest, ranging from tropical forest to snow covered peaks. It has important archaeological remains and five unique groups of indigenous people. Unfortunately, it also has problems of drug trafficking, guerrillas, unauthorized logging, and pressure on land from settler farmers. In this context an NGO, the Fundación Pro-Sierra Nevada de Santa Marta, has for the last decade been attempting to bring the diverse stakeholders together to search for achievable strategies for managing the Sierra Nevada. In addition, the Fundación carries out fundamental research through ecological field stations and provides technical expertise to support the dialogue.

Through a series of workshops with the Fundación, the project first explored the role that monitoring and assessment can play in the decision-making process of the Fundación. Using as a focus three draft booklets, "Questions of Survival," "Reflective Institutions," and "What are Strategies for Sustainability?," the senior staff of the Fundación attempted to clarify their vision of the future for the Sierra Nevada, the questions they were trying to answer through their projects, and their ability as an institution to absorb and learn from the answers to those questions. This process helped the Fundación to realize that monitoring and assessment could not be mere add-ons. If assessment is to be useful, it needs to be a central element of the institutional ethos. This realization led to an institutional restructuring which encouraged greater reflection and communication.

Once the institutional context for meaningful assessment had been established the Fundación's monitoring and assessment unit was able to focus more on the practical details of assessment. First this meant a reevaluation of the extensive store of data that had been collected over the previous decade. As with many development projects, much of this data had been accumulated largely for the sake of having data. But now, armed with a clearer idea of the questions that were being asked, the data could be revisited to identify the data gaps. Only then was a detailed work program in the field developed.

Work is now focusing on one municipality (an urban area with its rural hinterland). The emphasis is on RAMS and the production of simple maps that can communicate diverse and complex knowledge in a way that can be widely and rapidly understood. Fundación staff have been trained in the use of the Map Maker software. To increase the impact of the training, the opportunity was taken in a four-day training course to train staff from six field projects in Central America. By expanding the experience in this way, it is hoped to enrich the process of feedback in the continuing development of RAMS.

Tumkur, India

Development Alternatives (DA), an Indian NGO, is working with the District Government of Tumkur District in Karnataka State to develop a community-based strategy for sustainability. Through a program of dialogues, DA has discussed with villagers and government officials the issues that concern them. To all involved, the overriding issue is water. With a growing population and more intensive agriculture, the limited water supplies are even more strained and ground water levels are dropping. DA is using water as the key indicator of sustainability, since a system can be sustainable only when water demand is matched by supply. Water also has the advantage of being understood by all.

The agronomists and engineers of DA have developed maps to describe their view of optimal land use in Tumkur. Meanwhile, the community workers have worked with the villagers to develop conceptual maps of how they see future use of land around their villages. Inevitably, the two maps are different. The challenge for DA and the District Government is to work with both the agricultural "experts" and the local community so that both maps may slowly evolve into a common perspective of the vision for the future. Only once that vision of a sustainable future has been established can progress be assessed.

In this approach, the ability to make and modify maps easily and in the field is essential. Maps are the principal media for analysis, communication, and consensus. In the future, as the program moves from analysis to implementation, maps will also be the key to project design, implementation, and monitoring. DA has developed a resource atlas, which illustrates the state of the resource base for the region. This is being used as a project planning tool in Tumkur. In addition, to help develop a facility in map-making, IUCN supported a course, held in August 1995, on the use of the Map Maker software. The software is now being used in the field, not only by DA, but also by other local NGOs.

In addition, the booklet "Questions of Survival" has been translated into Hindi and Gujurati and used on an experimental basis by a number of small local NGOs. The booklet is used as a resource for workshops with village groups to focus discussion and help them to clarify in their own minds their situation with respect to their environment and their neighbors.

District Environmental Action Plans, Zimbabwe

Zimbabwe is preparing District Environmental Action Plans (DEAPs) in up to eight pilot districts. The lead agency is the Department of Natural Resources, IUCN is providing technical assistance, and the project is funded by the United Nations Development Programme. A national strategy team has been formed to help prepare the DEAPs, together with district strategy teams. These have been formed in the first three pilot districts: Umzingwane (Matebeleland South Province), Mberengwa (Midlands Province), and Hwange (Matabeleland North province).

Despite their name, the DEAPs are intended to be strategies for sustainable development. Their scope includes both human well-being and ecosystem well-being, and they will go beyond planning to include implementation. The strategies are being built from the ground up, starting in the villages.

Under the IUCN/IDRC assessment project, members of the international assessment team have been helping the national and district strategy teams develop and test a participatory method of assessing progress toward sustainability. IUCN's technical advisor to the project has provided training in Participatory Rural Assessment (PRA) tools and other members of the international team have provided training in using the tools to assess sustainability, the Barometer of Sustainability, indicators, and strategy development. The national and district strategy teams have conducted two-week assessments in villages in three of the districts (Umzingwane, Mberengwa, Hwange) and one-week action planning sessions in Umzingwane and Mberengwa. Assessments and action planning will resume in Hwange and other districts in 1996 once the main farming season is over.

This field testing has enabled the international, national, and district teams to work out the basic questions that need asking to assess human and ecosystem well-being, ways of asking the questions that are meaningful for the villagers, and the step-by-step guidance that is most helpful to the teams working with them. This information is distilled in the booklets, "Assessing Rural Sustainability" and "Planning Action for Rural Sustainability."

REFERENCES

Dudley, E., and A. Imbach. 1995. Asking questions of survival. IUCN, Gland, Switzerland. Draft.

Hodge, R. A. 1993. Reporting on sustainable and equitable development: Conceptual approach. Project paper no. 1. IDRC, Ottawa, Canada.

Hodge, R. A. 1995. Assessing progress toward sustainability: Development of a systemic framework and reporting structure. PhD (interdisciplinary) dissertation, School of Urban Planning, Faculty of Engineering, McGill University, Montreal, Canada.

Imbach, A., and E. Dudley. 1995. Rapid assessment mapping for sustainability (RAMS). IUCN, Gland, Switzerland. Draft.

IUCN/UNEP/WWF. 1980. *World conservation strategy: Living resource conservation for sustainable development.* IUCN, Gland, Switzerland.

IUCN/UNEP/WWF. 1991. *Caring for the earth: A strategy for sustainable living.* IUCN, Gland, Switzerland.

Lee-Smith, D., S. Chimbuya, C. Lue-Mbizvo, and R. Prescott-Allen. 1995. *Assessing and planning rural sustainability.* IUCN, Gland, Switzerland. Forthcoming.

Prescott-Allen, R. 1995. *Barometer of sustainability: A method of assessing progress toward sustainable societies.* PADATA, Victoria, Canada; IUCN, Gland, Switzerland.

Srinivasan, L. 1990. *Tools for community participation.* UNDP, New York.

UNDP. Annual (1990-). *Human development report.* Oxford University Press, New York and Oxford.

PART III

Indicators of Sustainability

Limitations in Measuring Ecosystem Sustainability

୯ଌ

RICHARD A. CARPENTER

Biophysical measurements by which to judge the sustainability of management practices in production and conservation ecosystems are inadequate except in cases of gross and obvious degradation. This unsatisfactory state of the science is due both to a lack of basic understanding of ecosystems and to the practical difficulties of ecological research. The expectations of participants from other disciplines in the implementation of "sustainable development" are that the environmental sciences can effectively monitor and predict the outcome of alternative strategies. Since this is generally *not* so, the limitations of biophysical measurements should be forthrightly communicated so that uncertainties are recognized and the opportunities for improvement can be pursued in a timely manner.

Introduction

There are at least four major obstacles to sustainable development: (1) population growth; (2) selfishness and other defects of human nature that deny equity within and among generations; (3) fundamental economic bias, especially in open-access resources; and (4) *inadequate measures of the condition of managed ecosystems* by which to judge whether they are stable or degrading. Nobel laureate Robert Solow (1992) suggests, "Talk without measurement is cheap. If we—the country, the government, the research community—are serious about doing the right thing for the resource endowment and the environment, then the proper measurement of stocks and flows ought to be high on the list of steps toward intelligent and foresighted decisions." This statement by an enlightened, and enlightening, economist represents the widely held expectations that natural scientists will provide the quantitative basis of sustainability strategies.

The IUCN Commission on Environmental Strategy and Planning is working on the process, or "how," of conservation and on the development of tools that are useful in progressing toward sustainability. Even when there is general acceptance of an ethic to do what Aldo Leopold (1968) defined as "right when it tends to preserve the integrity, stability, and beauty of the biotic community" (may that day come soon), practical implementation remains as the test of whatever we decide to do as stewards of the environment. Conservation is management, protection, and restoration: it is not leaving nature alone. Continuing human interventions are inevitable. Choices and actions for conservation require scientific biophysical measurements in order to address a myriad of questions such as:

□ What is right and how do we know?
□ What has happened, is happening, and will happen in the environment under varying conditions?
□ How can we accomplish what we decide is right? and,
□ How can we know if we are getting to where we want to be?

Inadequacy of Biophysical Measurement Capability

Of course, many elements besides objective facts go into policy and decision making for conservation, and ultimately, it is what we *can't* count that really counts. But those value-laden economic, social, political, and cultural components must be added upon a firm foundation of scientific understanding and quantification. This fundamental information is now substantially inadequate and uncertain. One reason is the great practical difficulties of gathering statistically significant data under field conditions, particularly in developing countries. For example, rates of soil erosion and sediment delivery are not measured accurately or frequently enough to allow reliable estimates of the useful life of dam-reservoir projects (Carpenter 1989 and 1991). Poor quality control of laboratory analyses, sampling errors, and estimates of natural variation introduce uncertainties. A different, and more profound, problem is the lack of explanatory paradigms or understanding of ecosystems that inhibits predictive modeling.

Unfortunately, as stated in my abridged paper in *Environmental Strategy,* "The capability to detect *un*sustainability far exceeds the capability to confirm or predict sustainability with confidence" (Carpenter, R. A., 1993). In fact, there are suggestions that "as a matter of practicality, *un*sustainability is easier to identify, measure, and address at the project level," and therefore a set of unsustainability indicators should be adopted as a tool for sustainability (Eckman 1993). Such a negative approach may improve early warnings but will not yield understanding of causal relationships or corrective actions.

The president of The Nature Conservancy (USA) recently described this challenge to their scientific program:

> "In short, we need to learn enough about how ecosystems function to improve preserve design and to intervene successfully in management. Similarly, we need to develop new ways of measuring success. No one's tried conservation on this scale before, and the methods for monitoring progress simply don't exist" (Sawhill 1991).

A review of two new books on conservation biology begins: "A major question sits at the heart of conservation biology: Is there a set of principles from which prediction and practice can be derived, or are conservation problems unique, such that their resolution requires new empirical investigations, constant verification, and ad hoc response?" (White 1993)

Managers of production ecosystems for agriculture, forestry, and fisheries also face this general inadequacy of biophysical measurements that are relevant and practically obtainable for use in judging whether current practices are sustainable or whether some alternative practice would be sustainable. For example, in the United States, the National Academy of Sciences (1994) has just advised that the ecological condition of range lands is so poorly understood due to inconsistent and fragmented data that a determination of how they should be managed cannot be made. A second, perhaps less important example concerns controlling wild mushroom collection. A U.S. Forest Service ecologist says, "We don't even know how abundant the resource is; are we picking ninety-five percent of the mushrooms? Are we picking five percent?" (Lipske 1994) I review some of the reasons for this alarming state of the science, what it should mean to the ongoing discussions of "sustainable development," and opportunities to improve the situation.

Sustainability Defined

Sustainability is whether (not the extent to which) *the productive potential of a certain natural system will continue* (for a long time, at least several decades) *under a particular management practice* (intensity and type of technical and social activities, e.g., inputs of energy, nutrients, genetic variety, harvesting procedures, and cyclic variations over time).

A natural system is a biome or ecosystem demarcated by changes in some biophysical characteristics at its boundaries, e.g., an upland agricultural area, lake, river basin, or island. The potential should relate to that quantity and mix of goods and services that is chosen to be produced by the society that owns or controls the natural system.

Sustainability is now an accepted constraint on economic development. It is a generalized obligation, not for every species or place, but a necessary direction toward a goal of continuity and stabilization. We certainly have the technological means to exhaust resources, and even modest discount rates (where natural growth of the harvestable product is slow) encourage exploitation to extinction. Thus, sustainability must be achieved through some combination of non-technological, non-economic motivations. The current cop-out, the "precautionary principle," or its thirty-year-old predecessor "safe minimum standard," asks that exploitation be voluntarily and drastically reduced in the face of uncertainty about thresholds of degradation. These formulations do not produce specific operating guidelines and are simply euphemisms for yet another value judgment as to what is the proper balance of risk between taking immediate gains and losing long-term potential.

Indicators of sustainability being suggested by a number of groups are quite diversified. The International Institute for Environment and Development offers a long list covering energy use, biological wealth, policy, economics, institutions, and society and culture. But only one criterion seems to deal with the definition at hand: "Renewable resources are increasingly used and harvested at rates within their capacity for renewal" (Dalal-Clayton 1992). Other attributes of sustainability are important but are subsidiary to production potential.

Sustainability Pertains to High Yields

No sophisticated measurements are needed to find that a management practice is *un*sustainable when gross and obvious damage occurs to the environment (such as gullies in fields and broken corals). Or, in contrast, when an ecosystem is thinly populated by humans, relatively inaccessible, shielded from external effects, and lightly managed, then it may be safely relegated to a sustainable category. But the majority of the land and near-shore ocean ecosystems are intensively managed for the maximum sustainable harvest yield, mainly because of the urgent needs of people living on them or nearby.

The fine-tuning of these generally highly productive ecosystems is where sustainable development will have meaning or become an empty phrase.

The real costs of acting with inadequate, erroneous, or uncertain information about the sustainable abundance of ecosystem products are incurred through two forms of management error: (1) urgent demand may increase risk-taking and drive over-exploitation that subsequently results in irreversible degradation; or, (2) unnecessarily conservative precautions may result in needlessly low harvests and deny some portion of basic human needs.

Sustainable development depends largely on renewable natural resources of air, water, soil, sunlight, and communities of plants and animals. The utility, or potential of these natural systems for producing goods and services, is to be continued. The absolute amount of production must be increased in order to maintain per capita flows since the human population will grow (or else the affluent must drastically, and improbably, reduce their consumption). These are the implications of sustainable development regardless of how arguments are settled about equities between or within generations, conversions among different kinds of capital, value judgments as to which goods and services are desired, or risk aversion as a function of economic status.

Expectations of Users of Biophysical Measurements

Economists, planners, and other development decision-makers turn to natural scientists for data with which to run models, calculate return-on-investment, and devise policies to manage land, water, and people. Their expectations for guidance from natural science may not be fulfilled, but they are unlikely to accept protestations of ignorance or impotence. Their frustration in finding little, and highly uncertain, information is exemplified in this passage from a recent report, "Economic Policies for Sustainable Development" (Asian Development Bank 1990):

> In the preparation of this report no task proved more daunting than the assembly of reliable statistical indicators of recent trends and the current state of the environment. Aside from the most glaring cases where officials and researchers are aware of what is happening and can describe conditions in general terms most eloquently, the lack of quantitative environmental information comparable with the statistics available regarding economic parameters is a major obstacle to integrated economic-cum-environmental planning. *Statistical information on the environment is scarce, often inaccurate, seldom comparable from country to country, and rarely available in a time series covering a sufficient number of years to indicate trends in a reliable way.* Thus, descriptions remain anecdotal and lack the hard edge of quantification which is necessary for analysis and policy formulation....
>
> Without question one of the most important findings of this study is that while reliable data on conventional economic parameters are plentiful, statistical information on the condition of the environment is scarce and poorly organized. [italics added]

Managers usually arrange for measurements that relate directly to their primary goal. Holling (1994) has studied a variety of managed ecosystems that failed or were unsustainable. He reports a sequence of events common to each of the systems studied. The management goal was always to reduce variability (for economic advantage) of some target parameter such as cattle grazing stocking density, fish population, or occurrence of fire or insects in forestry. In each case control was achieved as measured by the target variable. Natural capital increased and was stored. But slowly the total system changed to become more homogeneous, brittle, less resilient—an accident ready to happen. At the same time, management, having succeeded in its primary purpose, switched its concentration to improved efficiency in shifting cattle among paddocks, hatching fish, fighting fires, and spraying insects. Measures of the status and trends of conditions in the whole ecosystem were too difficult or too expensive. The stabilized managed systems were attractive to investors and were further developed. Meanwhile, these economic-social-ecological systems became increasingly vulnerable—to drought in pastures, inbreeding in fish hatcheries, contiguous forests that spread insect outbreaks and fires. Also, the other goods and services from the now-simplified ecosystems declined. Ultimately, each system could not sustain production of the target commodity, and the rigidified management and investment made reorganization and remediation more difficult. Measurements that might have guided adaptive management were not available.

Economic Valuation Techniques

Good progress has been made in monetizing environmental impacts and in bringing non-market valuation of environmental externalities into an extended and more complete financial account of the costs and benefits of development projects (Dixon and others 1988; Daly and Cobb 1989). National accounts such as the Gross National Product are being extended through similar techniques.

Expectations by economists also include some metaphors that have so far not proved helpful. Natural capital should somehow be analogous to financial capital and, therefore, if development can preserve natural capital and get along only on "natural interest," or if natural capital can be exchanged for an equal amount of technological or human capital, then a system is sustainable (Daly 1991). It is, however, difficult to define natural capital, to even tell the difference between stocks and flows in some instances. Another problem is how to aggregate quite different forms of natural capital that also differ in size of scale boundaries (Vitousek and Lubchenco 1994). Components of natural capital vary greatly as to the time when degradation or depletion is evident and in the time for recovery. For example, the lower atmosphere can be dirtied by a faulty damper in a flue but cleaned up with the next rain shower, while leaching of toxic chemicals from a landfill can slowly contaminate a drinking water aquifer for decades before finally reaching an unacceptable level. Salinization of soil through poor irrigation practices shows up slowly but may be rather quickly (if not cheaply) reversed. Global warming has yet to be detected but carbon dioxide resides in the atmosphere for hundreds of years. Modern agronomy "grows" the soil as surely as it grows the crop, so that soil is both a stock and flow resource. It is not clear how such diverse stocks, degrees of degradation, and recovery periods can be usefully combined into one expression of natural capital that is roughly equivalent to money.

The work of Paul Craig and others at the University of California at Davis (personal communication, 1994) emphasizes a "biophysical green account" because monetization requires aggregation that reduces data certainty and constrains policy insights.

No Simple Indicator

Another metaphor illustrates the "economics envy" of some natural scientists—the ecological equivalent of Gross National Product. Aggregation of biophysical measurements at the country level, as characterized by the reports of the United Nations and other international agencies, are not useful and may be misleading because political boundaries seldom coincide with natural demarcations of the landscape. Proposals for a GNP-like single indicator of the sustainability status of a natural system include Net Primary Productivity (as measured by remote sensing) and various Biodiversity Indices. Such integrating concepts could hide important qualitative differences among ecosystems that might show the same NPP or BI (and in fact, the GNP also is defective in this manner). For example, in forests there are "immense technical difficulties associated with measuring below-ground productivity" (Franklin 1994). And yet, the biomass of roots may have a high turnover rate.

Ecology is unlikely to develop any simplified single indicator of sustainability. However, a *minimum data set* for each type of managed ecosystem may be possible, as is suggested in a separate section below. A purely physical approach is to compare the total respiratory heat generated (as an expression of entropy) by an agricultural system with that of a natural climax vegetation. Assuming the latter is sustainable, then if the agricultural system generates the same or less heat, it too is sustainable (Hannon and others 1993).

"Health" is another proposed analogy; that is, just as a medical doctor checks a few "vital signs" and judges the health of an individual, so some similar datum should succinctly describe the health of an ecosystem. But the human body is much more tightly integrated than any ecosystem. The use of the term "ecosystem health" by Costanza (1991), Schaeffer (1988), and others is more qualitative and vague, and perhaps more realistic, than the temperature and blood pressure concept.

Is Science Possible in Complex Natural Systems?

Sustainability Is Inherently Uncertain

Nature, left alone, is self-organizing and is certainly sustainable in the sense that it has no discernible goals or purpose. Nature changes, responds, and evolves through a highly variable set of quasi-stable conditions over time. Ecosystems are self-controlled within larger scale constraints. For example, "natural systems may evolve toward increasing adaptability to environmental change and that adaptability is maximized when the system has evolved to the verge of chaos. This condition is analogous to that of a mature prairie or forest which is experiencing fires. The conditions for the support of occasional fire become optimal as the system reaches maturity" (Hannon and others 1993).

Human beings seek to impose some constancy and dependability of supply of needed products. Self-organizing systems evolve in a non-deterministic manner that changes their nature, not merely their behavior. The inference is that ecosystems, being far from equilibrium, and with future states highly dependent on random perturbations of initial conditions, are chaotic. "If the future is inherently unknowable, then technocratic control in the sense of management based on objective, scientific prediction of system behavior in response to alternative management inputs is impossible. . . . It also can be argued that attempts at technocratic control may be counterproductive in the long term" (Hollick 1993). Thus, sustainability is inherently uncertain and even its probability is uncertain. Sustainability may be only relative, not absolute; a given management practice is more or less sustainable at a certain location over a certain time with a certain mix of products.

A more familiar source of uncertainty is natural variation. Any "signal" that a change in condition is due to human action is often hidden in the "noise" of natural changes in the value measured. For example, no statistically significant change in the volume of water discharged by the Amazon river, or the amount of sediment delivered from the deforested Rondonia region, has yet been detected. A signal that deforestation has altered the hydrologic cycle or soil erosion in that basin is obscured by the high natural variability of rainfall, and El Niño events explain most of the occasional trends in the noise that are evident in the hundreds of gauging stations (Richey 1994).

Limitations of Ecological Research

Another gloomy argument in ecological circles is the extent to which research can contribute to better ecosystem management. Contributors to a forty-five page forum in the 1993 November-December issue of *Ecological Applications* debate whether basic ecological research—with its long-term experiments, difficulties of replication, control, and randomization, and the fact that the systems under study undergo evolutionary change—can test hypotheses and produce useful results quickly enough to affect the course of human perturbations of the biosphere. There is no way to learn how an ecosystem will respond to stress except to stress it. Properties of an ecosystem cannot be predicted from its components. It may not be possible to achieve the ninety-five percent confidence level that is generally regarded as essential for science (Hilborn 1992). The usual means of dealing with uncertainty through decision theory and models may not work in such a near-chaos situation.

The extreme of this line of thought appears to be close to the religious-like "deep ecology," where humankind is only another species, and to "environmental therapeutic nihilism" (Hargrove 1992), with its goal to do nothing overtly because we have no basis for action and because nature should be allowed to proceed alone. For conservation, this is the extreme "hands-off" policy. In contrast, most thoughtful ecologists accept an anthropocentric view where humankind is in charge of nature and had best get on with the job with due humility and purpose.

The more optimistic of the Ecological Society of America forum discussants argue that ecology can (only, or at least?) guide management in conducting economic development as a well-planned, but risky, *experiment.* Holling (1993) effectively restates his adaptive environmental management message of the 1970s: "There is an inherent unknowability, as well as unpredictability, concerning these evolving managed ecosystems and the societies with which they are linked [so that] . . . uncertainty and surprises become an integral part of an anticipated set of adaptive responses.

The U.S. National Research Council (1993) separates uncertainty into three categories: measurement problems of insufficient observations and natural variability; problems of extrapolating from the scale in time and space of observation to the scale of management; and inadequacy of models and fundamental knowledge of underlying mechanisms. More appropriate and better measurements can sometimes be obtained, and extrapolation errors can at least be quantified. Most important environmental problems, however, suffer from *true* uncertainty, i.e., indeterminacy, or events with an unknown probability, according to Costanza (1993). Uncertainties due to general scientific ignorance are hard to even quantify, much less reduce. Banks and other investors in development who expect dependable financial returns are likely to be aghast at such candid expressions of reality.

Long-term, Large-scale Research Needed

Ecological research has not emphasized investigations of large areas (regions such as the American Midwest agricultural heartland, large marine ecosystems, or the boreal forests), and that scale is most important in monitoring and predicting sustainability of management practices in economic development. The studies that have been made of ecoregions or biomes have revealed some of the sources of natural variation. Responses in nature to perturbations are non-linear, i.e., they involve lags, thresholds, and rapid transformations from one stable state to another. For example, despite considerable knowledge of atmospheric chemistry and years of monitoring the gradual build-up of CFCs, the appearance of the Antarctic ozone hole was a *surprise.* Mixtures of positive and negative feedbacks, each poorly understood, or perhaps not even known, make predictions difficult.

Very long-term effects sometimes become evident only after the original cause is no longer evident, and so explanation is confounded

(Magnuson 1990). The lament of the recent Sustainable Biosphere Initiative (SBI) report of the Ecological Society of America (1991) is that:

> Research programs exist to develop specific sustainable natural resources (e.g., sustainable forestry or sustainable agriculture). However, current research efforts are inadequate for dealing with sustainable systems that involve multiple resources, multiple ecosystems, and large spatial scales. Moreover, much of the current research focuses on commodity-based managed systems, with little attention paid to the sustainability of natural ecosystems whose goods and services currently lack a market value.
>
> [Current] efforts are not presently united in a comprehensive research framework. Such a framework is needed because ecological processes link natural and managed populations to ecosystems and because common ecological principles underlie effective management strategies.

Mooney notes that the SBI is now in a new phase under the administration of ICSU/SCOPE, beginning an interdisciplinary study to learn the reasons for successes and failures of managing sustainable systems. (Mooney and Sala 1993).

Concurrently, new research shows that combining large-scale experiments with long-term and comparative studies may obviate the necessity to tackle each ecosystem stress problem as if it were unique. "The challenge is not to eliminate uncertainty, for that is impossible, but to assign priorities to the tractable uncertainties and reduce them as rapidly as possible through targeted research" (Carpenter, S. R., 1993). B. A. Wilcox of the Institute for Sustainable Development expressed another view (personal communication with the author, 1992), namely, that risk expressions are useful. For example, specifying a ninety-five percent probability of persistence of a development strategy is a reasonable criterion for sustainability. Then it is possible to identify and evaluate the comparative risk (probability of frequency of occurrence and distribution of severity of consequences) of various threats (biotic and abiotic, stochastic and deterministic) to the system. In some applications to population biology such an exercise reveals the relative risk of different management strategies. Improved understanding may be on the way, but ecologists are cautioning all of the other participants in sustainable development against raising false expectations.

Measurement Problems Plague Management of Ecosystems

The following examples illustrate some of the practical difficulties in helping managers to get the most of what society demands from renewable resources without unacceptable damage to the production potential.

Agroecosystems

Food is so basic to human well-being that sustainable agriculture is the oldest and best-studied of all managed ecosystems. Fortunately, a large variety of cropping systems are sustainable. It is of interest to conservation that plant biodiversity is apparently actually higher on poorer soils than on fertile soils, where competition reduces the number of species (Huston 1993). Thus, he concludes, "Preservation of areas of high plant biodiversity does not require the sacrifice of productive agricultural lands."

The Green Revolution has been an agronomic, if not always a social, success. But population growth and concentrations are forcing more of marginal, usually sloping, lands into cultivation, and there the question of which, if any, practices are sustainable is in doubt. The most obvious measurement of sustainability is harvest over time. But the short-term production of specific commodities may mask the loss of potential in the system to yield a broad range of goods and services over a long period of time. Hidden subsidies, management inputs, and borrowing from adjacent systems can maintain harvest levels. Nevertheless, more effort is warranted to improve this traditional measurement because the crop does integrate many elements of the condition of the underlying ecosystem.

The year-to-year crop yield is the basic measurement, whether obtained from marketing data, actual sampling, or by interviewing farmers. In developing countries, rice harvests are usually not quantified by measuring weight or volume but merely estimated and negotiated between farmers and buyers. False, low yields are reported when taxes or government shares are related to harvests. Experiment stations are often few and far between. Yield variations due to weather and management can obscure subtle changes in productivity. Much economically oriented information is available about agroecosystems, but less is known about non-crop components such as soil organisms that ultimately affect sustainability. Faeth and others (1991) note that "in the field, erosion-induced productivity changes are almost impossible to isolate and measure accurately."

The Consultative Group on International Agricultural Research (CGIAR), based in Washington, D.C., has added the wider aspects of sustainability to its goal of sustained crop production. Measurements are not available at the regional level to evaluate the extent to which agricultural practices degrade, maintain, or enhance the total ecosystem. Major research areas are the reversibility of degradation, thresholds of decline, and the biodiversity necessary for the future genetic base of agriculture (CGIAR 1990).

Fisheries

The article that touched off the ecological debate on the relevance of research (referred to above) was a devastating review of failed fisheries management (Ludwig and others 1993). These authors conclude that "assigning causes to past events is problematical, future events cannot be predicted, and even well-meaning attempts to exploit responsibly may lead to disastrous consequences." They advise, "Distrust claims of sustainability. Because past resource exploitation has seldom been sustainable, any new plan that involves claims of sustainability should be suspect." In a mild rebuttal, Rosenberg and others (1993) note progress in the use of probabilistic advice to management through risk assessment in stock evaluations and alternative management actions. Fisheries may be uniquely vulnerable ecosystems because of the tragedy-of-the-commons syndrome, but a lack of scientific consensus about their condition and trends is an added barrier to sustainable management.

As in agriculture, the most important measure of sustainability is the level of catch, and fisheries management organizations concentrate on estimating abundance of stock. There is less concern with measuring the level of depletion of a fish community below which its potential for recovery and production is lost. Measurements relating stock size and composition to environmental stresses such as pollution, or to loss of spawning habitat, are not well-developed.

Even catch data are inadequate according to the International Center for Living Aquatic Resources Management (ICLARM) in the Philippines (MacKay 1991). Underestimation occurs because as much as twice the marketable catch may be consumed or processed locally without being measured. In developing countries, data on the species composition of the catch are rarely available.

Sherman (1994) calls for standardized sampling by trawlers of the large marine ecosystems around the world. He notes that a consistent data base over many decades is necessary to judge whether over fishing is the cause of changes in species composition. Few areas have such records as yet, the North Sea and the Georges Bank being notable exceptions. Even so, the closure of the Atlantic cod fishery by Canada in 1993 (at a cost of about US$1 billion and great social disruption) demonstrates the surprises that can occur in well-studied systems.

The difficulties in gaining international cooperation toward sustainable fisheries include a measurement problem. Regier and Bocking (1994) report that, historically, "networks of scientific researchers routinely shared information, sometimes even when such sharing was discouraged by a scientist's country. On occasion researchers informally provided relatively accurate data to their foreign peers while their countries were officially declaring inaccurate data for political purposes."

Forestry

The time between harvests in silviculture is usually many decades, so there are few places where sustainability, even just of saw logs, has been demonstrated. "It is not yet possible to demonstrate conclusively that any natural tropical forest anywhere has been successfully managed for the sustained production of timber" (Poore 1989). Botkin and Talbot (1992) could not find documentation of sustainability in any original forest under commercial harvest. For example, the block clear-cutting practice in the U.S. Pacific Northwest is now seen, after forty years, as unsustainable. "Clearly, defining sustainability in terms of the continuous yield of timber alone is a trap . . . timber yield is not a primary indicator of a forest ecosystem's health" (Johnson and Cabarle 1993).

For the future, American society is also demanding spotted owls and water for salmon from these forest lands. Franklin (1994) suggests that a reasonable assurance of sustainability of such a mix of forest products and services might require reducing the frequency of final harvest cut to 160 to 200 years from the current 80 to 100 years. This long rotation alternative management approach would reduce impacts on soil and water quality and maintain greater biodiversity. This is indicative of (1) the substantial sacrifices of economic production in order to achieve sustainability, and also (2) the considerable uncertainty involved. While the lower return-on-investment would only be acceptable on government forest lands, even there the sustainability outcome would not be known for certain for perhaps two-hundred years.

Grazing Lands

These are the ecosystems where the tragedy of the commons is most obvious, but even when the land and the ungulates have the same owner, it is difficult to set the right utilization rate. Pickup and Morton (1994) describe a method using remote sensing in arid lands to separate grazing-induced changes in forage biomass from rainfall-driven variations. "Grazing gradients" are patterns developed because sheep and cattle graze out only so far from water sources, and the areas where the vegetation is consumed can be detected. If the grazing gradient does not disappear with the recovery of vegetation after large infrequent rainfalls, the land has been more or less permanently damaged. If recovery does occur once, it does not mean that practice at that site is permanently sustainable. Large, unpredictable fluctuations in rainfall, and explosions of weeds and mammalian pests may yet ruin the pasture. They conclude that for Australia, "meshing of wealth-generating uses of land with ecological sustainability remains an unachieved goal."

Lusigi (1994) points out that African tropical range lands are not actually a managed production system but are responding to population pressures and political disruptions by shifting from a nomadic (plausibly sustainable) mode to a sedentary situation which is obviously rapidly degrading entire regions.

Risser (1994) suggests measures of range condition including biodiversity of plant species, peak standing crop, nitrogen content of foliage, and soil organic matter. (See also the discussion of minimum data sets below.) He proposes that the following values would indicate a sustainable situation: a high percentage (70 to 80 percent) of herbaceous cover species palatable to livestock; seasonal peak standing crop of greater than $300g/m^2$; plant species diversity exp. (H^1) not less than 5.0; soil organic carbon in the top 20 cm will be 3.0 kg/m^2 for sandy soils and 5.0 in silt-loam soils; and the nitrogen content of above-ground herbage is at least 0.6 g/100g dry biomass. These data might be difficult to obtain in developing countries.

Opportunities for Improving Biophysical Measurements

The most important scale for managing (and therefore for measuring) sustainability is at the landscape or regional level of perhaps thousands to millions of hectares. Local harvest-related data cannot be aggregated to give the needed information. Land use changes appear to be a fundamental cause of reduced ecosystem function and reduced sustainability of production of the goods and services desired. But ecosystems are naturally changing and adapting so that measures must discriminate effects of human activity against this background of change.

Over half the earth's surface has been transformed from its natural state by agriculture, forestry, urbanization, desertification, and other interventions. The altered landscape affects adjacent aquatic systems. One-third of the loss of species is ascribed to land-use change. For conservation, this implies that stringent restrictions on land use are necessary. The Society for Conservation Biology has outlined a vast system of core areas, corridors, and buffer zones in the Wildlands Project for the United States. The conservation of large fierce animals will require big reserves with big financial sacrifices, as the plans for the Florida panther and the Yellowstone grizzly bears are proving. The collection and analysis of the biophysical measurements to support these plans is a formidable task.

One new measurement approach is to combine growing capabilities in remote sensing, geographic information systems, and landscape ecology. The product is a set of data depicting land-use change that is practical, that is sensitive over time, and that can be interpreted in terms of sustainability (O'Neill and others 1994). Map-like outputs readily communicate to decision-makers about habitat coverage, ecotones, patch configuration, economic activity, water quality, and vegetation.

Supporting these measurements of landscape composition and pattern should be a selected data set for the particular type of managed ecosystem under consideration. Site-specific measurements (although individually unreliable for determining regional sustainability) can be gathered into status and trend reports. Integrating organisms and keystone species can be monitored—e.g., lake trout in Lake Superior. The research and monitoring agendas of management agencies and scientific organizations are beginning to focus on the broader conditions of ecosystems that relate to their sustainable utility.

Minimum Data Sets

Table 1 is an attempt to select a minimum set of data about environmental conditions in each type of managed ecosystem that would, taken together, inform management as to whether an ongoing practice was sustainable. This draft "minimum data set" derives from the United Nations University International Conference on the Definition and Measurement of Sustainability: The Biophysical Foundations, held June 22-25, 1992, in Washington, D.C. (Papers presented at this conference were published in Lovejoy 1994.) An asterisk in Table 1 indicates measurements that were judged by the participants to be the most important. Further development by panels of experts and managers should lead to a consensus on measures and their critical values that could be standardized for collection around the world. Eventually, a practical and at least partial approach to monitoring and predicting sustainability in these intensively managed ecosystems may result.

Summary: Can Sustainability Be Measured?

Sustainable development is being formulated, elaborated, interpreted, and debated in the abstract, but if it is ever to be implemented there must be great improvement in relevant, statistically reliable scientific measurements. This sobering conclusion is based on an extensive survey of recent literature (see Carpenter 1994 for excerpts), field work in Southeast Asia by various projects under the auspices of the East-West Center (Rerkasem and Rambo 1988; Carpenter and Harper 1989), and the recent UNU conference. Only with a foundation of useful biophysical measurements can the elegant models of ecological economics proceed to inform and influence policy and decision-making. Such quantifications will describe the conditions of natural systems under various management practices, monitor trends in the conditions and responses to natural and human-induced stresses, and predict the outcome of proposed alternative management practices.

Science is not completely incapable of measuring sustainability, and gross and obvious unsustainable practices need no measurements for their evaluation. Many subtle evidences of unsustainability also can be detected. Measurement inadequacies and uncertainties about ecosystem conditions are most important, however, when demands for goods and services from renewable natural resources are large and

Table 1

Suggested Minimum Data Sets for Managed Ecosystems

Measurement Category	Agriculture (common food crops)	Production Forests (natural and man-made)	Fisheries (marine and fresh-water)	Rangelands	Wildlife/Wildlands (including wetlands and coastal areas)
Landuse patterns and change	Size and mix of fields; *landuse conversion rate into and out of agriculture	*Landuse conversion rate into and out of forest	*Spawning and nursery habitats—changes	Grazing gradients	*Spatial variations of ecosystem types; patchiness/gaps
Production	Total biomass yield; *edible portion harvest; pest damage level	Growth rate and harvest of wood and other products; rotation period; pest damage level	*Catch—weight, composition, size, per unit effort, annual	Stocking density; *above-ground primary productivity; *N-content of vegetation	Hunting harvest
Biological diversity	*Crop diversity and genetic resources; diversity in soil organisms; pests and their predators	*Species richness and diversity of plant and animal indicator groups; soil organisms; pests and their predators	Species richness and diversity of indicator groups; *population size of keystone species	*Species diversity [exp (H')]; *percentage of palatable, non-palatable, and invading species of foliage	Ecologically viable population of sensitive, keystone, and link species; *proportion of species sensitive, and not, to human disturbance
Water quality and quantity	Pollutants in irrigation water	Pollutants in surface and subsurface waters; evapotranspiration	*Dissolved oxygen; nutrients; plankton; toxic chemicals	Pollutants in irrigation water	Pollutants in water
Soil properties	Classification; *erosion rate; organic matter; cation exchange capacity; *nutrients	Classification; erosion rate; *nutrients; parent rock	Sedimentation rate; suspended particulates	*Organic carbon	Erosion rate; organic carbon
Atmospheric composition	Acid precipitation; carbon dioxide	*Acid precipitation; carbon dioxide	*Pollutants (metals, pesticides); acid precipitation; UV-B irradiation	Carbon dioxide	Deposition of pollutants; *UV-B irradiation
Climate	Temperature mean and variability; *precipitation mean and variability; isolation	Temperature mean and variability; *precipitation mean and variability	Temperature mean and variability	Temperature mean and variability; *precipitation mean and variability	Temperature mean and variability; *precipitation mean and variability

*Measurements judged most important by participants in the United Nations University International Conference on the Definition and Measurement of Sustainability, held June 22-25, 1992, in Washington, D.C.

urgent, and the question is the maximum sustainable yield. To err in overstressing the natural production system will likely cause its partial, at least temporary, collapse. To err in foregoing too large a portion of yield in order to protect the basic resource will likely deprive some poor people of food and other needed natural products.

Measurement difficulties arise from:

(1) ignorance of how ecosystems behave and evolve at the regional scale;
(2) non-linearity of ecosystem response to stress;
(3) natural variability (signal-to-noise ratio);
(4) sampling and analytical errors under field conditions;
(5) inadequate monitoring and research over large areas and long times;
(6) deliberate falsification of data for sociocultural or political reasons; and
(7) inadequate research on the linkage of natural and managed ecosystems.

Opportunities to overcome these difficulties through improved monitoring and understanding of the structure and function of ecosystems are at hand. International development assistance agencies and investors should recognize that the current inadequate state-of-the-science of biophysical measurements threatens the financial soundness of their actions (to say nothing of the social and environmental soundness) and provide appropriate support to improve the situation. Such funding would appear to be highly cost-effective because better measurements will permit the realization of a greater and more dependable productive potential from natural resources and even, perhaps, sustainable development.

REFERENCES

Asian Development Bank. 1990. *Economic policies for sustainable development.* Asian Development Bank, Manila, Philippines.
Botkin, D., and L. Talbot. 1992. Biological diversity and forests. In *Managing the world's forests,* ed. N. P. Sharma. Kendall-Hunt, Dubuque, Iowa, USA.
Carpenter, R. A. 1989. Do we know what we are talking about? *Land Degradation and Rehabilitation* 1:1-3.

Carpenter, R. A. 1990. Biophysical measurement of sustainable development. *The Environmental Professional* 12:356-59.

Carpenter, R. A. 1991. Can we measure sustainable development? *Asian Society for Environmental Protection Newsletter* 7(2): 1-2.

Carpenter, R. A. 1993. Can sustainability be measured? *Environmental Strategy: Newsletter of the IUCN Commission on Environmental Strategy and Planning* 1(5): 13-16.

Carpenter, R. A. 1994. Limitations in measuring sustainability. In *Biophysical measures of sustainability. See* Lovejoy 1994.

Carpenter, R. A., and D. E. Harper. 1989. Towards a science of sustainable upland management in developing countries. *Environmental Management* 13:43-54.

Carpenter, S. R., and others. 1993. Complexity, cascades, and compensation in ecosystems. Paper presented at workshop, Biodiversity: Its Complexity and Role, 24-26 November at the National Institute for Environmental Studies, Tsukuba, Japan.

Consultative Group on International Agricultural Research (CGIAR). 1990. Report of the Committee on Sustainable Agriculture. Consultative Group Meeting, 21-25 May. CGIAR, The Hague, The Netherlands.

Costanza, R., ed. 1991. *Ecological economics: The science and management of sustainability.* Columbia University Press, New York.

Craig, P. P., and H. Glasser. 1994. Transfer models and explicit uncertainty: An approach to intergenerational "green accounting." In *Ecological Economics.* Forthcoming.

Dalal-Clayton, B. 1992. *Modified EIA and indicators of sustainability: First steps towards sustainability analysis.* International Institute for Environment and Development, London.

Daly, H. E. 1991. *Ecological economics and sustainable development.* World Bank Environment Department Paper No. 1991-24. World Bank, Washington, D.C.

Daly, H. E., and J. B. Cobb, Jr. 1989. *For the common good: Redirecting the economy toward community, the environment, and a sustainable future.* Beacon, Boston.

Dixon, J., R. Carpenter, L. Fallon, P. Sherman, and S. Manopimoke. 1988. *Economic analysis of the environmental impacts of development projects.* Earthscan, London.

Ecological Society of America. 1991. The Sustainable Biosphere Initiative: An ecological research agenda. *Ecology* 72:371-412.

Eckman, K. 1993. Using indicators of unsustainability in development programs. *Impact Assessment* 11(3): 275-88.

Faeth, P., R. Repetto, K. Kroll, Q. Dai, and G. Helmers. 1991. *Paying the farm bill: U.S. agricultural policy and the transition to sustainable agriculture.* World Resources Institute, Washington, D.C.

Franklin, J. F. 1994. Sustainability of managed temperate forest ecosystems. In *Biophysical measures of sustainability. See* Lovejoy 1994.

Hannon, B., M. Ruth, and E. Delucia. 1993. A physical view of sustainability. *Ecological Economics* 8(3): 253-68.

Hargrove, E. 1992. Environmental therapeutic nihilism. In *Ecosystem health: New goals for environmental management,* ed. R. Costanza, B. Norton, and B. Haskell. Island, Washington, D.C.

Hollick, M. 1993. Self-organizing systems and environmental management. *Environmental Management* 17(5): 621-28.

Holling, C. S. 1993. Investing in research for sustainability. *Ecological Applications* 3(4): 552-5.

Holling, C. S. 1994. Sustainability: The cross scale dimension. In *Biophysical measures of sustainability. See* Lovejoy 1994.

Huston, M. 1993. Biological diversity, soils, and economics. *Science* 262:1676-80.

Johnson, N., and B. Cabarle. 1993. *Surviving the cut: Natural forest management in the humid tropics.* World Resources Institute, Washington, D.C.

Leopold, A. 1968. *A Sand County almanac and sketches here and there.* Oxford University Press, New York.

Lipske, M. 1994. A new gold rush packs the woods in central Oregon. *Smithsonian* 1(January): 35.

Lovejoy, T. E., and others, eds. 1994. *Biophysical measures of sustainability.* United Nations University, New York.

Lusigi, W. J. 1994. Measuring sustainability in tropical rangelands: A case study from northern Kenya. In *Biophysical measures of sustainability. See* Lovejoy 1994.

MacKay, K. T. 1991. Global warming, fisheries and policy for sustainable development. Paper presented at the International Conference on Global Warming and Sustainable Development, 10-12 June, Bangkok.

Magnuson, J. J. 1990. Long-term ecological research and the invisible present. *BioScience* 40:495-501.

Mooney, H., and O. Sala. 1993. Science and sustainable use. *Ecological Applications* 3(4): 564-6.

National Research Council. 1993. *Issues in risk assessment.* National Academy Press, Washington, D.C.

National Research Council. 1994. Information on range lands too scarce for setting policy, study says. *Washington Post,* 8 January, Section A.

O'Neill, R. V., C. T. Hunsaker, and others. 1994. Sustainability at landscape and regional scales. In *Biophysical measures of sustainability. See* Lovejoy 1994.

Pickup, G., and S. R. Morton. 1994. Restoration of arid land. In *Biophysical measures of sustainability. See* Lovejoy 1994.

Poore, D. 1989. *No timber without trees: Sustainability in the tropical forest.* Earthscan, London.

Regier, H. A., and A. S. Bocking. 1994. Sustainability with temperate zone fisheries: biophysical foundations for its definition and measurement. In *Biophysical measures of sustainability. See* Lovejoy 1994.

Rerkasem, K., and A. T. Rambo. 1988. *Agroecosystem research for rural development.* Multiple Cropping Centre, Faculty of Agriculture, Chiang Mai University and Southeast Asia Universities Agroecosystem Network (SUAN), Chiang Mai, Thailand.

Richey, J. 1994. Tropical waste resources management. In *Biophysical measures of sustainability. See* Lovejoy 1994.

Risser, P. 1994. Indicators of grassland sustainability: A first approximation. In *Biophysical measures of sustainability. See* Lovejoy 1994.

Rosenberg, A. A., M. J. Fogarty, M. P. Sissenwine, J. R. Beddington, and others. 1993. Achieving sustainable use of renewable resources. *Science* 262:828-29.

Schaeffer, D. J., E. Herricks, and H. Kerster. 1988. Ecosystem Health I: Measuring ecosystem health. *Environmental Management* 12(4): 445-55.

Sawhill, J. C. 1991. Into the future. *Nature Conservancy* 1(Nov.-Dec.): 5-9.

Sherman, K. 1994. The definition and measurement of sustainability: The biophysical foundations of large marine ecosystems and fisheries. In *Biophysical measures of sustainability. See* Lovejoy 1994.

Solow, R. 1992. *An almost practical step toward sustainability.* Resources for the Future, Washington, D.C.

White, P. S. 1993. Review of *The balance of nature?* by S. L. Pimm, and *Conservation biology,* by P. L. Fiedler and S. K. Jain, eds. *American Scientist* 81(5): 488.

Vitousek, P., and J. Lubchenco. 1994. Limits to sustainable use of resources: From local effects to global change. In *Biophysical measures of sustainability. See* Lovejoy 1994.

Environmental Indicators for Latin America and the Caribbean: Tools for Sustainability

Cʒ

MANUEL WINOGRAD

The goal of the present work is to prepare a set of indicators that might be used in the evaluation and design of environmental policies.[1] Besides defining descriptive indicators that may allow a quantitative evaluation of a given situation, normative indicators are used to compare reference values and to show in what direction we must proceed. For this we used a rational methodology that will permit select retrospective and prospective environmental indicators in relation to the main issues related to the environment and development.

The model is based on the elaboration of three groups of indicators at different levels and scales: countries and bioregions, regional, and local. The first group is employed to observe the causes of the environmental problems (Pressure on the Environment); the second group of indicators is related to the quality of the environment in relation to the effects of the human actions (State of the Environment); and the third refers to the measures and responses taken by the society to ameliorate the environment (Response on the Environment). In addition, a fourth group of prospective indicators is elaborated related to the steps necessary for achieving sustainability in land use (Progress toward Sustainability). In this way, we are stressing the importance of considering the potential and limitations of land use and natural resources in the elaboration of policies and actions for a sustainable development.

Introduction

In the last few years there has been a rising level of consciousness about environmental problems as they relate to models of development and natural resource use. The conviction that people, countries, and regions ought to change their behavior with respect to the management and consumption of natural resources has become increasingly common. This serves as a starting point for the application of sustainable development models that allow for the preservation of the environment, the rational use of natural resources, and the betterment of the human quality of life.

The current world situation necessitates urgent changes in models of development—as much in socioeconomic terms as in environmental ones. These changes will not come about with conventional solutions, and they must transcend the sustainable development rhetoric in order to convert the idea into a reality. Nevertheless, modifying the current models of development in order to reach sustainability requires accelerating the coming together of the processes that lead to development. These processes, as well as time, imply enormous changes in development, land use, and natural resource policies. The application and elaboration of sustainable development therefore establishes new demands for its formulation and implementation. We must quantify and monitor the evolution of the process carefully and recognize the relationships between problems—their causes and effects, changes and progress—in order to create the necessary actions and responses.

This has led countries, international organizations, and nongovernmental organizations to reexamine the methods at their disposal to evaluate and watch over the evolution and trends in the state of the environment, the use of natural resources, and the processes of development (USAID/WRI 1993; Winograd 1992; WRI 1990, 1992). Environmental indicators have emerged as indispensable tools for following and defining actions and strategies leading to sustainable development and a cost benefit analysis.

For this we must appreciate and evaluate the impact of the human activities that cause pressure on the environment, on the condition of natural resources, on the measures that society generates to protect the environment, and the present and future potential and limitations for the application of models of sustainable development. Furthermore, one must consider that development policies and strategies are created and applied differently at different levels of society, and thus the consequences of such policies should be observed on different scales.

In Latin America and the Caribbean, despite the region's relative abundance of natural resources, the deterioration of the environment, both in urban and rural zones, is a common phenomenon. This situation is the result of the application of development models that have common characteristics at the regional level. For example, the problem of managing ecosystem diversity was addressed by establishing uniform use strategies, but these caused a loss of resilience and reduction in the capacity to absorb perturbations and respond to changes. One of the principal conclusions derived from studies done at the regional and local levels is that, in many cases, development models, productive activities, and use of natural resources lack one basic element: ecological sustainability.

Nevertheless, the impact, causes, and consequences of the development process on natural resources should be analyzed from a wider perspective, a perspective from which we can observe the interactions and synergistic effects among the different components of the process. This wider perspective can help people come up with alternatives and management strategies based on their potential effects, their limitations, and the necessities of the situation. That is to say, sustainable and unsustainable development must be analyzed as a function of ecological-environmental, economic-financial, social-cultural, and technological-scientific components.

The objective of this paper is to present a series of indicators which can be used to evaluate, follow, and design environmental policies. The series contains descriptive indicators intended for use in the quantitative evaluation of a given situation. In addition, it is possible to compare reference values and see the direction in which we must move. The series was constructed using a methodology that permits the rational selection of retrospective and prospective environmental indicators as a function of the main topics related to the environment and development at different levels and scales (countries and bioregions; regional and local).

The first group of indicators is used to observe the causes of environmental problems, the second describes the quality of the environment, and the third refers to societal actions and responses related to the environment. There is also a fourth group of prospective indicators that measure the necessary progress toward sustainability in the use of land. In this way, we emphasize the importance of considering the strengths and limitations in the use of land and natural resources in the creation of sustainable environmental policies.

Indicators and Sustainability

The creation of environmental indicators requires a conceptual framework that will enable the user to understand what he or she wants to monitor and what should be monitored. The indicators should be selected based on the levels and scales to be monitored and should be a function of the components and the steps of the process to be monitored. Furthermore, to analyze and monitor processes of development and the use of land and natural resources, it is necessary to classify the region from a wide perspective. This should allow the user to uncover socioeconomic differences as well as inequities resulting from differing endowments of natural resources and the weight that these exercise on economic processes and human activity. Depending on the level analyzed (country, ecoregion, ecosystem, or parcel of land), the factors that affect development and sustainability (economic, social, technological, or environmental) are different, and consequently, the indicators that are necessary to monitor the processes must be different. The same principle applies in the case of scales (global, regional, or local). Indicators' meaning and usage vary, therefore, in the monitoring and analysis of development processes.

Let us take for example the sustained use of a resource such as wood. At the level of a parcel of forest land, sustained use can be achieved through a volumetric increase in the harvest that does not supersede the overall growth rate of the forest. In this case, the indicators are of a physical nature and are obtained by a biological knowledge of the utilized resource and knowledge of the technology used for its exploitation (Dixon and Fallon 1991). To analyze sustainability at a higher level, such as the level of the ecosystem, we need to understand the behavior and interaction of other components of the system above the level of the individual resource. In practice, the sustainable management of an individual resource at this level could be unsustainable for the system as a whole. This is the case, for example, of reforestation using an exotic species (*Pinus sp.*), which could be sustainable with respect to productivity and production. However, problems of erosion, plagues, reduction in biodiversity, modification of hydrological cycles, and acidification of the soil must be considered against the variables of productivity and production and must be related to other existing activities within the zone. Indicators in this case are useful in evaluating the costs and benefits of obtaining the resource, considered in contrast to the deterioration of the ecosystem or river basin. If necessary, they can be used to determine compensation associated with maintaining the functioning and equilibrium of the system.

But the concept of sustainability is even bigger, and encompasses in its objective not only the sustained development of a physical reserve or of production within an ecosystem, but also sustained increase in the quality of human life. For this reason we need indicators which integrate in addition to physical and technological aspects, the sustainability of social and economic systems in their different levels and scales (Dixon and Fallon 1991).

Besides the characteristics and components of sustainability, we should incorporate spatial and temporal dimensions. Temporal dimensions are necessary in order to establish the evolution of components and activities over time. We observe that social and economic changes appear to have time spans that, from the ecological perspective, are extremely short. At the same time, technological changes can affect resources within a very short period of time, although their social and economic impact might only be considered over a longer term.

Specifying the spatial dimension is necessary for observing how development strategies and natural resource use affect the environment at its different levels. In practice, regions or regional groupings can be used as political units of growing integration in which development policies and strategies are created at a wide level. National borders can be used as administrative units in which political decisions that direct the process of development are made. Bioregions (or ecoregions) are areas with common ecological and productive characteristics where development actions and policies occur and where natural resources are found. Lastly, river basins and ecosystems are local units in which the causes and consequences of determined development policies are visualized on a short-term scale. They can serve as pilot areas.

What Is Sustainability?

The lack of a precise definition for the term "sustainable development" has its advantages and disadvantages. One of the advantages is that it permits a consensus to be reached supporting the morally and economically unsavory idea that the planet, the environment, and natural resources must be treated as a business in liquidation (Holmberg and others 1991). Another advantage is that the concept eliminates the dichotomy between economic growth and environmental protection, while the vagueness of the term enables people to incorporate values such as liberty, justice, and equity into the debate.

But the term presents inconveniences along with its advantages. The first is the sense in which one refers to a process (development), and a condition (sustainable) at which we want to arrive. For this we have different paths which should be chosen as a function of political options with different levels and scales, depending upon whether we refer to a community, a country, or a region. Second, one has to take into account the fact that differing definitions of the sustainability of development have already been created for diverse purposes; each existing definition therefore has concepts and applications with different reaches. For this reason, although it is not the purpose of this work to add one more definition to the many that already exist, I will delineate certain important aspects of sustainable development to serve as a reference for defining environmental indicators.

Sustainable development should be a process which allows for the satisfaction of human necessities without compromising the basis of that development, which is to say, the environment.

The objectives of development are to achieve an equitable process economically, a just and participative one socially, one that reorients and is efficient with technology, and, finally, one which uses, conserves, and improves the environment (Winograd 1991, 1993a). To do this, sustainable development must comply with the following requirements:

(1) In economic terms, it must not impoverish one group as it enriches another. Sustainable development should avoid the exclusion of important social sectors from the benefits generated by development. A structure characterized by a growing inequality could become sustainable in purely biophysical terms, but not in socioeconomic ones (Gallopín and others 1989; Saunier 1987).

(2) In ecological terms, it must not degrade the diversity and biological productivity of ecosystems nor ecological processes and vital systems (IUCN/UNEP/WWF 1991). It should maintain, recover, and restore the natural resource base of the areas of the highest productive potential as well as those of marginalized, deteriorated zones through adequate productive management.

(3) In social and political terms, the roles of solidarity, coordination of action, participation by all sectors and individuals, and international cooperation are necessary aspects for the achievement of sustainability. For this type of development to become a reality at the global and regional levels (and not only at the level of isolated communities), the action and respect of all parties is required. Currently, all societies (save for a few) are strongly integrated into the capitalist market. If the system as a whole does not support the practices and objectives of sustainability, a community or isolated country that moves forward in adopting sustainable policies runs the risk of being penalized by higher costs or lower benefits in the short-run economic point of view (Gallopín and others 1989; Preston 1990).

(4) In technological terms, sustainable development must increase the capacity to respond to change and maintain or increase available options for self-reliant adaptation. In the current world situation—with great changes occurring at the level of production and technological innovation, the continual appearance of new products and markets, and growing interdependence and interconnection—sustainability can no longer limit itself to only the increase of productivity or to sectoral self-reliance that might guarantee long-term production of a given product (Gallopín and others 1989). Technology will have to be rooted in the more efficient use of natural resources and the possibility of putting aside or increasing productive options, and not be limited to increases in productivity.

(5) Lastly, the existence of diverse socioeconomic, cultural, productive, and ecological systems must be seen not as an impediment to development, but as a guarantee that the system will be able to respond to change. Homogenization leads to the loss of options (cultural, social, and economic), and this loss goes against productive and ecological diversity. Although it is extremely difficult to foresee what will be the most socially and economically sustainable activities or what the value of resources will be in the long run, what should be sought in sustain-

able development is to preserve options and opportunities (Winograd 1991, 1993a).

Definition of Indicators

In general terms, environmental indicators should perform the following functions: simplify, quantify, analyze, and communicate. That is to say that the indicators should faciltate understanding by depicting issues in less complex terms and should make them quantifiable so that they can be analyzed in a given context and communicated to the different levels of society (Adriaanse 1993). The purpose is to make different aspects of the environment and development stand out, thus reducing the level of uncertainty in the formulation of strategies and actions and enabling decision-makers to better define their priorities.

Although a series of common elements exists in the elaboration of environmental information, the selection and development of environmental indicators makes it necessary to define a model for structuring and integrating that information. Structuring different sources of information improves access to information that is generally diverse and scattered. Integrating data permits one to interpret information in such a way as to understand the connections and synergistic effects among problems.

The model of indicators adopted here consists of three types of indicators that are intended to provide a clear view of the condition of the environment and of natural resources, development trends, and responses to and progress toward sustainability (Adriaanse 1992, 1993; Winograd 1993a, 1993b). In Table 1, the first group refers to the indicators of the causes of environmental problems and relates them to human activities that exert pressure on the environment. The second group has to do with the quality of the environment as affected by human actions and relates them to the condition of the environment. A third group of indicators refers to the measures that society takes to improve its environment and relates these to political actions and responses.

In addition, the indicators should be useful in predicting and anticipating aspects of non-sustainable development, as well as the limitations and opportunities for applying sustainable development (Winograd 1993a). This fourth set of indicators is concerned with progress toward sustainability. Although the indicators are of the same type as the "Pressure" and "State" indicators, they are presented in a separate section since they are based on data from simulations and projections of land use. Our objective is to present data in a manner of analysis whose limits we can manipulate in the application of alternative models of development. In this way, the collection of indicators as a whole can be useful for diagnosing where we stand with respect to a given threshold. It can also be used for designing policies based on objectives which reorient actions and responses toward the implementation of sustainable development. In the same way, we will be able to monitor the progress of certain actions and determine what policies should be created, reinforced, or eliminated to stop the causes of environmental degradation.

Selection of Indicators

Given the diversity of situations within the region and the great variation in the availability of environmental information, it is not an easy task to identify the most important and urgent aspects of the environment and development situation. Any categorization of problems, opportunities, and indicators selected will inevitably contain a certain amount of arbitrariness.

A first approximation allows us to analyze the development process as a function of its interaction with the environment and natural resources. Based on the principal studies on the environment and development in the region (BID/PNUD 1990; Gallopín and others 1991; PNUMA/AECI/MOPU 1990; USAID/WRI 1993; WRI 1990), one can conclude that the most important environmental problems are:

- ☐ Erosion and loss of soil fertility
- ☐ Desertification
- ☐ Deforestation and the fate of land
- ☐ Rural migration and land ownership
- ☐ Exploitation and use of forests
- ☐ Degradation of river basins
- ☐ Loss of genetic resources and ecosystems
- ☐ Deterioration of marine and coastal resources
- ☐ Water and air pollution
- ☐ Quality of life in human settlements.

But these problems can also be analyzed as a function of the magnitude of the affected area, of transformations which impact natural systems in the affected area, and of populations and economic activities in the affected area. From this perspective, two overreaching topics help us to explain and analyze the past, present, and future evolution in the region with respect to the environment and development. These are (1) land use, and (2) urbanization.

These topics affect the environment, population, and economic activity in different ways. For example, the urbanization process affects more than half of the population of a region, but it is limited in space and with respect to some natural resources. Land use, meanwhile, affects all natural resources and almost all of the regional surface area, though it affects a limited amount of the population. Within the context of these problems and regional environmental themes, and although these are interrelated, it is important to separate the topic of land use from that of urbanization for the analysis and elaboration of indicators. Urban environmental problems are more related with the quality of life and health of cities (Linares and others 1992). Problems of land use refers mainly to the use of natural resources. Land use in terms of opportunities and alternatives for sustainable development is also emerging as a priority topic for the region. For this reason, for the first stage of creating environmental indicators, we select land use.

Within this context, the necessary indicators are chosen based on:

☐ The availability and quality of data
☐ Its application and connection with the problem being analyzed
☐ Its geographic coverage
☐ Its importance for analysis
☐ Its relation to the sustainability or non-sustainability of development
☐ Personal judgment, which permits the interrelation of the different levels and scales used in this work (Winograd 1993a).

Using the Pressure-State-Response model adopted in this work, one can identify different variables for measuring up to what point the system is or is not affected in its sustainability in land and natural resource use at the level of the country and bioregions, as well as at the regional or local scale (de Camino and Miller 1993; IIE 1993; Winograd 1993a) (See Table 1).

Table 1

Pressure-State-Response Model for Indicators of Sustainability in Land and Natural Resource Use

Indicators are developed to show (1) *Pressure*, or causes of environmental problems; (2) the *State* of the environment and effects of human activities; and (3) *Response* by society in the form of measures taken to improve the condition of the environment. Variables and their associated indicators are grouped according to these three categories in the table below.

Variable	Element	Descriptor	Indicator	Level and Scale
Population[1]	Population Growth	Measure of Increase	Total Population	Country, Bioregion, Region, Local
	Pressure on Land	Ratio with Surface Area	Density	Country, Bioregion, Region, Local
	Population Distribution	Urban-Rural Ratio	% Urban and Rural	Country, Bioregion, Region, Local
Development Socio-economics[1]	Production Increase	Measure of Increase	Annual Growth Rate of GDP	Country, Region
	Production Increase	Ratio with Population	GDP per capita	Country, Region
	Purchasing Power	Purchasing Power Parity	Real GNP per capita	Country, Region
	Employment	Level of Employment	% of Unemployment	Country, Region
	External Debt	External Debt-Export Ratio	External Debt and Debt Service as % of Exports	Country, Region
	International Prices	Exports-Imports Price Ratio	Terms of Trade Ratio	Country, Region
	Social Welfare	Level of Human Development	Index of Human Development	Country, Region
	Health Conditions	Life and Mortality Expectancy	Life Expectancy and Infant Mortality Rate	Country, Region
	Conditions of Nutrition	Malnutrition and Calorie Intake	% of Malnourished Children and Daily Caloric Intake	Country, Region
	Condition of Education	Male and Female Literacy	% of Literacy	Country, Region
	State of the Population	Population-Poverty Ratio	% of Incidence of Poverty	Country, Region
Agriculture and Food[1]	Food Production	Measure of Increase	Change in Production and Yield	Country, Region
	Food Production	Measure of Increase	Index of Food Production	Country, Region
	Food Consumption	Change in Calorie Intake	Calories per capita and % Change in Calorie Supply	Country, Region, Local
	Agricultural Inputs	Growth in Use of Inputs	Annual Fertilizer and Pesticide Use	Country, Region
	Land Availability	Agricultural Land and Population	Agricultural Land per capita	Country, Region
	Land Concentration	Inequality of Land Distribution	GINI Coefficient	Country, Region

continued→

Pressure-State-Response Model for Indicators of Sustainability in Land and Natural Resource Use, *continued*

Variable	Element	Descriptor	Indicator	Level and Scale
Agriculture and Food[1] *(continued)*	Production Orientation	Grain Production and Destination Ratio	% of Grain Consumed by Livestock	Country, Region
	Soil Condition	Ratio with Hillside Lands	% of Agricultural Lands	Country, Region
	Condition of Hillside Soil	Soil Limitations	% of Soil with Limitations	Country, Region
	Condition of Hillside Soils	Soil Potential	Potential Agricultural Land	Country, Bioregion, Region
	Production Potential	Agricultural Land, Population, and Level of Inputs Ratio	Necessary Agricultural Land	Country, Bioregion, Region
	Land Availability	Agricultural Land and Potential Population Ratio	Agricultural Land Potential per capita	Country, Bioregion, Region
	Land Availability	Potential and Current Agricultural Land Ratio	Potential for Land Expansion	Country, Bioregion, Region
	Load Capacity	Population Potential and Level of Inputs Ratio	Ratio of Support Capacity	Country, Bioregion, Region
	Production Orientation	Production of Drugs and Employment Ratio	Production of Drugs	Country, Region, Local
	Orientation of Production	Changes in Food Consumption	Food Sources	Country, Local
Energy and Materials[1]	Production of Bioenergy	Firewood and Coal Production-Population Ratio	Firewood and Coal per capita	Country, Region
	Bioenergy Production	Production and Requirement Ratio	Traditional Fuels as a % of Total Requirements	Country, Region
	Production Potential	Production of Bioenergy	Bioenergetic Potential	Country, Region
	Hydroelectric Resources	Generation Capacity	Installed Hydroelectric Capacity	Country, Region
	Hydroelectric Production	Production and Capacity Ratio	% of the Capacity Generated	Country, Region
	Hydroelectric Potential	Generation Potential	Exploitable Hydroelectric Potential	Country, Region
	Hydroelectric Production	Generation and Surface Area Ratio	Kilowatts Generated per flooded hectare	Country, Region
	Materials Consumption	Consumption and Population to Surface Area Ratio	Per capita Materials Consumption	Country, Region

continued →

Pressure-State-Response Model for Indicators of Sustainability in Land and Natural Resource Use, *continued*

Variable	Element	Descriptor	Indicator	Level and Scale
Ecosystems and Land Use[2]	Change in Primary Productivity	Measurement of Primary Production	Current and Natural Primary Production	Bioregion, Region
	Change in Land Use	Measurement of the Change in Patterns of Use	% Change	Country, Bioregion, Region, Local
	Employment and Production	Relationship Among Jobs and Surface Area, People Fed	Jobs per hectare	Country, Bioregion, Local
	Land Production	Economic Production	Annual Production and Value	Country, Bioregion, Local
	Impact of Land Use	Measure of Emissions and Changes in Use Intensity	Net Emissions, Species Used And Years of Use	Country, Bioregion, Local
	Impact of Land Use	Urban and Rural Emissions Relationship	Equivalent People Using Fossil Fuels	Country, Bioregion, Local
Forests and Pastures[2]	Cover of Vegetation	Type of Forest	Surface Area of Dense and Open Forests	Country, Bioregion, Region
	Decrease of Forests	Deforestation of Dense and Open Forests	Annual Deforestation	Country, Bioregion, Region
	Earnings from Forests	Reforestation in Dense and Open Forests	Annual Reforestation	Country, Bioregion, Region
	Change in Forest Surface Area	Annual Deforestation	Annual Deforestation Rate	Country, Bioregion, Region
	Change in Forest Surface Area	Ratio of Deforestation and Reforestation	Ratio of Deforestation and Reforestation	Country, Bioregion, Region
	Production of Forests	Relationship of Production and Population	Wood Production per capita	Country, Bioregion, Region
	Forest Potential	Ratio of Wood Reserves and Population	Wood Reserves per capita and by hectare	Country, Bioregion, Region
	Forest Potential	Ratio of Production and Reserves	Ratio of Production/Reserves	Country, Bioregion, Region
	Cover of Vegetation	Change in Surface Area of Pastures	% Change in Pastures	Country, Bioregion, Region
	Livestock Population	Measurement of Increase	% Change in Livestock Population	Country, Bioregion, Region
	Load Capacity	Measurement of Increase	Index of Load Capacity	Country, Bioregion, Region
	Production of Pastures	Measurement of Increase in Meat Production	% Change in Meat Production	Country, Bioregion, Region
	Economic Value	Ratio of Surface Area and Export Value	Dollars per hectare	Country, Local

continued →

Pressure-State-Response Model for Indicators of Sustainability in Land and Natural Resource Use, *continued*

Variable	Element	Descriptor	Indicator	Level and Scale
Biological Diversity[2]	Decrease in Number of Species	Ratio of Threatened Species to Total	% Threatened Animal Species	Country, Region
	Decrease in Number of Species	Ratio of Threatened Species to Total	% Threatened Plants Species	Country, Region
	Decrease in Number of Species	Ratio of Threatened Species to Surface Area	Threatened Plants per 1000 km^2	Country, Region
	System of Protected Areas	Ratio of Protected Areas to Total	% of Protected Areas	Country, Bioregion, Region
	Use of Biodiversity	Ratio of Used Species to Total	Index of Vegetation Use	Country, Bioregion, Local
	Risk of Species Disappearance	Relationship of Habitat and Species Disappearance	Index of Species Disappearance	Country, Bioregion, Local
	Investment in Protection	Relationship of Investment and Surface Area	Risk Dollars per 1000 hectares	Country, Region
	Economic Value	Economic Production	Protected Value of Production	Country, Local
	Economic Value	Profitability of Investment	Current Net Value	Country, Local
Waters and Coasts[2]	Coastal Resources	Ratio of Coastline and Coastal Resources	Ratio of Coastline, Mangroves, and Meadowlands	Country, Region
	Protection of Coastal Resources	Protected Areas	Number of Protected Coastal Areas	Country, Region
	Load Capacity	Population Growth in Coastal Areas	Population in Coastal Cities	Country, Region
	Fresh Water Reserves	Ratio of Total Water to Population	Renewable Water Resources per capita	Country, Region
	Fresh Water Use	Ratio of Total Resources to Population	% of Water Extraction per capita	Country, Region
	Distribution of Water Use	Ratio of Water Extraction by Sector	Sectoral Water Extraction	Country, Region
	Value of Coastal Resources	Ratio of Jobs and Income	Jobs and Income in Mangroves	Country, Local
Atmosphere and Climate[2]	Emissions of Greenhouse Gases	Increase in Emissions Through Change in Land Use	Emissions of CO_2 Eq. Carbon Total and per capita	Country, Bioregion, Region
	Emissions of Greenhouse Gases	Increase in Total Emissions	Emissions of CO_2 Eq. Carbon Total, per capita and per GNP	Country, Region
	Emissions of Greenhouse Gases	Relationship of Activities and Change in Land Use	Emissions of CO_2 Eq. Carbon by Activity	Bioregion, Region

continued →

Pressure-State-Response Model for Indicators of Sustainability in Land and Natural Resource Use, *continued*

Variable	Element	Descriptor	Indicator	Level and Scale
Atmosphere and Climate[2] (continued)	Emissions of Greenhouse Gases	Ratio of Current and Accumulated Emissions	Current and Accumulated Emissions of CO_2 per capita	Country, Region
	Climate	Incidence of Natural Disasters	Population Affected and Economic Losses	Country, Region
Information and Participation[3]	Environmental Information	Countries with Environmental Profiles and Inventories	Number of Environmental Profiles and Inventories	Country, Region
	Societal Participation	Possibility of Participation in Decisions	Number of NGOs per Area of Activity	Country, Region
	Public Opinion	Importance of Environment	Perception of Environmental Problems	Country, Region
Treaties and Agreements[3]	Environmental Policy	Participation in Treaties and Agreements	Signing and Ratification of International Treaties	Country, Region
	Sources of Financing for Conservation	Debt-for-Nature Swaps	Funds Generated for Conservation	Country, Region, Local
Land Use Projections[3]	Land Use Potential	Ratio of Potential Productive Land to Population	Potential Productive Land per capita	Bioregion, Region
	Land Need	Ratio of Needed Agricultural Land to Level of Inputs	Agricultural Land Necessary in 2030	Bioregion, Region
	Current and Potential Use	Ratio of Current to Potential Productive Land	Index of Land Use	Bioregion, Region
	Vegetation	Ratio of Gains to Losses of Forests	Deforestation Rate and Ratio of Reforestation/Deforestation	Bioregion, Region
	Land Use	Ratio of Land Use to Population	Agricultural Land and Forests per capita	Bioregion, Region
	Consequences of Land Use	Additions to Greenhouse Gases	Net, Total, and per capita Additions	Bioregion, Region
	Cost and Investment for Development	Ratio of Necessary Surface Area and Cost of Land Use	Average Annual Investment	Bioregion, Region
	Potential Land Use	Ratio of Actual to Potential Use Cost	Cost and Benefit of Rehabilitation	Bioregion, Local
Agro-forestry[3]	Potential for Mitigating the Consequences of Land Use	Ratio of Potential Surface Area to Absorption of Carbon	Carbon Absorption Through Reforestation and Agroforestry	Bioregion, Local

For the elaboration of indicators, we have selected variables for each category of analysis that allows us to measure and describe the situation and evolution with respect to land and natural resource use. Each of the variables is composed of different elements that should be chosen based on their significance for sustainability. Each element has significant characteristics, which we will call "descriptors," with respect to the path to sustainability that should be chosen. Furthermore, for each descriptor selected, one should define one or various indicators to measure its effect on the system. Lastly, in order to understand the significance of some indicators, we need statistical data on the effect of the variables and the elements on the system. Table 1 shows the selected variables as well as the elements, descriptors, and indicators that are necessary for each of the categories in relation to the environment and sustainability of land use (Winograd 1993a, 1993b).

NOTES

1. This paper was completed with the collaboration of the World Resources Institute (Washington, D.C.), the IICA/GTZ project (Costa Rica), and the Organization of American States (Washington, D.C.). It has been translated from the Spanish version, "Indicadores Ambientales para América Latina y el Caribe: Herramientas para la Sustentabilidad."

REFERENCES

Adriaanse, A. 1992. *Some views on environmental performance indicators at a global scale.* Netherlands Ministry of Housing, Physical Planning and Environment. The Hague, The Netherlands.

Adriaanse, A. 1993. *Environmental policy performance indicators: A study on the development of indicators for environmental policy in the Netherlands.* Netherlands Ministry of Housing, Physical Planning, and Environment. The Hague, The Netherlands.

de Camino, R., and S. Muller. 1993. *La definición de sostenibilidad, las variables principales y bases para establecer indicadores.* Proyecto IICA-GTZ sobre Agricultura, Recursos Naturales y Desarrollo Sostenible, San José, Costa Rica. Manuscript.

Dixon, J., and L. Fallon. 1991. El concepto de sustentabilidad: Sus orígenes, alcances y utilidad en la formulación de políticas. In *Desarrollo y medio ambiente: Hacia un enfoque integrador,* ed. J. Vial. CIEPLAN, Santiago, Chile.

Gallopín, G., P. Gutman, and H. Maletta. 1989. Global impoverishment, sustainable development, and the environment: A conceptual approach. *International Social Sciences Journal* 121:375-97.

Gallopín, G., M. Winograd, and I. Gómez. 1991. *Ambiente y desarrollo en América Latina y el Caribe: Problemas, oportunidades y prioridades*. Grupo de Análisis de Sistemas Ecológicos (GASE), Fundación Bariloche, Bariloche, Argentina.

Holmberg, J., S. Bass, and L. Timberlake. 1991. *Defending the future: A guide to sustainable development*. Earthscan, London.

Instituto de Investigaciones Económicas (IIE). 1993. *Principales problemas que afectan el desarrollo sostenible en América Latina y el Caribe con enfasis en los sectores agrícola y de recursos naturales*. Consultoria para el Proyecto IICA/GTZ, Documento Borrador, IIE-University of Costa Rica, San José, Costa Rica.

IUCN/UNEP/WWF. 1991. *Caring for the earth: A strategy for sustainable living*. IUCN, Gland, Switzerland.

Latin American and Caribbean Commission on Development and Environment. 1990. *Our Own Agenda*. Latin American and Caribbean Commission on Development and Environment, Inter-American Development Bank, Washington, D.C.; United Nations Development Programme, New York.

Linares, C., D. Seligman, and D. Tunstall. 1992. *Developing urban environmental indicators in third world cities*. Final draft report to USAID, Center for International Development and Environment at the World Resources Institute, Washington, D.C.

Preston, T. R. 1990. Future strategies for livestock production in tropical third world countries. *Ambio* 18(8): 390-93.

PNUMA/AECI/MOPU. 1990. *Desarrollo y medio ambiente en América Latina y el Caribe: Una visión evolutiva*. Ministerio de Obras Publicas y Urbanismo (MOPU), Madrid.

Saunier, R. 1987. *Conceptos de manejo ambiental*, Taller Avanzado sobre Planificación Regional y Medio Ambiente, 2-14 November, Organization of American States (OAS), Bariloche, Argentina.

USAID/WRI. 1993. *Green guidance for Latin America and the Caribbean*. Bureau for Latin America and the Caribbean (USAID) and Center for International Development and Environment (WRI), Washington, D.C.

Winograd, M. 1991. *Indicators for Latin America: Indicators for the sustainability or non-sustainability of development*. Paper for Discussion, World Resources Institute, Washington, D.C.

Winograd, M. 1992. *Environmetal indicators for Latin America: Trends and progress toward land use sustainability*. Workshop on Global Environmental Indicators, 6-8 December. World Resources Institute, Washington D.C.

Winograd, M. 1993a. *Indicadores ambientales para Latinoamérica y el Caribe: Hacia la sustentabilidad en el uso de tierras* [Environmental indicators for Latin America and the Caribbean: Toward land use sustainability]. Grupo de Análisis de Sistemas Ecológicos (GASE) in collaboration with Project IICA-GTZ (CostaRica), Organization of American States and World Resources Institute.Washington, D.C.

Winograd, M. 1993b. *Indicadores ambientales para las Américas: Análisis comparativo en el uso de los recursos naturales*. Grupo de Análisis de Sistemas

Ecológicos (GASE), Organization of American States (OAS), Bariloche, Argentina; Washington, D.C.

WRI. 1990. *World resources 1990-91: A guide to the global environment.* Oxford University Press, New York.

WRI. 1992. *World resources 1992-93: A guide to the global environment.* Oxford University Press, New York.

National Economic Indicators and Sustainable Development

Cஃ

FULAI SHENG

Introduction

We start with sustainable development.[1] We agree that sustainable development has ecological, social, and economic dimensions. Accordingly, sustainable development should be measured along these three dimensions at local, national, and international levels. In this context, we look at economic indicators at the national level in relation to sustainable development (see Table 1).

National economic performance is measured by Gross Domestic Product (GDP), Gross National Product (GNP), or National Income under the United Nations System of National Accounts (SNA). These indicators measure the market value of goods and services produced in an economy in a given time. Looking from the other side, they measure the amount of income generated from the production of goods and provision of services. Formal definitions of these concepts are given in Table 2.

What these indicators are supposed to measure is true income or economic sustainability, and therefore, economies' real contributions

Table 1

Aspects and Levels of Sustainable Development

		Aspects		
		Ecological	**Social**	**Economic**
	Local			
Levels	National			X
	International			

to sustainable development. Income is defined by Sir John Hicks and accepted by most economists as the maximum amount that one can consume without eventual impoverishment.[2] "True income"—or simply "income"—is therefore *by definition* economically sustainable.

This economic sustainability, however, is not to be confused with sustainable development. Income figures cannot capture many social and ecological aspects of sustainable development, such as wealth distribution, women's education, the extent of industrial pollution, and biological diversity. For these aspects, we need social and ecological indicators of sustainability.

Nevertheless, economic sustainability is an integral part of overall sustainability. Income is not only economic, but also social and ecological in terms of the ways in which it is generated, distributed, and spent. When income is miscalculated, and spending (therefore resource use activities) misguided and inappropriately promoted due to the omission of environmental values, eventual impoverishment will affect all dimensions of sustainability.

Problems with National Economic Indicators

In their present form, national economic indicators fail to even measure economic sustainability, let alone accurately reflect social and ecological aspects of sustainable development. They often fail to capture a large part of economic activities. Transactions that take place in informal sectors, such as subsistence farming and household work, do not enter into these indicators. Yet informal activities can be significant in developing countries in terms of income generation, expenditures, and "eventual impoverishment" that resource use for such activities might bring about. In Bangladesh, for example, forty percent of the population is in informal sectors.[3] In Papua New Guinea, subsistence fishing, which amounts to thirteen percent of GDP, is normally excluded from national accounts (Bartelmus, Lutz, and Schweinfest 1992).

From an environmental viewpoint, these indicators overstate true income. The first problem is that expenditures incurred by governments and households for dealing with negative effects of investment, production, and consumption are treated fully as income in national accounts, although those incurred by industry are treated as production costs (United Nations Environment Programme 1992). Household medical spending due to exposure to air pollution represents a source of revenue for hospitals and is entered into national accounts as income. Government spending on oil spills is transformed into goods and services, and along with these, wages, rents, and profits, which together boost the level of national income; the damages to marine environment and its potential income-generating capacity are not counted at all. In terms of economic sustainability, these expenditures should properly be treated as the costs of preventing eventual impoverishment that can result from pollution.

Table 2

Major Concepts under the System of National Accounts

Gross Domestic Product (GDP)
GDP is an indicator that records the market transaction value (often in US dollars for purpose of comparison) of all goods and services for final use produced in an economy in a given period (normally a year). For example, the GDP in the U.K. in 1990 was measured at US$975.15 billion. (World Bank 1992)

Net Domestic Product (NDP)
NDP is GDP adjusted for the depreciation of manmade capital, such as machine equipment and factory buildings.

Gross National Product (GNP)
GNP comprises GDP plus net income received from abroad on labor and capital, i.e., the income people at home have received from abroad for labor services and capital investments, minus similar payments to people abroad. In the UK in 1990, for example, the GNP amounted to US$924.14 billion. (World Bank 1992)

National Income
National Income measures the total income generated from the production of goods and provision of services. It is the sum of all wages, rents, interests, and profits that are brought about by economic activities. Technically, it equals GNP minus manmade-capital depreciation and tax on final product. For simplicity, GNP and GDP are often used to mean national income.

These "defensive expenditures" are necessitated by the externalities that take place at investment, production, and consumption levels.[4] Had air pollution been controlled at the source, there would have been no need for household medical spending for that purpose. Had the full costs of an oil spill been placed on oil companies, there would have been incentives for reducing the risk of spillage and the related public funds could have been used for public health and education. The accounting of such expenditures fully as national income permits externalities to occur at microeconomic levels.

The second problem with these indicators is that the revenues generated from resource depletion and environmental degradation are counted not as costs of economic activities, but fully as income (although the depreciation of manmade capital is sometimes deducted from GNP to arrive at Net Domestic Product or NDP) (United Nations Environment Programme 1992). An example is the logging of timber, which is reflected in national accounts as an income-generating activity in terms of the market value of timber products sold for final consumption; the related loss of the forest's other economic functions, such as habitats for wildlife and non-timber products, is not calculated and deducted from income calculation.

The failure of these indicators to account for the values of natural resources and environmental quality reflects the externalities taking place at microeconomic levels. Loggers are not required by market forces to consider the costs of logging other than those of logging concession fees, labor, transportation, and logging equipment; the related environmental costs are largely externalized. Economic activities that bring about resource depletion and environmental degradation acquire market values which are then written up as national income, but market values do not capture externalized costs.

Implications for Sustainable Development

Why should we be worried about these problems with national economic indicators? We are worried because they lead to unsustainable use of natural resources, which in turn contributes to overall unsustainability in social, economic, and ecological terms.

These indicators conceal the true costs of economic activities and encourage policies and activities that are superficially contributory to the economy, but actually destructive to the environment, the basis for both economic sustainability and overall sustainability. Most economic decisions are based on a comparison of costs and benefits. An underestimation of costs encourages activities that are most damaging to the environment, the costs to which do not normally get counted in the cost-benefit calculations. This partly explains why many developing countries heavily rely on extractive activities for income generation. In rich countries, seventy percent of economic growth comes from thirty percent of economic activities that are environmentally destructive (Tinbergen and Hueting 1991, 42).

The indicators also give an illusory picture about the true wealth of a country and places the national economy on an unreal and vulnerable basis. Under the prevailing accounting system, unsustainable resource use activities inflate true GNP or "the maximum amount of income that can be spent without eventual impoverishment." Since most governments worship the growth of GNP and pursue it as a political objective, they have every reason to promote unsustainable activities. By engaging in unsustainable activities, however, a country weakens the prospect for both economic growth and sustainable development.

From a social viewpoint, the present system of national economic indicators does not do justice to future generations. It does not account for the values of many goods and services provided by the ecosystem that are essential for the survival and welfare of the many generations to come. Specifically, it fails to allow for any compensation to future generations for the reduction of natural resources and for deterioration of environmental quality caused by present generations.

From the viewpoint of economics, as mentioned before, the national income as currently measured is not true income, which is by definition economically sustainable. Under the existing system, a significant part of national income is achieved through depletion and degradation of natural resources without replenishment and restoration. Future income-generating capacity is therefore permanently lost, leading to eventual impoverishment.

Thus, national economic indicators under the SNA have not only failed to measure economic sustainability, but also contributed to economic unsustainability and, therefore, unsustainable development. These flaws must be corrected before we can use the SNA to measure economic sustainability, and therefore economy's true contributions to sustainable development.

Methodologies

Data on defensive expenditures are more readily available; the question is whether they should all be deducted from national income. It is argued that almost all expenditures can be regarded as defending against something: expenditures on food for defending against hunger, on clothing against weather (Hicks 1946). The treatment of national defense expenditures is also a disputable issue. Categorization is needed for charging appropriate amounts against national income. We leave this to a separate discussion.

We focus here on environmental degradation and resource depletion. There are two major approaches for estimating the money value of degradation. In the *compensation approach,* compensation paid by polluters to resource owners is taken as an approximate value for degradation. For this to be meaningful, resource ownership must be clarified and a regulatory mechanism for applying the "polluter-pays principle" must be put in place. In the *avoidance cost approach,* the costs of avoiding the degradation are used as an approximation. These hypothetical costs are then used for gauging the actual costs that have already occurred in terms of the effects of pollution.

The money value of depletion may be estimated with the depreciation approach, also known as the *net price approach.* As a resource is extracted, the capacity of the remaining stock of the resource to generate income is weakened. A depreciation allowance from current sales of the resource is calculated, and supposed to be invested, to make up for the lost income-generating capacity of the remaining stock. The allowance amounts to the physical quantity of depletion times the net price (ie., market price minus all production costs, including interest payments on loans and dividends to shareholders, among other things.)

Depletion can also be valued with the *user cost approach.* The net revenues (net of all production costs) from the current sale of a resource, instead of being counted fully as income, is split into two components: a user cost allowance and a true income. The user cost allowance is calculated, and supposed to be invested, in such a way that the extraction and sale of the remaining stock of the resource plus the proceeds from the investment of the user cost throughout the lifetime of the resource will together yield a stream of annual true income at least equal to what we have in the current period.

The pros and cons of these methodologies are yet to be analyzed. In the case of valuation for degradation, for example, the amount of compensation and the hypothetical costs of avoidance may still be far short of reflecting the full costs to the environment. In the case of depletion, the depreciation method may overlook the resource advantages of some countries over others by taking the entire depreciation amount off national income, and the user cost approach may involve choosing an arbitrary discount rate for estimating investment revenues of user cost.

International agencies have played key roles in researching the methodologies for environmental valuation. In the last ten years, UNEP, the World Bank, and the UN Statistical Division have held workshops that triggered enormous efforts in seeking ways of internalizing environmental costs in national accounts.

In early 1994 the UN Statistical Division released a *Handbook on Integrated Environmental and Economic Accounting (IEEA)*. It provides a broad framework for data classification, accounting standards, and environmental valuation methodologies. Governments are expected to use the *Handbook* in their efforts to adjust economic indicators for environmental values.

But the *Handbook* does not correct distortions in the SNA directly. It advocates a satellite approach where national income may be adjusted for the environment in different ways by countries, but the existing SNA is left intact. This permits existing indicators to continue to misguide policies, encourage unsustainable resource use activities, and contribute to overall unsustainability. The SNA is the most influential system of economic indicators. The satellite approach, which leaves the SNA intact, does not have the same policy impact as we would have from a reformed SNA. Cost internalization does not take place as long as environmental accounting is not fully integrated into the SNA.

The methodologies have yet to be improved and the satellite approach surpassed by an integrated approach. But compared to the previous situation when environmental values were never considered, the state of the art represents a leap forward in terms of better reflecting the costs of economic activities and better guiding planning and decisions. We should not wait for perfect methodologies before we act on reforming the existing economic indicators. They will never come. The sooner we internalize costs in the SNA, using techniques that are available, the better for the environment, for the economy itself, and for sustainable development.

Impediments to the Reform of National Economic Indicators

The flaws of the existing indicators are obvious, and the methodologies for correcting the flaws, though not perfect, have nevertheless become available. Why have governments and international organizations thus far been slow to internalize environmental costs in national accounts and apply environmentally adjusted economic indicators to their decision-making processes?

First, it is politically difficult for some governments to formally adjust national accounts for the real costs of economic activities. In many cases, doing so would mean a major reduction in the level of GNP. Since GNP is often seen as the yardstick for measuring government performance, few governments would want to present a poor grade report to the public. At stake is the very basis for governments to stay in power.

Second, some countries still regard natural resources as free and inexhaustible gifts of nature. To use a Chinese idiom, natural resources are often considered as so abundant that they can be "drawn without an end, used without exhaustion." Such misconceptions have led governments and the general public to believe that accounting for natural resources is not necessary.

Third, it is difficult to collect needed data and to value many goods and services provided by the environment. Baseline data on natural resources are often not available in many countries. Environmental goods and services are typically not traded in market place. Even when they are, market prices do not internalize all the values. The complex interactions between the environment and economy and within the ecosystems, together with different preferences of individuals, further make it a difficult task to classify defensive expenditures, identify environmental goods and services, and give an appropriate valuation of natural resources.

Fourth, in many developing countries, both the necessary financial resources and institutional capacity are lacking for internalizing environmental costs in national accounts. Data collection and analysis, establishment and maintenance of databases all need money and professional expertise. For low-income countries which are struggling with poverty, famine, debt, and depressed terms of trade and commodity prices, these are no less than luxuries. For others, the engagement in the reform of economic indicators would mean a diversion of limited financial and human resources from activities that are deemed more of a priority.

Fifth, national accountants, environmental statisticians, and natural resource economists do not share the view on the need to internalize costs in national accounts. National accountants see the existing SNA as a well-established system and want no alterations of it. Environmental statisticians believe that physical environmental data are sufficient for decision-making purposes, and that it is not worth the effort to monetarize environmental information. Natural resource economists insist, however, that there are serious flaws in the existing SNA and that these flaws should be corrected for sustainable management of both the environment and the economy.

Lastly, although international organizations have been involved in methodological development of resource valuation, they are reluctant to place the issue on their policy agenda and start applying environmentally adjusted economic indicators in their own policies, official economic data publications, operational guidelines, and project analyses. This partly reflects institutional inertia driven by traditional economists and partly the lack of political will on the part of their member governments. The lack of international coordination also hampers the development of a universally comparable framework for internalization, which prompts many governments to take a wait-and-see attitude.

Despite these difficulties, a number of countries have started to experiment with various approaches in an effort to provide a solid and scientific basis for economic planning. The experiences of ten countries are briefly presented in Table 3. Some countries have only worked on physical environmental accounts. Overall, however, these experiences demonstrate that even at this unfinished stage of methodological development, actions not only should, but also can, be taken to start correcting the errors in the existing system of national economic indicators. Even when the existing SNA remains in place, efforts to internalize environmental costs in economic indicators can at least provide information on the real costs of economic growth which was not available before.

Conclusions and Recommendations

The externalized environmental costs must be internalized into the existing system of economic indicators. The current SNA conceals the true costs of economic activities, gives an illusory picture of the true wealth of a country, discriminates against future generations, and

---

Table 3

Reforming SNA: Country Experiences[1]

Costa Rica
Physical accounts were set up for soils, forests, and fisheries. The depreciation of forests and fisheries was based on the market values that could have been reaped had these resources been harvested sustainably. The depreciation of soils was based on the cost of replacing principal nutrients lost through erosion. The depreciation of these resources for 1970-89 exceeded $4.1 billion, the average of the country's annual GDP.

France
On top of physical accounts like those in Norway, the French system records expenditures on resource management (as Japan did). The interactions among resources and between resources and human activities, together with the social, economic, and ecological values affected, are also captured.

Indonesia
Physical accounts were compiled for petroleum, timber and soils. Deducted from GDP was the value of their net depletion measured by net economic rent (market prices minus the costs of production). The costs of erosion in terms of productivity losses were estimated and deducted from GDP. The adjusted GDP growth for 1971-84 was 4.0% rather than 7.1% as conventionally calculated.

Japan
In 1973, Net National Welfare was calculated as an adjusted GNP. Actual pollution abatement costs were identified and deducted from GNP, so were the potential costs of meeting environmental standards for specific pollution problems. The value of non-market activities was added to GNP.

Mexico
Physical accounts were constructed for oil, forests, groundwater, land, and the quality of air and water. Using a combination of valuation techniques, such as those used in PNG, Mexico's environmentally adjusted NDP for 1985 was estimated at 36,448 million pesos, compared to 42,060 million pesos calculated under the conventional system.

The Netherlands
Existing unsustainable activities are identified and environmental standards set up for these activities. The costs of technical, economic, and social measures required to meet the standards are then deducted from GNP. In the Netherlands, a shift from unsustainable activities to sustainable ones by 1% (measured in labor volume) would reduce national income by at least 1.5% on average. For details of the Dutch approach, see Hueting 1992.

Norway
In 1975, Norway started to compile physical resource accounts as a supplement to the conventional national income accounts. The stock, flow, quality, and use of various natural resources have been recorded for budgeting future use of the resources.

Papua New Guinea
The SEEA approach was tested. Environmental spending was 0.31% of GDP in 1990. Based on the net-price approach (market prices minus all production costs, multiplied by the quantity of a depleted resource) for minerals, the willingness-to-accept approach for degradation due to agriculture and energy, and the avoidance cost approach for degradation due to mining and forestry, the adjusted NDP for 1990 was 2,526 million Kina instead

[1]This table draws on Abaza 1992.

continued →

of 2,760 million Kina as conventionally measured. For technical details, see Abaza 1992 and "Methodologies Used in Papua New Guinea," below.

The Philippines
The depreciation of forests and soils were estimated as in Indonesia and Costa Rica. Between 1970-87, annual depreciation of forests was 3.3% of GDP. The depreciation of dryland farm soils was 2.5% of GDP.

The United States
Efforts have been made to collect data on pollution abatement expenditures. Physical accounts have been constructed for oil, gas, and timber. The avoidance cost approach has been experimented for the Chesapeake Bay Region to estimate the costs that would have incurred to resource users had they been forced to avoid using the resources or reducing the use to an ecologically sustainable level. At present, the Bureau of Economic Affairs within the US Department of Commerce is trying to produce a prototype of environmentally adjusted national income figures before April 1994.

Methodologies Used in Papua New Guinea

Environmental expenditures were not deducted from GDP due to the difficulties in obtaining data from other sectors and in defining which of these expenditures are final for the purpose of proper accounting. Physical accounts were compiled for all major natural assets, but no value was assigned to the known stock of natural assets. Depletion and degradation of these assets, however, are valued and deducted from GDP.

Two different valuation techniques, user-cost approach and depreciation method, were used. In the former, a calculated portion of the revenues from the current sale of mineral resources is taken away from GDP and invested as a "user cost," the accumulation of which would, when the resource in question is fully depleted, start generating a stream of income equal to the remaining portion of the current revenues. According to this approach, the depletion of mineral resources accounted for 0.3 to 1.4 percent of conventional GDP in PNG for the period 1985-1990.

Using the depreciation method, the quantity of a depleted resource multiplies the net price (market price minus all production costs) gives an indication of the potential income-generating capacity of the depleted resource. According to this method, the depletion of mineral resources in PNG accounted for 0.8 to 7.0 percent of traditional GDP during 1985-1990.

For estimating the costs of environmental quality degradation, a compensation approach (polluters paying compensation to the resource owners) was adopted for agriculture and energy, and an avoidance cost approach (costs of preventing pollution) for forestry and mining. For 1986-90, the total annual costs of degradation from these sources averaged 2.0 (low estimate) to 10.4 (high estimate) percent of NDP (GDP minus depreciation of manmade capital).

represents anything but true income which—by definition—must be sustainable.

To correct these fundamental flaws in the existing SNA, governments must have the political will to support the reform of national accounts, the public must be educated to realize that the supply of natural resources are not infinite, and international organizations must provide technical and financial support to developing countries for the implementation of the reform.

Many countries have already started experimenting with various approaches to reforming the existing national accounting system; but in order for these reforms to have a real impact on development policy-making process, a concerted effort at the international level has to be made to change the core of the existing system. The satellite approach would have only limited effect on policy because it leaves the fundamentally flawed traditional accounts intact. GNP, GDP, or National Income as traditionally defined would continue to be used as the basis for development planning if the reform of the existing system is allowed to be obstructed by a system of satellite accounts.

With the establishment of a universally accepted new system of national accounts as an ultimate objective, what should and can be done immediately and simultaneously includes:

(1) Disseminating related information to governments, development agencies, national statistical offices, research institutes, the NGO community and other concerned parties. Providing education on the necessity and possibility of reforming the existing system.

(2) Facilitating open debates on methodological issues and on policy application of environmentally adjusted economic indicators.

(3) Integrating environmental accounting into the SNA and developing an internationally comparable framework for measuring the economic aspect of sustainability. Adjusting national income for the most serious distortions to start with.

(4) Strengthening coordination among international organizations in research activities, pilot projects, country or regional focus, and application of adjusted economic indicators within each organization.

(5) Linking environmental data collection with monetary valuation to the extent possible and facilitating dialogues among natural scientists, national accountants, economists, and environmental statisticians.

(6) Providing financial, technical, and institutional support to national statistical offices, including data collection, compilation of environmental physical accounts (particularly for most seriously threatened resources), environmental monitoring, training of national accountants, pilot projects, and the provision of regional and subregional centers of expertise.

(7) Including environmental accounting in national sustainability strategies and reports and using adjusted economic indicators in decision-making processes and for guiding economic policies with a view to contributing to overall sustainability.

(8) Applying environmental accounting techniques at micro and international economic levels(i.e., in cost-benefit analyses of projects and in the calculation of international balance of payment).

International organizations, national governments, academic institutions, non-governmental organizations, statisticians, economists, and natural scientists should combine their efforts to reform the SNA to better reflect the environmental costs of economic activities. Among international organizations, the World Bank, given its institutional capacity and political leverage, must continue to play a leading role. NGOs must not be excluded from this process. They can play a unique role in environmental education and dissemination of information to generate a momentum for the reform. Moreover, the various resource valuation techniques are of high value to the field activities of NGOs themselves.

NOTES

1. This paper uses the definition of sustainable development provided by *Caring for the Earth* (IUCN/UNEP/WWF 1991, 10): "improving the quality of human life within the carrying capacity of supporting ecosystems." For detailed discussions of conceptual issues related to sustainable development, see WWF 1993.
2. "The purpose of income calculation in practical affairs is to give people an indication of the amount which they can consume without impoverishing themselves. Following out this idea, it would seem that we ought to define a man's income as the maximum value which he can consume during a week, and still expect to be as well off at the end of the week as he was at the beginning. Thus when a person saves he plans to be better off in the future; when he lives beyond his income he plans to be worse off. Remembering that the practical purpose of income is to serve as a guide for prudent conduct. I think it is fairly clear that is what the conceptual meaning must be." (Hicks 1946,172). See also Daly 1989.

3. Data published by Bangladesh Centre for Advanced Studies, 1990.
4. "Externality" is here defined as the effects of anything (on other things) for which monetary compensation is not automatically effected through market forces.

REFERENCES

Abaza, H., and others. 1992. *The present state of environmental and resource accounting and its potential application in developing countries.* Environmental Economics Series Paper No.1. United Nations Environment Programme, Nairobi.

Bartelmus, P., E. Lutz, and S. Schweinfest. 1992. *Integrated environmental and economic accounting: A case study for Papua New Guinea.* Environment Working Paper No. 54. World Bank, Washington, D.C.

Daly, H. E. 1989. Toward a measure of sustainable social net national product. In *Environmental accounting for sustainable development,* ed. Y. J. Ahmad and others. World Bank, Washington, D.C.

Hicks, J. R. 1946. *Value and capital.* 2nd ed. Oxford University Press, Oxford.

IUCN/UNEP/WWF. 1991. *Caring for the earth: A strategy for sustainable living.* IUCN, Gland, Switzerland.

Tinbergen, J., and R. Hueting. 1991. GNP and market prices: Wrong signals for sustainable economic success that mask environmental destruction. In *Building on Brundtland,* ed. R. Goodland, H. Daly, and S. El Serafy. World Bank, Washington, D.C. Draft.

WWF International. 1993. *Sustainable use of natural resources: Concepts, issues, and criteria.* World Wide Fund for Nature International, Gland, Switzerland.

Poverty Alleviation and Sustainability: The Case of Zimbabwe

CꙄ

CALVIN NHIRA

Introduction

Attempts at designing indicators for poverty alleviation and sustainability might provide explanations on why and how sustainability can or cannot be achieved. However, these attempts need to incorporate the impacts of macro policies on people's survival strategies and, in turn, the impact of the survival strategies on local environments and the changes over time for fuller explanations to be drawn. Empirical descriptions of indicators for poverty and sustainability, while essential, cannot provide a fuller picture of what lies behind local motivations that have an impact on the environment. Thus, this paper is less concerned with the development of indicators, but rather the task is to address the impacts of policy instruments employed with regard to the rural communal agricultural sector in Zimbabwe, where poverty is concentrated, and the environmental effects over time. The assumption is that poverty alleviation and increased levels of human welfare should lead to sustainable development and the converse would lead to unsustainability.

This paper attempts to address the problems of poverty and sustainability as they affect Zimbabwe in particular, using secondary sources. It takes a long time scale, dealing with both the colonial period and the post-independence period (after 1980) to argue that over time, attempts at poverty alleviation have not yielded self-sustaining growth in the rural communal agricultural sector such that sustainability of both rural livelihoods and the environment are not assured. Alleviation measures have had little impact on the pervasive historical patterns of poverty in the rural communal agricultural sector. The focus is broadly on the role of the state and the impacts of its policy instruments and their environmental effects and, conversely, the reaction to the policy instruments by rural people and the environmental effects. The contours that policy instruments have taken over time correspond broadly to the colonial period and the post-independence period. I deal with the colonial period to show that its legacy has not been surmounted. The post-independence period is further divided into the "growth with equity" phase, the economic liberalization phase, and the economic nationalism phase.

The Colonial Period

At the broader macroeconomic level, the countries in the Southern African subregion have been termed the Africa of the Labor Reserve Economies (Amin 1972). The principal modes through which indigenous people were incorporated into the developing capitalist social formations in these economies resulted from the expropriation of rich land in favor of European settlers or companies. Indigenous people were relegated to unproductive land (the "native reserves"); agriculture and pastoralism in the "native reserves" were partially commercialized; and labor was extracted from the indigenous agricultural sector to work in the towns, mines, and plantations (Blaikie 1987). The "native reserves" also suffered discrimination in terms of taxation, distortion of markets, allocation and access to input supplies, marketing services, infrastructure, and so on (Arrighi 1970; Palmer and Parsons 1977; Riddell 1978; Mumbengegwi 1986; Moyo 1986; Phimister 1988). Thus the overall aim was to marginalize indigenous people.

With specific reference to land allocation in Zimbabwe, the percentage of land under "native reserves" at specific points in time was as follows: twenty-two percent in 1911, forty percent in 1965, and forty-two percent in 1992 (Moyo 1992). The increased allocations of land to "native reserves" after 1931 were achieved primarily through taking land away from state holdings. The increased allocations are telling of the failure of colonial state policies that were designed for the "native reserves" to hold more people. These policies are dealt with below showing their environmental impacts that were clearly unsustainable despite draconian measures to alleviate the latter.

Colonial state interventions started off as taxation and religious conversion and then gradually shifted to agricultural improvement programs.[1] It is important to note that these interventions began after conquest of indigenous people and alienation of their land, leading to "instant 'over-population'" (Blaikie 1987). A "villagization" program was adopted in the 1930s that was intended to locate linear villages along watersheds and separate grazing from agricultural land. It was designed to squeeze more people into the "native reserves" and to impose order with conservation as a by product. Conservationist arguments later became more important to justify its forcible implementation. Centralization resulted in large-scale clearance of woodland in demarcated fields, and use of timber for construction of new homes in the new linear villages. Force was used following the enactment of the Natural Resources Act of 1941, under which people could be prosecuted if they failed to contour land, voluntarily destock, abandon wetland fields, stop cultivation of land outside the arable block, and stop cutting live trees.

The Native Husbandry Act of 1951 went through more or less similar stages, relying on persuasion and then compulsion because of conservationist concerns (Bruce 1990). The distinguishing characteristic of the Act was that it was intended to individualize rights to arable land and enforce conservation measures. The implementation of the Act was abandoned in the 1960s because of resistance from rural people. Its collapse allowed for more land to be cleared for cultivation. This has prompted Blaikie (1987) to observe that when many African farmers were faced by coercive conservation policies imposed by the colonial authorities, the problem was diagnosed as one of alienation of land by settlers, and the political solution of ridding themselves of the British appealed more than costly conservation works. Indeed, the success of the mobilization of the peasantry for the liberation struggle in Zimbabwe hinged on the demand for land.

The commons were further invaded for arable land just before and after independence. Scoones and Wilson (1989, 85-87) have specified the methods by which invasion was done *viz.* incorporation of lands adjacent to existing holdings, opening up of new fields in grazing areas, annexation of woodlands to private holdings, direct squatting by outsiders on grazing land with local permission and expansion of homefields into grazing land. Land owned by the state and the large scale commercial sector was also subject to squatting and resource poaching (Moyo 1992; Herbst 1990).

At independence, the situation in the "native reserves," now called communal areas, was as follows:

☐ seventy-four percent of all peasant land was in areas where droughts were frequent and where normal levels of rainfall were inadequate for intensive crop production (Herbst 1990);

☐ population density in communal areas was at twenty-eight people per sq. km. in contrast to nine people per sq. km. in commercial areas (Herbst 1990); and

☐ the population in the communal areas exceeded their carrying capacity by approximately two million people (Jordan 1979).[2]

The nature of incorporation of indigenous people in the economy of Zimbabwe, pointed out above, created widespread poverty and undermined traditional coping strategies and strategies for managing the environment in both the technical and the institutional sense. Local strategies and objectives for ensuring a livelihood for large sections of the rural population lay outside the realm of the rural environment (eg., labor migration and survival on remittances from wage labor). The struggle for survival meant that ensuring household food and income security took primacy over environmental concerns. In cases where the household economy revolved around wage labor rather than agriculture, knowledge about household economics and not agriculture (and the inputs from nature) became more appropriate (Blaikie 1987).

The Post Colonial Period

"Growth with Equity"

The need for land redistribution was recognized at independence. By 1982 the government had set a target of 162,000 families (twenty percent of 800,000 peasant families with severe land pressures) for resettlement (Herbst 1990). These plans were to be coupled with greatly expanded services to the communal agricultural sector in terms of extension and input supplies, credit availability, development of infrastructure including roads, expansion of social services (health, education, water), marketing facilities and attractive grain prices, etc.

In the resettlement program, government was restricted by the "willing-seller willing-buyer" rule put in place in the independence agreement (Herbst 1990). This early phase of the resettlement program lagged behind in terms of its own objectives. Over time the plans were scaled down, primarily because of the government's lack of will and resources. By 1985, the year by which the target of 162,000 families was to have been achieved, only 35,000 had actually been given new land (Moyo 1990). The inability to achieve these resettlement targets led to peasant farmers with severe land shortages seizing land in the commercial farms ("squatting") and migration to marginal areas of the country where the ecosystems are fragile and population densities were low, thus accelerating environmental degradation.

Over time the emphasis reverted to communal area reorganization (Herbst 1990). In 1986 the "villagization" program was initiated (Cousins 1992). District Councils were empowered through the Communal Land (Model) (Land Use and Conservation) Bylaws of 1985 to specify the maximum number of livestock that may be grazed. The program has been resisted throughout the country given that land access has not greatly improved.

The expansion of services to the peasant agricultural sector led to what has been termed Zimbabwe's agricultural success story (Bratton, *mimeo*). However, a number of studies, summarized by Cousins (1993) have looked at this period more critically.

Moyo (1986, 188-189), for example, shows how the bulk of marketed grain from communal areas comes from the high potential regions, where only a small proportion of the communal land population lives. Jackson and others (1987) show that the top ten percent of households in their survey controlled forty percent of all cereal production, and the bottom fifty percent accounted for only ten percent of all crop incomes. Weiner and Moyo (forthcoming) find wage income to be more important than agricultural income in all agro-ecological regions except for the most productive. Finally, Adams (1987) shows that there is a significant degree of reliance on both permanent and casual wage labor on the part of households with little or no access to the means of agricultural production—principally land and draft power.

Land pressures in the communal areas have continued to exacerbate. Moyo and others (1991) estimate that about 100,000 hectares of woodland is cleared annually. In the mid-1980s, environmental degradation in the countryside was graphically set in the popular mind through the silting of the Save river, one of the major river systems in the country that flows into the Indian ocean. There has been a lack of monitoring of environmental impacts of the resettlement program in both the source and destination areas, even though the role of resettlement is sometimes justified in terms of relief of population pressure and development of communal areas (Elliott). However, because more often than not resettlement areas are located next to communal areas, they have also been subject to resource poaching (sometimes for commercial purposes) by communal area inhabitants.

Economic Liberalization

The expansion of services in the country could not be maintained over time given the very low growth rates of the economy as a whole. Thus government was forced to endorse an economic liberalization program. The program involves export-oriented trade policies, removal of subsidies on inputs into crop production, cutbacks on credit and extension services, reduction in crop marketing depots, and shedding of "excess" labor in the industrial, commercial, and state sectors, among others (Sapem Editorial 1989; Sachikonye 1992). Of recent, Zimbabwe has experienced a drought that has decimated crops and livestock. Until 1993 the country was a net importer of food from being an exporter. Given the nature of the economy pointed out above, shedding of "excess" labor has meant that remittances to rural areas dwindle and more people resort to their rural homes on leaving employment. This phenomenon adds even more pressure in the communal areas.

Associated with the economic liberalization program has been a change in the criteria for resettlement. Government now insists that the resettlement program should be a strategy to increase economic productivity rather than a social welfare mechanism for the landless and the resource poor. Thus the focus is now on master farmers (a kulak class) and agricultural graduates (i.e., those that benefitted from the expansion of agricultural and social services). Thus the resettlement program is no longer a poverty alleviation measure, unless if one assumes that the poor will benefit from the movement of the "rich" from the communal areas.

Economic Nationalism

This phase was signalled by the passing of the Land Acquisition Act of 1992, under which government wishes to acquire five million of the eleven million hectares under the large-scale commercial sector and to democratize the commercial farming sector by allowing the entry of more blacks into the sector. Other signals include the polarization and politicization of commercial and industrial interests along black-white lines. The Five-Year Plan, going along with these measures, restates the focus on rural development, especially on the improvement of water resources and rural housing. However, given the policy foci pointed out above, it is unlikely that the situation of the poorer sections of communal area residents will be addressed.

Conclusion

This paper took a historical approach to examine policy instruments with environmental-poverty consequences. It was pointed out that during the colonial period the policy instruments adopted were designed to marginalize the "native reserves" and their inhabitants leading to serious adverse environmental consequences. In the post colonial period, a battery of poverty alleviation measures were adopted, but have been eroded over time. The legacy of the colonial period is still largely intact. In the absence of an expansion of access to land, the environmental crisis in the communal areas has continued. Lately, policy instruments have shifted to addressing elite interests to the detriment of the poorer sections of communal area residents.

If sustainability is taken to mean the ability over a long period of time to provide for the increased welfare of people and the ability to protect and enhance the environmental base, then poverty alleviation measures in Zimbabwe have not been sustainable.

NOTES

1. I rely on McGregor (1991) for much of this section.
2. I am aware of the controversy over the concept of carrying capacity. Its use here follows that of the author.

REFERENCES

Adams, J. 1987. *Wage labour in Mutirikwi communal land, Masvingo.* Occasional Paper, Centre for Applied Social Sciences. University of Zimbabwe, Harare.

Amin, S. 1972. Underdevelopment and dependence in black Africa. *Journal of Modern African Studies* 10(4).

Arrighi, G. 1970. Labour supplies in historical perspective: A study of the proletarianisation of the African peasantry in Rhodesia. *Journal of Development Studies* 6(3): 197-234.

Blaikie, P. 1987. The SADCC countries' historical experience of soil conservation and peoples' participation in it: Some lessons for future policy. In *History of soil conservation in the SADCC region,* Coordination Unit Report no.8, Soil, Water Conservation and Land Utilization Program. Southern African Development Coordination Conference, Maseru, Lesotho.

Bratton, M. n.d. Drought, food and the social organisation of small farmers in Zimbabwe. Mimeo.

Bruce, J. W. 1990. *Legal issues in land use and resettlement.* Background paper presented for World Bank Zimbabwe Agriculture Sector Memorandum.

Cousins, B. 1992. *Room for dancing on: Grazing schemes in the communal areas of Zimbabwe.* Occasional Paper NRM 4/1992, Centre for Applied Social Sciences. University of Zimbabwe, Harare.

Cousins, B. 1993. *Community, class and grazing management in Zimbabwe's communal lands.* Occasional Paper NRM 1993, Centre for Applied Social Sciences. University of Zimbabwe, Harare.

Elliott, J. n.d. *The sustainability of household responses to fuelwood needs in the resettlement areas of Zimbabwe: A preliminary report of survey findings.* Department of Geography, University of Zimbabwe, Harare and Staffordshire University, Stoke-on-Trent, England.

Herbst, J. 1990. *State politics in Zimbabwe.* University of California Press, Berkeley, California, USA.

Jackson, J. C., and others. 1987. *Rural development policies and food security in Zimbabwe: Part II.* International Labour Organisation, Geneva.

Jordan, J. D. 1979. The land question in Zimbabwe. *Zimbabwe Journal of Economics* 1:134.

McGregor, J. 1991. *Woodland resources: Ecology, policy and ideology: An historical case study of woodland use in Shurugwi Communal Area, Zimbabwe.* Doctoral thesis submitted in partial fulfillment of the requirements of Loughborough University of Technology, U.K.

Moyo, S. 1986. The land question. In *Zimbabwe: The political economy of transition 1980-1986,* ed. I. Mandaza. Codesria, Dakar, Senegal.

Moyo, S. 1990. The promised land! Why reform has been slow. *Sapem* 3(7).

Moyo, S. 1992. Land tenure issues in Zimbabwe during the 1990s. Draft.

Moyo, S., and others. 1991. *Zimbabwe's environmental dilemma: Balancing resource inequities.* ZERO, Harare.

Mumbengegwi, C. 1986. Continuity and change in agricultural policy. In *Zimbabwe: The political economy of transition 1980-1986,* ed. I. Mandaza. Codesria, Dakar, Senegal.

Palmer, R., and Q. N. Parsons. 1977. *The roots of rural poverty.* Heinemann, London.

Phimister, I. 1988. Commodity relations and class formation in the Zimbabwean countryside, 1898-1920. *Journal of Peasant Studies* 13(4): 240-257.

Riddell, R. C. 1978. *The land problem in Rhodesia: Alternatives for the future.* Mambo Press, Harare.

Sachikonye, L. M. 1992. Peasants, politics and structural adjustment. *Sapem* 5(9).

Sapem Editorial. 1989. *Sapem* 3(1).

Scoones, I., and K. Wilson. 1988. Households, lineage groups and ecological dynamics: Issues for livestock research and development in Zimbabwe's communal lands. In *Socio-economic dimensions of livestock production in the communal lands of Zimbabwe,* ed. B. Cousins, C. Jackson, and I. Scoones. Centre for Applied Social Sciences, University of Zimbabwe/GTZ, Harare.

Weiner, D., and S. Moyo. *Wage labour, environment and peasant agriculture.* Forthcoming.

Learning Our Way Out: Indicators of Social Environmental Learning

CЗ

MATTHIAS FINGER AND JAMES KILCOYNE, JR.

This article develops a rationale for social environmental learning, conceptualizes the key elements and stages of this process, and derives criteria for assessment or indicators from them. We see such indicators as a means to determine progress toward a more sustainable society.

Rationale

There seems to be agreement that our present society—whether it is viewed from the global, national, or even local perspective—is far from being sustainable (Tolba and others 1992). Furthermore, most indicators, especially global ones, show that this unsustainability is increasing, often exponentially. Generally, these indicators pertain to ecological degradation such as resource depletion, deforestation, and various forms of pollution and waste generation, as well as global environmental changes, including ozone depletion and climate change. There are, to our knowledge, very few indicators that measure the often parallel degradation of society or, as we call it, "sociocultural erosion."

This is due in part to profound disagreement about what constitutes sociocultural erosion and to the lack of conceptualization of the relation between societal and ecological degradation.

If one claims, however, as many people do, that ecological degradation has societal origins or causes, then it is important to measure those societal factors. More importantly, we need to measure progress away from these societal dysfunctions toward activities that are socially, culturally, and ecologically more sustainable.[1] Here is where indicators of social environmental learning come into play. Such indicators are needed to measure and assess the dynamics and changes that lead communities, organizations, and entire societies to diminish and ultimately to reverse their ecologically (and socioculturally) degrading behaviors. We think that such behaviors necessarily result from a collective learning process, a process we call "social environmental learning" (Princen and Finger 1994; Finger and Verlaan 1995). By formulating corresponding indicators, we establish benchmarks to assess the collective learning process that will lead to such behaviors. Thus, the indicators will pertain to the process and not to the behavior itself.

We are aware that in developing such indicators, we are moving on ideological grounds that are quite slippery. We will present in detail, therefore, the kind of analysis and argumentation on which our indicators are based. In the first section of this paper, we will outline the nature and main causes of today's unsustainability. Next, we will develop a rationale for why collective learning constitutes a necessary first step to address this sociocultural and ecological unsustainability. In the third section, we will conceptualize this learning process. This will lead us, in the final section, to identifying the main indicators of social environmental learning.

This paper is, above all, conceptual in nature. It is rooted in a theoretical analysis of the present situation, aimed at a collective learning process that will lead to a way out of growing global ecological and sociocultural unsustainability. The criteria that will measure progress along this collective learning process are therefore not empirically grounded, but again, conceptual in nature. Translating these criteria into empirical measurements remains to be done and will constitute another step in our research beyond this paper.

Our Analysis

Generally, people in advanced industrial societies assign problems to either the environmental or societal realms. Most of the time, they do not establish a link between ecological degradation, on the one hand, and societal problems on the other. In this section we will argue, with many others (e.g., Chambers 1984; Ghai 1994), that unsustainability is not an exclusively environmental phenomenon: rather, it is entire communities, organizations, and societies that are unsustainable, both in their ecological and social dimensions.

The roots of both ecological and societal unsustainability lie in the process of industrial development, largely characterized, in our view, by techno-scientific progress, capital accumulation, and the accumulation of power. Though the initial ecological consequences of industrial development were once clearly separable from its societal effects, we have now reached a point where both types of consequences reinforce each other in an ever-accelerating vicious circle (Figure 1). Social environmental learning examines the ecologically and societally degrading consequences of industrial development, not as separate entities, but rather in terms of the vicious circle and the dynamic of the interaction of its components.

Limits and Growth

Along with many other authors (e.g., Brown, Kane, and Roodman 1994), we work with the assumption of a deepening ecological crisis of increasingly global proportions. Three stages and three types of limits must be distinguished in this process: first, before the political ecology movement of the 1970s, industrialized nations were mostly concerned with species extinction and then, increasingly, with natural resource depletion. Society thus became concerned with input limits to growth (Meadows and others 1972). Second, as a result of the political ecology movement of the 1970s and early 1980s, industrial societies of the North became increasingly concerned with pollution and waste problems. The limits at that time were seen in political terms; that is, unfavorable political will or insufficient political management capacity would place the upper limits on growth. Since the middle of the 1980s, as the concept of global ecology (see Malone and Roederer 1985) and global changes such as ozone depletion and climate change have gained

---

Figure 1

The Vicious Circle

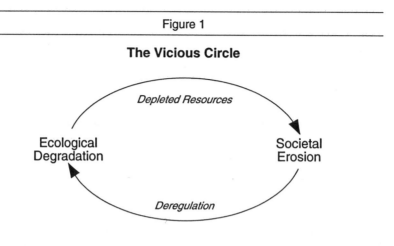

---

recognition, we have begun to talk about a third type of limits, namely, output limits to growth. These might actually be far more serious than the input and management limits that received attention earlier on. What is more, global change is exacerbating the problems caused by input and management limits.

Industrial development, which is characterized by technological and scientific progress, capital accumulation, and the accumulation of power, both draws from the global ecological resource base and impacts the biosphere. In this way, it restricts rather than expands the three kinds of limits described above. Technological progress in areas of ecological efficiency and pollution control, environmental education (seeking to foster environmentally responsible behavior), and corresponding environmental politics can help to slow down the process of ecological degradation and thus stretch (to a certain extent) these input, management, and output limits to industrial development. This is, in fact, the idea behind the concept of "sustainable development," as promoted at the 1992 Earth Summit (Chatterjee and Finger 1994).

But because the pace of industrial development is currently accelerating all over the planet, such efficiency gains are quickly offset by further industrial expansion. In short, further industrial development, by its very nature, and because of its exponential expansion, is rapidly degrading the biosphere and limiting our ecological and societal options—not only for further development, but for survival (Figure 2). With the emergence of global ecology, this becomes a planetary—and no longer simply a local, national, or regional—process.

Figure 2

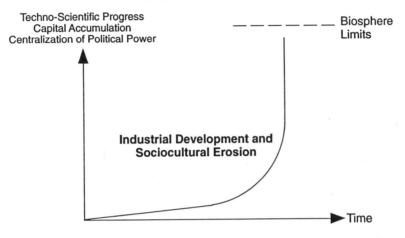

Acceleration of Industrial Development and Sociocultural Erosion

Techno-Scientific Progress
Capital Accumulation
Centralization of Political Power

— — — — — — Biosphere
Limits

**Industrial Development and
Sociocultural Erosion**

Time

From Sociocultural Modernization to Sociocultural Erosion

As well as leading to ecological degradation, industrial development leads to what we call "sociocultural erosion." Until recently, this process has been viewed in a positive light and has been characterized by terms such as "individualization," "emancipation," and sociocultural and political "modernization." This modernization—exemplified in the concepts of the building of the "modern self" or the creation of nation-states—has itself been a significant factor in further promoting industrial development. Moreover, there has been a parallel erosion of "traditional" communities, worldviews, and cultures, which is manifested in growing individualization, loss of spiritual, social, and cultural roots, and subsequent slackening of social responsibility. The erosion has become a necessary condition for further industrial progress. Indeed, many features of modern (or post-modern) societies (such as individualism, loss of tradition, democracy, and so forth) both result from and are a necessary condition for further industrial development. Until recently, most of these features were seen as highly positive and desirable; in fact, many people still view them that way.

_ocultural modernization and sociocultural erosion
same process, separated only by perspective. The lat-
t the perversion of the former (as many maintain) but
ing, only seen in a different context and, subsequently,
perspective (Adorno and Horkheimer 1947).

ural modernization was seen as beneficial mainly be-
c_   sequences of industrial development, in particular its ecological cc. sequences, were often not (yet) visible. In any case, these
consequences were and still are exported and shifted to others. That is,
the sociocultural modernization of Europe, North America, and other
highly industrialized regions of the world was—and still is—achieved
at the expense of the non-industrialized South, future generations of
both North and South, and the biosphere.

However, with exponential expansion and acceleration of industrial development, the emergence of global ecological (output) limits
and the end of unlimited expansion, the ecological and sociocultural
consequences of industrial development have suddenly hit home. Seen
against the background of global limits and our current social and ecological unsustainability, sociocultural modernization becomes a process of increasing counterproductivity—where too much of the same
development style destroys the very foundations for growth and de-
forms what was once positive. This change in perspective, from sociocultural modernization to sociocultural erosion, allows us to see a
vicious circle, where sociocultural erosion furthers ecological degradation, which in turn hastens sociocultural erosion, and so on.

The Vicious Circle

Once a critical spread of industrial development and corresponding
consumption patterns is reached, ecological degradation on scales large
enough to challenge the biosphere's input and output limits is the inevitable result. Awareness increased in the late 1980s when the end of
the Cold War and the subsequent acceleration of global trade through
deregulation and liberalization gave a new push to industrial development. This push further eroded communities, societies, and entire
countries—especially in the South and Eastern Europe—opening the
way for even faster industrial development and sociocultural erosion.

At the same time, global ecological degradation has started to reinforce societal trends that are counterproductive in this age of ecologi-

Figure 3

The Vicious Circle in Full Motion

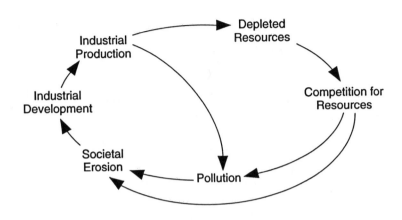

cally imposed input and output limits to continued industrial development. For example, individualism, besides being an ecological problem (e.g., when it becomes an excuse for irresponsible consumption), furthers societal problems (e.g., the weakening sense of responsibility and withdrawal from participation in society). The same is true for population growth, migration, and conflict, all of which are trends that contribute to increasingly rapid sociocultural erosion. Further erosion of society and culture will in turn accelerate the destruction of the biosphere. The direct causes will be wars, conflicts, individualistic and nationalistic behavior, and other ecologically destructive activity. Perhaps more powerful, however, is the indirect cause—namely, that eroded society has lost the last cultural and ethical impediments to global capital accumulation, techno-scientific progress, and growing political power. With nothing left to rein in development, the vicious circle is in full motion. Figure 3 summarizes this process graphically.

The Challenge: Learning Our Way Out

We thus face a vicious circle where ecological degradation fuels sociocultural erosion, which in turn accelerates ecological destruction. It is this vicious circle that now has come to restrict any positive possibilities for further sociocultural modernization. The challenge before us is to slow down and ultimately reverse the circle's spin—a process which requires collective learning, in both social and ecological matters.

Unfortunately, many so-called solutions to social and environmental degradation and the vicious circle they generate still speak in terms of industrial development. The concept of sustainable development, as promoted by the United Nations system and the global business community since the Earth Summit in 1992, is a perfect illustration of this (Chatterjee and Finger 1994). This concept does not take into account the emerging limits to growth and instead proposes more of the same. These include technological "quick-fixes," and other ideas which depend on more development for answers. We can predict that these will only further accelerate the vicious circle.

Indeed, the popular problem-solving devices of the day, such as national policies, executive management, science-based technologies, and even institutional education (awareness-raising and skills development), have become subservient to an overall objective of industrial development. This happened in two stages. *First,* these devices became increasingly specialized, isolated, and technical, and as a result, removed from any socially and culturally relevant unit. Education, technology, policy, management, and economic growth have become goals in themselves, making it easier for them to be incorporated into an overall industrial development process. For example, the nation-state, originally conceived as a means to assure a just society of free individuals, has increasingly become a development agency. Correspondingly, national policies have become more and more geared to promoting economic growth. A similar evolution can be observed in universities and technical schools, and even NGOs engaged in development work.

In the *second* stage, these units themselves became eroded, as industrial development no longer depended on their active role. This is particularly visible in the case of the state and its functions in public service. The state, after having developed schemes of transportation, communication, education, and more, is now increasingly being side-stepped by the global processes of liberalization and deregulation, which lead to the erosion of state power (Martin 1993).

Industry, having appropriated national infrastructure, uses these to move on to its own multinational purposes, unhampered by national regulation. Similarly, NGOs are increasingly taken over or co-opted by global development agencies such as the World Bank and the United

Nations Development Programme (Danaher 1994). Even science and technology are removed from the public sector and made to serve transnational corporations, who then become owners of intellectual property that belonged to the people.

In short, the main societal actors—government, business and industry, academia, the media, and, to a certain extent, NGOs—remain mired in the problem because their solutions are predicated on further industrial development. Although they seek to address some of the sociocultural and ecological consequences of industrial development, such actions generally only accelerate and exacerbate the circle.

Today's actors and the solutions they propose, then, will not adequately address the combined dynamics of ecological degradation and sociocultural erosion. The dominant problem-solving devices and the industrial development process of which they are a part will only further accelerate the vicious circle. We must therefore work to transform the perspective of today's actors. Only by stepping outside of the growth paradigm can we see modernization as sociocultural erosion and development as ecological degradation. By looking for solutions outside of the "development spiral," will we be able to gain the leverage and time to halt this degradation.

Learning our way out is therefore not about directly managing the sociocultural and ecological consequences of the vicious circle. It is not about better policies, more efficient technologies, improved science, better management, or increased public awareness (though these can certainly be useful in earning precious time). Moreover, there is no individual way out, as we all are collectively caught up in the circle. Indeed, it is about collectively breaking out of the circle. We must gain control by slowing it down and ultimately reversing its direction.

The challenge of learning our way out means, therefore, building sustainable sociocultural learning units—units such as communities, organizations, and societies—that are not part and parcel of this vicious circle. To recall the discussion of limits and growth, this goal must be achieved within a context of restricting rather than expanding limits.

Conceptualizing the Process: Social Environmental Learning

As we have seen, traditional problem-solving devices and the actors that promote them will not get us out of the vicious circle. Similarly, the social units such as communities, organizations, and societies that at one time could have slowed down the industrial development process are eroding. If and when these social units address any consequences of industrial development, we can expect their behaviors to be reactive, defensive, and at times even fundamentalist. These eroded social units, cogs in the wheel of a development-oriented culture, need to be made socioculturally and ecologically more sustainable. New, sustainable units need to be created.

The challenge of learning our way out is therefore to involve all relevant and critical actors in building such socioculturally and ecologically more sustainable units. We see this as a process of collective and collaborative learning, organized around concrete problems, and linking theory and practice. In other words, a process of reflection and action. This process, which we call social environmental learning, should of course be actively fostered by educational institutions. But this is not the object of this paper.

The ultimate objective of building such ecologically and socioculturally sustainable units is, of course, to slow down the vicious circle. This will be achieved because, as part of these new units, existing actors and problem-solving devices will become transformed through a perspective that will be more anchored socioculturally and biophysically. This perspective will face the now-clear input and output limits of the planet. As a result, these actors' understanding of their own roles will gradually change. The actors will undertake organizational change (structural and cultural) and become themselves more environmentally sustainable units.

In order to be successful, this social environmental learning process must involve all relevant and critical actors. In other words, all actors currently part of the problem must become part of the transformative process that might lead to a way out. This means involving the various sectors—government, business and industry, academia, NGOs, the media—as well as the various levels—local, regional, national, and global.

Indicators of Social Environmental Learning

This conceptualization lays the ground for defining theory-based indicators of social environmental learning—the process that should lead out of the vicious circle. It is important to note the distinction between indicators of sustainability and indicators of social environmental learning. Social environmental learning may ultimately lead to ecological sustainability via the building of sustainable learning communities and societies, but there is no immediate and linear correlation between them.

We distinguish three types of indicators of social environmental learning: indicators of involvement, of transformation, and of community-building. They are related to each other because they assess three measurable steps in the process of social environmental learning. Of course, the indicators proposed here are still sketchy. They are theoretical in nature, and seek to measure aspects of social environmental learning as it is not now being practiced. At a later stage, we plan to make these indicators more concrete and more operational.

Indicators of Involvement

There are in our view two types of indicators of involvement: one measures the amount and the diversity of the various actors involved in social environmental learning; the other measures the actors' readiness to change (i.e., the degree to which they are meaningfully involved). As stated above, learning our way out will only be successful if the main relevant and critical actors—the ones that are problematic in terms of sustainability—are involved. These actors should be from the various sectors, including the private and public sectors, and from various political levels (local, regional, national, and global). To start, those actors who are most problematic in terms of sustainability should be most urgently involved in learning our way out. Corresponding indicators will have to measure this.

One or several indicators should measure how many relevant actors are involved and how diverse they are. This may involve an initial inventory of stakeholders in a given situation, a list that can then be cross-checked against a list of those participating in the collective effort to learn a way out. As the list of all people concerned comes to match more closely the list of those collaborating on the solution, progress toward social environmental learning is marked. Knowing that select populations are often marginalized in decision-making, and that organizations truly learn only as people at every level learn, the diversity of participants must be measured in light of all possible participants. As more and various levels are included, we note the steps taken toward learning our way out.

Other indicators must measure to what extent their involvement is serious—to what extent these actors are ready to change as opposed to being solely interested in pursuing their agenda and influencing others. Most social units in their current state cannot be expected to willingly enter a matrix of involvement with others that promises from the outset to transform them. Therefore, participants will bring to the collective learning table different levels of flexibility, sincerity, and readiness to change. Accounting for these different drives will bring greater understanding of how productive the process of collaborative learning will be. These indicators will apply mainly to social units, as opposed to individuals. Indeed, it is usually social units that need to be transformed, and individuals are simply part of them. As said above, there is no individual, but only a collective, way out.

Indicators of Community-building

As we have said, building socially and culturally more sustainable learning units is a prerequisite for sociocultural and ecological sustainability. All currently existing social units are still very much part of the problem and need to be transformed (see below). We foresee two types of indicators here: indicators that measure the degree and the nature of the collaboration of the various actors (individuals and organizations), and indicators that measure the extent to which new units (formal and informal ones) are emerging as a result of this collaboration.

The first set of indicators should help us measure whether and to what extent the various sectors, actors, and political levels are effectively collaborating to collectively learn our way out. This, of course, is highly complex, since collaboration can take place among individuals and organizations. Communities are complex by nature, however, and intentionally collaborating on new social structures calls for a high level of sophistication about the interactions of diverse groups. These indicators are not to be confused with the measurement of actors' readiness-to-change (seen in the drives that actors bring to the discussion table), described above. They are intended, instead, to assess actual collaborative work as it is accomplished by all involved.

The second set of indicators should assess whether new, socioculturally and ecologically more sustainable units are emerging as a result of this. New social units, resulting from collective and collaborative learning, must be examined to see if they in fact escape the dominant forces of industrial development, contribute to transforming individual perspectives, and are more sustainable. These indicators will also assess the nature and solidity of these emerging units.

Indicators of Transformation

More so than the previous two types of indicators, indicators of transformation raise the question of the relationship between the individual and larger social units. We therefore distinguish here between indicators at three levels: individual, organizational, and societal. The latter will mainly be limited to countries, at this point.

At the individual level, indicators of transformation will measure skills and acquisition of knowledge about sustainability: awareness of sustainability issues, both societal and ecological; cognitive style; critical and holistic thinking; leadership; professional orientation; and institutional dimension (career changes), collaboration, and impact upon institutions. Compared to all other indicators, these changes are the easiest to measure. Individuals will undergo transformation through participation in the process of learning our way out. These indicators will assess their ability to work, play, and live a more sustainable lifestyle in general. Such a lifestyle, as we anticipate it, will require personal understanding of the ecological limits to certain activities. This understanding will be reflected in the individual's actions. This growth can be measured in both positive and negative terms, such as the eschewing of certain activities (e.g., overconsumption) and adoption of necessary practices (e.g., recycling).

At the organizational level, indicators will measure whether present organizations become socioculturally and ecologically more sustainable through their experience as involved actors. Just as individuals can be transformed through a new perspective, so too must organizations. We think of this process as being one of organizational learning and believe that the literature in that field should help us further conceptualize such indicators, for example, by distinguishing between structural changes, cultural transformations, and emerging leadership. Though it is easy to define benchmark outcomes of such organizational transformations (such as ecological solvency) little work has been done on defining criteria of progress along the process of organizational transformation. Therefore, considerable effort will need to be put into developing good criteria of organizational transformation.

At the societal level, we suggest using countries as relevant units of transformation—at least at this point. Like organizations, countries must become socioculturally and ecologically more sustainable, and corresponding indicators should be able to measure this transformation. More precisely, we suggest identifying indicators of the policy environment (i.e., to what extent is the environment favorable to societal transformation?); indicators of policy-making with respect to sociocultural and ecological sustainability (i.e., what kind of policies have been made to promote such societal transformation?), and indicators measuring practices in a given country with respect to achieving sociocultural and ecological sustainability.

Let us explore these three indicators. The first seeks to examine in measurable terms the macro-climate of a particular society. To what extent are the various pertinent actors participating positively in the country's sustainability matters? To what extent are they responsible actors? When individuals and organizations collaborate, are there means for them to have an impact on policy? Is ground-up, inclusive policy encouraged? Does the society see itself as moving toward policy that recognizes limits to industrial development? Apart from the climate surrounding policy in a given country, how is national policy actually set? A second indicator of societal transformation should look at actual policy formulation. This must be distinguished from the previous measurement of policy environment. Transforming societies will have to work through impediments to sustainability, and their ability to do so is an important reflection of their progress in social environmental learning. Once sustainability is given priority on the national agenda, can policy be enacted to accomplish this goal? Finally, are steps toward sustainability carried out at the national level? A third indicator of societal transformation should thus look at changes in practice that reflect a coherent understanding of sustainable practices and the extent to which these are acted out. Table 1 outlines all of these indicators.

Conclusion

Indicators of social environmental learning will play an important role in evaluating progress toward sustainability. Against the backdrop of input, management, and output limits to industrial development, and a dearth of solutions that are not themselves predicated on further industrial development, we must begin to collectively learn our way out. This learning process will be greatly facilitated by the development of markers by which we can measure progress. Although theoretical at present,

---

Table 1

Summary of Indicators

1. Indicators of involvement
- Amount and diversity of involvement
- Readiness to change

2. Indicators of community-building
- Degree of collaboration among critical actors
- Degree of emerging sustainable units

3. Indicators of transformation
- Indicators of individual transformation
  - Skills and knowledge acquisition
  - Awareness of sustainability issues
  - Cognitive style (critical and holistic thinking)
  - Leadership
  - Professional orientation
  - Institutional dimension (career changes)
  - Collaboration
  - Impact upon others and other institutions
- Indicators of organizational transformation
  - Leadership / management
  - Organizational structure
  - Organizational culture
- Indicators of societal transformation
  - Policy environment
  - Policy-making
  - Practice

---

these indicators will help to shape the collaborative work necessary to begin this learning. At the same time, they will provide meaningful feedback, even as we attempt to define new structures and methods for learning. This paper is based on the idea that indicators of social environmental learning do not make sense apart from a necessarily ideological view of the current situation and how to get out of it. We see our situation as increasingly unsustainable, and believe that as time passes our options become fewer and more limited. We feel that the indicators we propose must not be judged or changed independently of it.

These indicators should be discussed and refined. Only through collaborative discussion will they take on the necessary dimensions to adequately measure social environmental learning. We hope that at a later stage an institution will take up these indicators and use them to measure progress toward a sustainable world.

NOTES

1. Unfortunately, the term "dysfunction" is misleading, for it seems to indicate a malfunction, an unintended step or series of steps leading away from the desired result. While social factors (such as the push for industrial development) can indeed be seen to undermine society's quality of life, they do so only while appearing normal and healthy, and not dysfunctional. Yet, as we shall see, industrial development is often a malignant process; it is "dysfunctional" in that while fulfilling one of society's aims (increased production), it diminishes another (sustainability or quality of life). Hence, societal dysfunctions that are clearly counterproductive are often seen as beneficial. This contradiction is explored further in the discussion of perspective and transformation, below.

REFERENCES

Adorno, T., and M. Horkheimer. [1947] 1994. *Dialectic of enlightenment.* Continuum, New York.

Brown, L., H. Kane, and D. M. Roodman. 1994. *Vital signs: The trends that are shaping our future.* Norton, New York.

Chambers, R. 1984. *Rural development: Putting the last first.* Longman, London and New York.

Chatterjee, P., and M. Finger. 1994. *The earth brokers: Power, politics, and world development.* Routledge, London.

Danaher, K., ed. 1994. *Fifty years is enough: The case against the World Bank and the International Monetary Fund.* South End Press, Boston.

Finger, M., and P. Verlaan. 1995. Learning our way out: A conceptual framework for social environmental learning. *World Development* 23(3).

Ghai, D., ed. 1994. *Development and environment: Sustaining people and nature.* Blackwell, Oxford.

Malone, T. F., and J. G. Roederer, eds. 1985. *Global change.* Cambridge University Press, Cambridge.

Martin, B. 1993. *In the public interest? Privatization and public sector reform.* Zed Books, London.

Meadows, D., D. Meadows, E. Zahn, and P. Milling. 1972. *The limits to growth.* Universe Books, New York.

Nader, R., and others. 1993. *The case against "free trade": GATT, NAFTA, and the globalization of corporate power.* Earth Island, San Francisco.

Princen, T., and M. Finger. 1994. *Environmental NGOs in world politics: Linking the local and the global.* Routledge, London.

Tolba, M., O. El-Kholy, E. El-Hinnawi, M. W. Holdgate, D. F. McMichael, and R. E. Munn, eds. 1992. *The world environment 1972-1992: Two decades of challenge.* Chapman and Hall, London.

Linking Sustainability Levels to Performance Goals at National and Subnational Levels

C ∝

WALTER H. CORSON

A survey of works on the topic suggests that sustainability is a multidimensional concept with a number of interrelated aspects, including ecological, environmental, economic, technological, social, cultural, ethical, and political factors. Studies of sustainability have focused on various levels, ranging from individual households to municipalities, states and provinces, nations, and the global level (Corson 1993; Corson forthcoming). This paper gives several examples of programs at the community, state, and national level that use numerical indicators and goals to measure performance on environmental, economic, social, and political dimensions of sustainability.

Example Programs in Operation

Community Programs

A number of urban areas around the world are using numerical indicators and goals to assess the quality of life and progress toward sustainability; in the United States these include Jacksonville, Florida and Pasadena, California.

Jacksonville's program has used seventy-four indicators to monitor the quality of life on an annual basis since 1983. The indicators reflect trends in nine areas: the economy, public safety, health, education, natural environment, travel mobility, government and politics, social environment, and culture and recreation. From 1983 to 1992, thirty-five of the indicators showed improvement, twenty-three worsened, and sixteen exhibited no clear trend (Jacksonville Community Council 1993).

Of the seventy-two indicators for which targets for the year 2000 have been established, the extent to which current data for the indicators approached or exceeded the target level (a measure of performance expressed as a percentage of the target figure) varied from a high of 123% (for septic tank permits) down to a low of -86% (for net job growth). The average performance rating for all seventy-two indicators was 64%. Of the nine areas, the natural environment had the highest average rating of 96%; the social environment had the lowest average rating of 29%. Of the seventy-two indicators, 42% had values that were at least 80% of the target figure.

Pasadena's program includes 112 indicators covering ten areas: environment, health, drugs, education, the economy, housing, arts and culture, recreation and open space, transportation, and community safety. The environmental indicators include air quality, water conservation, energy efficiency, solid waste and recycling, trees, and environmental education. Many of the indicators are compared with other local, state, and national data. Quantitative targets have been established for more than a third of the indicators (City of Pasadena 1992).

The report gives trend data for a number of the indicators: of the twenty-one showing clear trends, thirteen were positive and eight negative. Of the six environmental indicators, three improved and three showed no clear trend. The extent to which current data for eighteen of the indicators approached or exceeded the designated target level (a measure of performance expressed as a percentage of the target figure) varied from a high of 138% (for vehicle deaths) down to a low of -210% (for syphilis cases). The average performance rating for the eighteen indicators was 57%. Of the eighteen indicators, half had values that were at least 80% of the target figure.

The Jacksonville and Pasadena programs both involve public-private partnerships. The Jacksonville report is prepared for the Chamber of Commerce by the city's community council and funded by the

Department of Housing and Urban Development. Pasadena's report is part of the California Healthy Cities Project, sponsored by the Pasadena City Council, and carried out by the city's Public Health Department.

State Programs

In the United States, several states are using indicators and setting numerical targets; they include Minnesota and Oregon. Minnesota's Milestones program includes twenty general descriptive goals and seventy-nine indicators with quantitative targets for the years 1995, 2000, 2010, and 2020, designed to measure progress in a number of areas. These areas include economic viability, health, education, community safety, community services, housing, environmental quality, recreation, participation in government, and government effectiveness. For thirty-one of the seventy-nine indicators, the data show trends from 1980 to 1990; fifteen of these demonstrated progress toward the targets, eleven exhibited movement away from the targets, and five displayed no clear trend (Minnesota Planning 1992).

The extent to which current data for forty-nine of the indicators approached or exceeded the designated target level (a measure of performance expressed as a percentage of the target figure) varied from a high of 110% (for hazardous waste generation) to a low of 0% (for highway litter). The average performance rating for all forty-nine indicators was 75%. The average rating for thirteen environmental indicators was 69%. Of the forty-nine indicators, 61% had values that were at least 80% of the target figure.

Oregon's Benchmarks program includes 272 indicators pertaining to people, quality of life, and the economy, with data for some indicators from 1970 to 1992, and numerical targets for 1995, 2000, and 2010. Areas covered include health, education and worker training, housing, crime, transportation, cultural activities, environmental quality, civic and political participation, government effectiveness, economic viability and diversity, income, employment, and energy use. Many of the 272 indicators are designated as critical measures of Oregon's human, environmental, and economic well-being. Of the thirty-seven critical indicators for which trend data is given, seventeen showed progress toward the targets, thirteen reflected movement away from the targets, and seven displayed no clear trend. Of the five critical environmental indicators, two improved, two worsened, and one showed no trend (Oregon Progress Board 1992).

Of the fifty-one critical indicators that included both current data and a target value for the year 2000, the extent to which data approached or exceeded the designated target level (a measure of performance expressed as a percentage of the target figure) varied from a high of 101% (the percentage of forest land and the percentage of agricultural land preserved) to a low of -41% (teenage pregnancy rate); the average performance rating for all fifty-one indicators was 69%. The average rating for six environmental indicators was 78%. Of the fifty-one indicators, 53% had values that were at least 80% of the target figure.

Both the Minnesota and Oregon programs are endorsed by the state governor. The Minnesota program is sponsored by the governor's Minnesota Milestones Advisory Committee and carried out by Minnesota Planning, an agency charged with coordinating public policy among the various units of government. Oregon Benchmarks is produced by the Oregon Progress Board (chaired by the governor) and is a report to the state legislature.

National Programs

A number of nations are establishing goals and using indicators to monitor environmental trends. Canada, France, The Netherlands, Norway, and the United Kingdom have all developed national environmental plans that include targets for reducing solid waste generation and emissions of carbon dioxide (CO_2), sulfur dioxide (SO_2), nitrogen oxides (NO_x), and ozone-depleting chemicals. In the analysis that follows, information on national targets is from Julie Hill, "National Environment Plans" (1992); the data on emissions, waste generation, and recycling is from the *OECD Environmental Data Compendium* (1993).

Carbon dioxide emissions. All five nations have established targets to stabilize CO_2 emissions by 2005 or earlier. The Dutch plan calls for stabilization by 1994-95. Of the five nations, Canada has by far the highest per capita CO_2 emissions (16.5 tons per year) and showed the greatest increase in emissions (+27%) since 1971. The Netherlands, with the most rigorous goal for reducing emissions, has the second highest per capita CO_2 emissions (12.8 tons) and the second highest increase in emissions since 1971 (+19%). France, which (along with the U.K.) has the least rigorous target for reducing emissions, has (along with Norway) the lowest per capita emissions (7.1 tons) and the greatest decrease in emissions since 1971 (-12%). The Dutch commitment to reducing CO_2 emissions may be related to its vulnerability to sea level rise from global warming.

Sulfur dioxide emissions. Canada and Norway have the most rigorous targets for SO_2 emissions; both plan 50% reductions by 1993 or 1994. Of the five nations, Canada has by far the highest per capita SO_2 emissions (123 tons), while Norway has the lowest (10.7 tons); both countries are incurring significant acid damage from emissions in neighboring countries. The Netherlands, with the second lowest per capita emissions, has the least rigorous target, which calls for a cap on emissions rather than a reduction by 2000. Among the five nations, The Netherlands and Norway have achieved the largest reductions in SO_2 emissions since 1971 (-75% and -73% respectively), compared with reductions of between -44% and -56% for the other three nations.

Nitrogen oxide emissions. The national plans for Canada and France omit targets for NO_x reduction; the Dutch plan calls for a cap on emissions, and both Norway and the U.K. plan 30% reductions. Of the five nations, Canada showed the greatest emissions increase between 1970 and 1991 (+41%) and has by far the highest per capita emissions (72.3 tons). With its large nuclear power program, France exhibited the smallest emissions increase (+14%) and has the lowest per capita emissions (26.6 tons). Norway's target of a 30% cut may reflect its relatively high per capita emissions (50.7 tons) and relatively large emissions increase since 1970 (37%).

Municipal waste and recycling. All five national plans include a goal of reducing waste and/or increasing recycling of materials. Only the Canadian plan contains a specific waste reduction target of 50%; France and the U.K. set 50% recycling targets, and the Dutch plan calls for increasing the overall recycling rate from 20% to 33%. In terms of indicators, Canada has the highest per capita municipal waste generation (601 kg), the second highest increase in waste generation between 1980 and 1990 (27%), and the lowest recycling rates for paper (20%) and glass (12%). France has the lowest rate of waste generation per capita (328 kg) and the second highest recycling rates for paper (46%) and glass (29%). While The Netherlands is relatively high on per capita waste generation (497 kg), it showed the smallest increase in generation between 1980 and 1990 (5%) and has the highest recycling rates for paper (50%) and glass (67%).

The targets in these five national plans reflect the varying importance each country attaches to the different issues; the targets also represent varying degrees of commitment to their achievement. Although the Canadian plan contains national initiatives, the federal government shares authority with the provincial governments. The French plan is not a document of the entire government, and its course of implementation is uncertain. The Dutch plan may have the broadest political acceptance of all the plans. The Norwegian plan lacks a concrete program for implementation, and compared with the others, the U.K. plan is less detailed regarding specific measures and probable costs (Hill 1992).

Conclusion

At the community and state levels, indicators and goals have usually resulted from the participation of major interest groups in a process to envision a desired future. The resulting indicators and goals thus represent a diversity of interests and reflect a community's values and priority concerns. For example, the Jacksonville indicators stress education, the economy, and public safety; Pasadena's indicators highlight health concerns and drug use. The Minnesota program emphasizes education, job training, and environmental issues, while Oregon's priorities include employment, education, and economic viability.

At the national level, national environmental plans also reflect priority concerns. In addition to the issues of climate change, ozone depletion, acidification, and wastes, goals in the five national plans reviewed show a concern for toxic and radioactive substances, water quality, and noise. The variety of issues represented in indicator projects at the community, national, and global levels is illustrated in Table 1.

The programs reviewed above suggest that indicators and numerical goals can be used to compare current environmental, economic, and social conditions with desired performance levels. This information can also be used to show trends over time and to allow comparisons between different regions. The choice of indicators reflects a community's priority concerns and values. Indicators and goals can help define and publicize new standards and measures for assessing progress, and can help judge the effectiveness of policies and programs. If combined with adequate resources and political commitment, programs employing indicators and targets can help move communities and societies toward a sustainable future.

Table 1

Indicators of sustainability: selected examples

<u>**Dimension**</u>   <u>**Indicator**</u>   (G, R, N, and L denote global, regional, national, and local level)

Natural resources and environment

Energy
  Energy use, total and per person[1](G,N,L)
  Energy efficiency index[1](N), Percent of energy from renewable sources[1](G,N,L)
  Energy imports as percent of consumption[1](N), Fossil fuel reserves[1](G,N)

Nonfuel minerals
  Aluminum consumption per person, Percent of aluminum recycled[2](N)
  Metal reserves[1](G), Metal reserves index[1](N)

Solid waste
  Municipal solid waste, total and per person[1,4](G,N,L)
  Percent of glass and paper recycled[2,4](N,L)

Hazardous waste
  Hazardous waste generated, total, per person, and per square kilometer[2,4](N,L)
  Emissions of selected gaseous, liquid, and solid toxic substances (N,L)

Atmosphere and climate
  Greenhouse gas emissions, total and per person[1](G,N)
  Carbon emissions from energy use (G,N,L)
  Atmospheric concentration of carbon dioxide[1](G), Average global air temperature[5](G)

Acidification
  Emissions of sulfur and nitrogen oxides, total and per person[1,2](N)
  Acidity of rainfall, surface water, soil[2](L)

Air pollution
  Emissions of traditional air pollutants[4](N)
  Concentrations of carbon monoxide, nitrogen and sulfur oxides, ozone[2](L)

Ozone layer depletion
  Consumption of ozone-depleting chemicals, total and per person[2](G,N,L)
  Atmospheric concentrations of ozone-depleting chemicals[1](G)
  Ozone layer depletion, global average and regional (G,R,N)
  Ultraviolet radiation levels (N,L)

Noise
  Percent of population disturbed by traffic noise[3](N,L)

Fresh water supply
  Water withdrawals, total and per person[1,4](G,N,L)
  Water withdrawals as percent of water resources[1](N,L)
  Renewable water supply per person[1](N), Groundwater levels (L)

Fresh water quality
  Nitrogen and phosphorus concentration in major rivers[1,3](R)
  Concentration of nitrogen, phosphorus, and organic chemicals in surface and groundwater[2](L)
  Biological and chemical oxygen demand[2](L)

Food and agriculture
  Index of food production per person[1,4](G,N), Grain production per person (G,N)
  Food import dependency ratio[4](N), Percent of food consumption produced locally (L)
  Pesticide use[1,2](N), Percent of food produced without chemical pesticides (L)

continued →

Indicators of sustainability: selected examples, *continued*

Land and soil
Rate of rural to urban conversion (G,N); Percent of area in parks, gardens, open space (L)
Land degradation as percent of vegetated land[1](G,R)
Rate of soil loss from water and wind erosion (G,N)

Forests
Percent of land area in forest and woodland[1](G,N,L)
Deforestation rate[1,4](G,N), Reforested area as percent of deforested area[1](G,N)

Natural habitat
Percent of land under protected status[1](G,N)
Number and extent of protected areas[1](G,N,L), Protected area index[1](N)

Wildlife
Percent of wildlife species at risk[1](G,N,L), Species risk index[1](N)

Marine resources, fisheries
Marine fish catch as percent of estimated sustainable yield[1,5](G,R)
Coastal ocean pollution index[1](N), Municipal and industrial discharges to coastal waters[2](L)
Total suspended solids and biological and chemical oxygen demand in coastal waters[2](L)

Transportation
Total production of automobiles, bicycles[5](G,N); Passenger cars per 1000 people[4](G,N,L)
Percent of people using public transportation (L), Percent of people using carpools (L)
Measures of passengers and freight carried by air, rail, and road[1,5](G,N)

Economy
Gross world product per person[4](G), Gross domestic product (GDP) per person[4](N)
Domestic national product corrected for harm to human and natural resources (N)
Unemployment rate[4](N,L), inflation rate[4](N)
Budget deficit or surplus and export-import ratio as percent of GDP (N)

Socioeconomic equity
Percent of population living in absolute poverty[4](G)
Income ratio of highest 20% of households to lowest 20%[4,5](G,N)
GDP per person for developing nations as percent of GDP for industrial nations[6](G)
Years of schooling, females as percent of males[4](N); Percent of parliament seats held by women[4](N)

Social environment

Human development
Human development index[4](N,L), Life expectancy at birth[4](G,N),
Expenditures for education and health per person and as percent of GNP[6](G,N,L)

Housing
Average number of persons per room in housing units[1](N,L)

Utilities
Percent of households without electricity[1](N,L), Telephones per 1000 people[4](N,L)

Security
Intentional homicides per 100,000 people[4](N,L), War-related deaths[6](G,N)
Military expenditures as percent of combined expenditures for education and health[4,6](G,N)

continued →

Indicators of sustainability: selected examples, *continued*

Population
Annual rate of population increase, Birth rate per 1000 people, Population density[10](G,N,L)
Access to birth control index[7](N), Percent of married couples using birth control[1,4](G,N)

Health
Life expectancy at birth[1,4](G,N,L), Infant death rate and child death rate[1,4](G,N,L)
Calorie supply and protein consumption per person, Access to safe drinking water[1](N)

Education
Literacy index[4](N), Schooling index[4](N), Environmental awareness index (N)
Percent of population over age 25 with high school education (N,L)

Culture
Daily newspaper circulation per 1000 people[4](G,N), Radios per 1000 people[4](G,N)
Book titles published per 100,000 people[4](N), Circulation of library materials per person (L)

Recreation
Public park area per 1000 people (N,L)

Political participation and involvement
Percent of population registered to vote (N,L)
Percent of population voting in elections[11](N,L)
Political freedom index[9](N)
Civil rights index[9](N)

Governmental stability and effectiveness
Changes of government indicator[8](N), Communal violence indicator[8](N)
Government efficiency index[11](N), Government employees as percent of total population (N)
Perceived responsiveness and effectiveness of government (N,L)

Data sources for the indicators

1. World Resources Institute. 1992. *World resources 1992-93.* Oxford University Press, New York. World Resources Data Base.

2. United Nations Environment Programme. 1991. *Environmental data report 1991-92.* Basil Blackwell, Cambridge, Massachusetts, USA.

3. Organization for Economic Cooperation and Development. 1993. *OECD environmental data compendium.* OECD, Paris.

4. United Nations Development Programme. 1993. *Human development report.* Oxford University Press, New York.

5. Brown, L. R., H. Kane, and E. Ayres. 1992. *Vital signs 1992.* W.W. Norton, New York. And Brown, L. R., H. Kane, and E. Ayres. 1993. *Vital signs 1993.* W.W. Norton, New York.

6. Sivard, R. 1993. *World military and social expenditures 1993.* World Priorities, Washington, D.C.

7. Population Crisis Committee. 1992. *World access to birth control.* Washington, D.C.

8. Population Crisis Committee. 1990. *Population pressures: Threat to democracy.* Washington, D.C.

9. Population Crisis Committee. 1992. *The international human suffering index.* Washington, D.C.

10. Population Reference Bureau. 1993. *World population data sheet.* Washington, D.C.

11. Shapiro, A. 1992. *We're number one: Where America stands and falls in the new world order.* Vintage Books, New York.

REFERENCES

City of Pasadena. 1992. *The quality of life in Pasadena: An index for the 90s and beyond.* Pasadena Public Health Department, Pasadena, California, USA.

Corson, W. H. 1993. *Measuring urban sustainability.* Global Tomorrow Coalition, Washington, D.C.

Corson, W. H. Measuring sustainability: Indicators, trends, and performance goals at the community, national, and global levels. In *Footsteps to sustainability,* ed. D. Pirages. Forthcoming.

Hill, Julie. 1992. *National environment plans: A comparative survey of the national plans of Canada, France, The Netherlands, Norway, and the United Kingdom.* Green Alliance, London.

Jacksonville Community Council. 1993. *Quality indicators of progress.* Jacksonville, Florida, USA.

Minnesota Planning. 1992. *Minnesota milestones.* St. Paul, Minnesota, USA.

Oregon Progress Board. 1992. *Oregon benchmarks: Standards for measuring statewide progress and government performance.* Salem, Oregon, USA.

Organisation for Economic Cooperation and Development (OECD). 1993. *Environmental data compendium.* OECD, Paris.

Bibliography

This is not meant to be a comprehensive bibliography of materials on defining and measuring sustainability and sustainable development, but rather a list of the chief sources that were consulted by the editor and his colleagues in the course of the project, as well as works cited in the introduction. See also the references in each chapter.

Beckerman, Wilfred. 1994. "Sustainable development": Is it a useful concept? *Environmental Values* 3:191-209.

Bergh, Jeroen C.J.M. van den, and Jan van der Straaten, eds. 1994. *Toward sustainable development: Concepts, methods, and policy.* Island, Washington, D.C.

Brown, Donald A., conf. dir. 1994. *The ethical dimensions of the United Nations program on environment and development.* Earth Ethics Research Group, Inc., n.p.

Brown, Lester R., and others. Annual (1984-). *State of the world: A Worldwatch Institute report on progress toward a sustainable society.* Essays focus on a different set of themes each year, for example, oceanic fisheries, solar power, or a country or region.

Brown, Lester R., and others. Annual (1992-). *Vital signs: The trends that are shaping our future.* Norton, New York and London. Presents concise information on some forty key indicators of world environmental, economic, and social health. A project of the Worldwatch Institute.

Brown, Noel, and Pierre Kuiblier, eds. 1994. *Ethics and Agenda 21: Moral implications of a global consensus.* United Nations, New York.

Carew-Reid, Jeremy, and others. 1994. *Strategies for national sustainable development: A handbook for their planning and implementation.* Earthscan, London.

Commission on Global Governance. 1995. *Our global neighborhood: The report of the Commission on Global Governance.* Oxford University Press, Oxford and New York.

Conroy, Czech, and Miles Litvinoff, eds. 1988. *The greening of aid: Sustainable livelihoods in practice.* Earthscan, London.

Corson, Walter H., ed. [1990.] *Citizen's guide to sustainable development.* Global Tomorrow Coalition, Washington, D.C.

Daly, Herman E., and John B. Cobb, Jr. 1989. *For the common good: Redirecting the economy toward community, the environment, and a sustainable future.* Beacon, Boston.

Engel, J. Ronald, and Julie Denny-Hughes, eds. 1994. *Advancing ethics for living sustainably: Report of the IUCN ethics workshop, April 1993, Indiana National Lakeshore, USA.* International Center for the Environment and Public Policy, Sacramento, California, USA. Published for the IUCN Ethics Working Group.

Engel, J. Ronald, and Joan Gibb Engel. 1990. *Ethics of environment and development: Global challenge, international response.* Belhaven, London; University of Arizona Press, Tucson, Arizona, USA.

Forum: Science and sustainability. 1993. *Ecological Applications* 3(4): 545-89.

Gastil, Raymond D. Annual (1978-). *Freedom in the world: Political rights and civil liberties.* Freedom House, New York. Country summaries and ratings on civil liberties and political rights, along with essays on current issues.

Goodland, Robert. 1995. Environmental sustainability: Universal and rigorous. Environment Department, World Bank, Washington. Draft, January 30, 1995.

Goodland, Robert, and Herman Daly. 1991. Approaching global environmental sustainability. Environment Department, World Bank, Washington, D.C.

Goodland, Robert, Herman Daly, and Salah El Sarafy, eds. and comps. 1991. *Environmentally sustainable economic development: Building on Brundtland.* Environment Department, World Bank, Washington, D.C.

Goulet, Denis. 1992. Development indicators: A research problem, a policy problem. *Journal of Socio-Economics* 21(3): 245-60.

Goulet, Denis. 1986. Three rationalities in development decision-making. *World Development* 14(2): 301-317.

Harrison, Paul. 1987. *The greening of Africa: Breaking through in the battle for land and food.* Paladin Grafton, London.

Holdgate, Martin W., and others. 1982. *The world environment 1972-1982: A report by the United Nations Environment Programme.* Tycooly, New York. Reports on environmental and policy changes in the decade. A follow-up for 1982-1992 is in preparation.

Holmberg, Johan. 1992. *Making development sustainable: Redefining institutions, policy, and economics.* Earthscan, London; Island, Washington, D.C.

Human Rights Watch and Natural Resources Defense Council. 1992. *Defending the earth: Abuses of human rights and the environment.* HRW and NRDC, New York.

Humana, Charles, comp. 1992. *World human rights guide.* 3d ed. Oxford University Press, New York and Oxford. First published in 1983, this is a country-by-country assessment of the state of human rights in most countries of the world.

IUCN/UNEP/WWF. 1980. *World conservation strategy.* IUCN, Gland, Switzerland.

IUCN/UNEP/WWF. 1991. *Caring for the earth: A strategy for sustainable living.* IUCN, Gland, Switzerland.

Jacobs, Peter, and David A. Munro. 1987. *Conservation with equity: Strategies for sustainable development: Proceedings of the Conference on Conservation and Development: Implementing the World Conservation Strategy, Ottawa, Canada, May 31-June 5, 1986.* IUCN, Gland, Switzerland.

Jayal, Nalni D. 1993. *Ecology and human rights.* Indian National Trust for Art and Cultural Heritage, New Delhi.

Kidd, Charles V. 1992. The evolution of sustainability. *Journal of Agricultural and Environmental Ethics* 5(1): 1-26. Explores the roots of the concept of sustainability.

Korten, David C. 1992. A deeper look at "sustainable development." *World Business Academy Perspectives* 6(2): 25-36.

Lebel, Gregory G., and Hal Jane. 1989. *Sustainable development: A guide to "Our common future: The report of the World Commission on Environment and Development."* Global Tomorrow Coalition, Washington, D.C.

Lélé, Sharachchandra M. 1991. Sustainable development: A critical review. *World Development.* 10(6): 607-21.

McKenzie-Mohr, Doug, and Michael Marien, eds. 1994. Special issue: Visions of sustainability. *Futures* 26(2).

MacRae, Duncan, Jr. 1985. *Policy indicators.* University of North Carolina Press, Chapel Hill, North Carolina, USA.

Marien, Michael. 1992. Environmental problems and sustainable futures: Major literature from WCED to UNCED. *Futures* 24 (8): 731-757.

Merideth, Robert W., Jr., and Laurie S. Z. Goldberg. 1990. *Global sustainability: A selected, annotated bibliography.* Institute for Environmental Studies (University of Wisconsin) Report no. 137. IES, Madison, Wisconsin, USA.

Myers, Norman, ed. 1984. *Gaia: An atlas of planet management.* Anchor, New York.

Niu, Wen-Yuan, Jonathan J. Lu, and Abdullah A. Khan. 1993. Spatial systems approach to sustainable development: A conceptual framework. *Environmental Management* 17(2): 179-86.

Organisation for Economic Co-operation and Development. 1994. *Environmental indicators: OECD core set.* OECD, Paris. The indicators, designed to evaluate countries' environmental performance and progress toward sustainable development, are organized by issues, such as climate change and biodiversity.

Organisation for Economic Co-operation and Development. 1993-. OECD environmental performance reviews (series). Separate, systematic peer reviews of environmental conditions and progress in OECD member countries. OECD, Paris.

Organisation for Economic Co-operation and Development. 1991-1993. Various working papers on environmental, economic, social, and science and technology indicators. OECD, Paris.

Pearce, David, and others. 1993. *Blueprint 3: Measuring sustainable development.* Earthscan, London.

Redclift, Michael R. 1987. *Sustainable development: Exploring the contradictions.* Methuen, New York.

Reid, Walter V., and others. 1993. *Biodiversity indicators for policy-makers.* World Resources Institute, Washington, D.C.

Robinson, John G. 1993. The limits to caring: Sustainable living and the loss of biodiversity. *Conservation Biology* 7(1): 20-28.

Rockefeller, Steven C., and John C. Elder, eds. 1992. *Spirit and nature: Why the environment is a religious issue.* Beacon, Boston. Papers from a conference held in part to discuss the ethical component of *Caring for the earth* (IUCN/UNEP/WWF 1991).

Sachs, Wolfgang, ed. 1992. *The development dictionary: A guide to knowledge as power.* Zed, London and Atlantic Highlands, New Jersey, USA.

Serageldin, Ismail, and Andrew Steer, eds. 1994. *Valuing the environment: Proceedings of the first annual international conference on environmentally sustainable development.* World Bank, Washington, D.C.

Slocombe, D. Scott, and others, eds. 1993. *What works: An annotated bibliography of case studies of sustainable development.* International Center for the Environment and Public Policy, Sacramento, California, USA. Published for the IUCN Commission on Environmental Strategy and Planning.

Stockholm International Peace Research Institute. Annual. *SIPRI yearbook: World armaments and disarmament.* Oxford University Press, New York and London.

Toman, Michael A. 1992. The difficulty in defining sustainability. *Resources* (Resources for the Future), Winter 1992.

UNED-UK. *See* United Nations Environment and Development UK Committee.

United Nations. 1993. *Agenda 21: Programme of action for sustainable development.* United Nations, New York.

United Nations Development Programme. Annual (1990-). *Human development report.* Oxford University Press, New York and Oxford. Provides detailed human development indicators and ranks all countries in a Human Development Index.

United Nations Environment and Development UK Committee. 1994. Values for a sustainable future: Report of a symposium held on 2 June 1994 to celebrate World Environment Day. UNED-UK, London.

United Nations Environment Programme. Biennial. *Environmental data report.* UNEP, Nairobi. Published in alternating years with the World Resources Institute's publication, *World resources.*

United Nations Environment Programme. Annual. *The state of the environment.* UNEP, Nairobi.

WCED. *See* World Commission on Environment and Development.

Wilkes, Brian, ed. 1989. *Sustainable development and a quality environment: Proceedings of a workshop, June 4, 1988, Smithers, B.C.* Northern Institute for Conservation Research, Smithers, British Columbia, Canada.

World Bank. Annual (1990-). *Making development sustainable: The World Bank Group and the environment.* World Bank, Washington, D.C.

World Bank. Annual. *Social indicators of development.* Johns Hopkins University Press, Baltimore and London. Statistics by country.

World Bank. Annual (1989-). *Trends in developing economies 1992.* World Bank, Washington, D.C. Statistics and analysis by country.

World Bank. Annual (1978-). *World development report.* World Bank, Washington, D.C. Includes the World Development Indicators, which give comprehensive, current data on social and economic development in the countries of the world. Three of these annual reports constitute a "trilogy on the goals and means of development": their themes are poverty (1990), development strategies (1991), and development and the environment (1992).

World Commission on Environment and Development. 1987. *Our common future.* Oxford University Press, Oxford and New York.

World Conservation Monitoring Centre. 1992. *Global biodiversity: Status of the world's living resources.* Chapman & Hall, London. A systematic, detailed compilation of information on the status of species and ecosystems and their use.

World Resources Institute. Biennial (1984-). *World resources.* Oxford University Press, New York and Oxford. Published by WRI in collaboration with the United Nations Environment Programme and the United Nations Development Programme. A detailed presentation of environmental indicators. Includes a bibliography of sources of published global and regional environmental information. Published in alternating years with UNEP's *Environmental data report.*

World Wide Fund for Nature International. [1993.] *Sustainable use of natural resources: Concepts, issues, and criteria.* Sustainable Resource Use Programme, WWF International, Gland, Switzerland.

Yanarella, Ernest J., and Richard S. Levine. 1992. Does sustainable development lead to sustainability? *Futures,* October 1992.

Index

Aalborg (Denmark), 115-151
ABC-indicator model®, 118-120
Adriaanse, A., 101
Agenda 21, 15, 61
Agricultural systems, 187-188, 208-209, 261
Air quality, 131-133, 211-212, 258-260, 261
Amsterdam, 115-151
Angers (France), 115-151
Asking Questions of Survival, 157, 164-168
Assessing and Planning Rural Sustainability, 157, 162-164
Assessment, of progress toward sustainability, 152-172
Authentic development, 50-57

Barometer of Sustainability, 157-160, 163
Basic Human Needs, 47-49
Belgium, 115-151
Biophysical green account, 182
Biodiversity, 182, 211, 262
Brandt Commission. *See* Independent Commission on International Development Issues
Breda (Netherlands), 115-151
Brooks, Harvey, 36
Brundtland Commission. *See* World Commission on Environment and Development
Brussels, 115-151

Cobb, John B., Jr., 53
California (USA), 256
California Institute of Public Affairs, 12
Canada, 258-260
Canadian International Development Agency, 152
Caribbean, 60-73, 198-213
Caring for the Earth, 15, 27-35, 158
Carrying capacity, 29-31, 100

Cars, 126-127, 133-136; *see also* Transportation
Chatterjee, Ashoke, 153
Chimbuya, Sam, 153
Chrematistics, 53
Climate change, 211-212, 261
Colombia, 160, 170
Commoner, Barry, 37
Complexity theory, 108
Consultative Group on International Agricultural Research, 188
Container issue, 119
Convention on International Trade in Endangered Species, 81
Craig, Paul, 182
Crime, 137-138
Culture, 50-52

Daly, Herman, 9, 53
Decision-making processes, 9
Deep ecology, 184
Denmark, 115-151
Depletion, resource, methods of valuing, 221-223
Development, defined, 28, 47-57; *see also,* Sustainable development
Development Alternatives, 20, 152, 170-171
Dudley, Eric, 153

Earth Summit. *See* United Nations Conference on Environment and Development
East-West Center, 192
Ecodevelopment, 7
Ecological sustainability, 29-31, 52-56, 77-86, 87-112, 115-151, 175-197, 198-215, 255-263
Economic sustainability, 33-34, 44-58, 93-98, 128-129, 115-151, 176, 255-263; national economic indicators, 216-228
Economics, limits of, 39-43, 63-64

Economy, globalized, 56-57
Education, 263; *see also* Learning
Egg of Sustainability, 155, 163
Energy, 143-144, 209, 261
Environmental Almanacs, 78
Environmental Data Report, 78
Environmental impact assessment, 64-65
Environmentally Adjusted Product, 94
Esteva, Gustavo, 50
European Sustainability Index, 115-151
Evaluation, of strategies, 152

Famine Early Warning System, 80
Finger, Matthias, 40
Fisheries, 188-189, 262
Florida (USA), 256
Food and Agriculture Organization (of the UN), 79, 81
Forests and forestry, 189-190, 201-202, 210, 262
France, 258-260
Freiburg (Germany), 115-151
Fromm, Erich, 45-46
Full-life paradigm, 51
Fundación Pro-Sierra Nevada de Santa Marta, 170
Funtowicz, S., 38, 42

Gandhi, Mohandas, 49
Geographic scale (of data), 82-83, 106-108, 191, 202
Germany, 115-151
Global Atmosphere Watch, 79
Global Environment Facility, 70
Global Environment Monitoring System, 81, 84
Global Information and Early Warning System, 81
Globalization, 70-71; economy, 56-57
Grazing lands, 190, 210
Griffin, Keith, 47
Gross Domestic Product, 216-228
Gross National Product, 94, 181, 182, 216-228
Growth, 47-48

Hague, The (Den Haag), 115-151
Hannover (Germany), 115-151
Health, 263; as analogy, 183; *see also*

Social sustainability indicators
Henderson, Hazel, 9
History, 43, 55
Hodge, Tony, 153
Holling, C.S., 180-181
Human Development Index, 102
Humility principle, 38

Illich, Ivan, 50
Imbach, Alejandro, 153
Independent Commission on International Development Issues, 52
India, 170-171
Indicators, generally, Part III (173-264), also Part II (77-151); colors for, 104; composite vs. "gripping," 91; ecological, *see* Ecological sustainability; economic, *see* Economic sustainability; five-point scale for, 103; of learning, 239-254; no simple, 182-183; pass/fail, 103; political, *see* Political indicators; social, *see* Social sustainablility; typology, 205; *see also* Performance indicators, individual indicators
Industrial ecology, 40
Institutional change, 67-68
International Center for Living Aquatic Resources Management, 188
International Center for the Environment and Public Policy, 12
International Development Research Centre, 152-154
International Institute for Environment and Development, 8
International Institute for the Urban Environment, 115-151
Italy, 115-151
IUCN - The World Conservation Union, 7-8, 11, 152-154
IUCN Commission on Environmental Strategy and Planning, 8, 11, 20, 176

Jacksonville (Florida, USA), 256
Justice, 50

Karnataka (India), 170-171
Keeling, Charles, 82
Knowledge, and sustainability, 36-43
Kumar, C. Ashok, 153

Landscape scale, 191
Land use, 191, 207, 210, 212, 262; in
   Zimbabwe, 231-236
Latin America, 60-73, 198-213
Latouch, Serge, 49
Laws, environmental, 68-69, 212
Learning, indicators of environmental,
   129-131, 239-253
Lee-Smith, Diana, 153
LeGuin, Ursula, 50
Leicester (UK), 115-151
Leipzig (Germany), 115-151
Lue-Mbizvo, Carmel, 153

MacPherson, Nancy, 154
Makha, Elliott, 153
Map Maker, 168
Marine environments, 211, 262
Materials, 209, 261
Minnesota (USA), 257
Monitoring, of strategies, 152; of sus-
   tainability, 77-86, 152-172
Montreal Protocol, 102
Mumford, Lewis, 45
Munro, David A., 7-8, 37
Mussel Watch, 81

Najam, Adil, 153
National accounts, 181, 216-228
National Income, 216-228
Natural capital, defining, 181-182
Nature, access to, 140-141
Netherlands, 85, 101-103, 115-151,
   258-260
Net Domestic Product, 216-228
Net National Product, 94
Net Primary Productivity, 182
Noise, 134, 261
Non-governmental organizations, 71,
   131, 228
Norway, 258-260
"NUSAP" approach, 109-110

Oikonomia, 53
Oregon (USA), 257
Organisation for Economic Co-opera-
   tion and Development, 92, 95
Orr, David, 38
Ortíz, Natalia, 153
Our Common Future, 8, 15, 27

Panikkar, Raimundo, 54-56
Papua New Guinea, 226
Participation, 138-139, 249-250, 263
Pasadena (California, USA), 256
Performance indicators, 99-105, 110-
   111, 152-172, 255-263
Pillai, Vijay, 153
Policy relevance, of indicators, 79, 83,
   86, 89-91, 116-118, 150-151, 219-
   220, 227-228, 260
Political indicators of sustainability,
   138-139, 212, 249-252, 255-263;
   community-building, 250-252; in-
   volvement, 249-250; "transform-
   ation," 251-252; *see also*
   Participation, Social sustainability
Politics, 62-63, 66-67
Population, 78, 125, 175, 179, 208,
   263; *see also* Social sustainability
Poverty, 57, 230-236
Precautionary principle, 40, 178
Prescott-Allen, Robert, 153
Pressure-state-response (PSR) ap-
   proach, 90-93, 198-213
Privatization, 69-70
Protocol for assessing sustainability, 34
Pyramid of Action, 163, 169

Quality, of data, 77-84, 103-105, 107-
   110, 176-178, 179-180

Rapid Assessment Mapping for Sus-
   tainability, 157, 160-162
Ravetz, A., 38, 42
Redistribution, 48
Research, need for, 71, 185-186
Reversibility principle, 40

Sachs, Ignacy, 52
Safe minimum standard, 178
Sanchez, Hernando, 153
Sanyal, Sriparna, 153
Save River, 235
Scale, *see* Geographic scale, Time scale
Science, limits of, 36-43, 183-187
Silk, Leonard, 57
Sierra Nevada de Santa Marta, 170
Social sustainability, 9, 31-33, 93-98,
   115-151, 152-172, 208, 212, 230-
   236, 239-253, 255-263; *see also*

Political indicators, Population
Society for Conservation Biology, 191
Soil, 262
Solow, Robert, 176
Spain, 115-151
Statistical offices, 228
Strategies, *see* Evaluation of, Monitoring of
Sustainability, defined, 15, 37, 178-179, 201-202
Sustainable authentic development, 44-58
Sustainable Biosphere Initiative (ESA), 186
Sustainable Biosphere Project (ICSU/SCOPE), 22, 186
Sustainable development, ambiguity of term, 15-16, 203; casual use of term, 72-73; as cross-cutting concept, 19-20; defined, 28-29, 203, 242; as moral principle, 21, 36-43; origin of term, 7-8, 15; as social process, 20-21
Systemic User-driven Sustainability Assessment, 152-172

Technocratic approaches, 65-66
Technology, 37
Terni (Italy), 115-151
Time scale, 82, 102, 111, 150-151
Trade, international, 56-57, 71-72
Traditional values, 49-50
Transportation, 147-148, 262; *see also* Cars
Tumkur (India), 170-171

UNEP/UNSTAT Consultative Expert Group, 91
United Kingdom, 115-151, 258-260
United Nations Conference on Environment and Development, 8, 68, 70; *see also* Agenda 21
United Nations Conference on the Human Environment (1972), 7
United Nations Development Programme, 9
United Nations Environment Programme, 7, 9, 78, 81
United Nations System of Economic and Environmental Accounts, 93-99

United Nations System of National Accounts, 216-228
United Nations University, 192
United States, 255-263
United States Agency for International Development, 80
United States Forest Service, 84
Unsustainability, 241; ability to detect, 177, 180-181
Urban areas, 115-151, 255-263

Valencia (Spain), 115-151
Valuation, 91; of degradation and depletion, 221-222
Values, human, 21, 243-244, 251
Varughese, George C., 153

Waste and recycling, 141-142, 144, 258-260, 261
Water, 143, 211
Wealth, 45-47
Well-being, 148; as goal, 156
White, Robert, 37
Wilcox, B.A., 186
World Bank, 9, 87-112, 228
World Bank Atlas, 87
World Commission on Environment and Development, 8; *see also Our Common Future*
World Conservation Monitoring Centre, 81
World Conservation Strategy, 7, 15, 20, 27, 158
World Development Index, 9
World Development Indicators, 93
World Development Report, 9, 87
World Health Organization, 101
World Resources, 78, 87
World Resources Institute, 9, 78
Worldwatch Institute, 9
World Weather Watch, 79
World Wide Fund for Nature, 7
World Wildlife Fund. *See* World Wide Fund for Nature

Zimbabwe, 160, 164, 171-172, 230-236